THE MYTH OF ETHNIC WAR

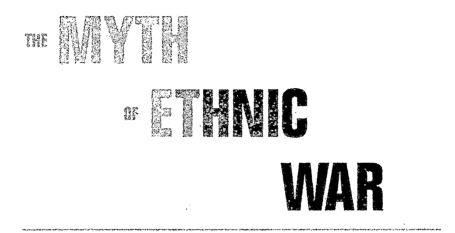

THE MYTH OF ETHNIC WAR

SERBIA AND CROATIA IN THE 1990s

V. P. GAGNON JR.

CORNELL UNIVERSITY PRESS
ITHACA AND LONDON

First published 2004 by Cornell University Press
First printing, Cornell Paperbacks, 2006

Gagnon, V. P. (Valère Philip), Jr.
  The myth of ethnic war : Serbia and Croatia in the 1990s / V. P. Gagnon Jr.
    p. cm.
  Includes bibliographical references and index.
  ISBN-13: 978-0-8014-7291-6 (pbk. : alk. paper)
  1. Yugoslav War, 1991–1995—Causes. I. Title.
  DR1313.G34   2004
  949.703—dc22   2004010399

Cornell University Press strives to use environmentally responsible suppliers and materials to the fullest extent possible in the publishing of its books. Such materials include vegetable-based, low-VOC inks and acid-free papers that are recycled, totally chlorine-free, or partly composed of nonwood fibers. For further information, visit our website at www.cornellpress.cornell.edu.

Paperback printing   10 9 8 7 6 5 4 3

CONTENTS

ABBREVIATIONS

BH   Bosnia and Herzegovina

HDZ   Croatian Democratic Community (Hrvatska Demokratska Zajednica)

HDZBH   Croatian Democratic Community of Bosnia-Herzegovina

SDS   Serbian Democratic Party (Srpska Demokratska Stranka)

SDSBH   Serbian Democratic Party of Bosnia-Herzegovina

SIV   Federal Executive Council (federal government) (Savezni izvršni već)

SKBH   League of Communists of Bosnia-Herzegovina (Savez komunista
        Bosne i Hercegovine)

SKH   League of Communists of Croatia (Savez komunista Hrvatske)

SKJ   League of Communists of Yugoslavia (Savez komunista Jugoslavije)

SKS   League of Communists of Serbia (Savez komunista Srbije)

SPO   Serbian Renewal Movement (Srpski pokret obnove)

SPS   Socialist Party of Serbia (Socijalistička partija Srbije)

SRS   Serbian Radical Party (Srpska Radikalna Stranka)

ACKNOWLEDGMENTS

This project has been long in the making, and in that time I have become indebted to many people.

I thank the institutions that have funded my research. The U.S. Department of State-administered Title VIII (Research and Training Act) Postdoctoral Fellowship in Russian and East European Studies at the Hoover Institution of Stanford University provided me with time to begin thinking about this project. I am also grateful to the Social Science Research Council–MacArthur Foundation Postdoctoral Fellowship Program on Peace and Security in a Changing World for three years of funding that gave me the opportunity to read deeply in the field of ethnicity, ethnic conflict, and identity. This fellowship also provided me with the chance to meet and interact with colleagues from disciplines other than my own. The impact of that intellectual exchange was enormously positive and proved crucial to my further development of this project. The SSRC-MacArthur fellowship also made it possible for me to spend an academic year in Croatia and Serbia, as well as a follow up year to begin digesting and synthesizing the experiences and data from my field research with the theoretical literature.

Thanks also go to the Sociology Department at the University of Zagreb, and to Vesna Pusić, who was chair at that time, for providing me with an intellectual home and for giving me the opportunity to share my research and thinking on issues of ethnicity. The Institute for Philosophy and Social Theory in Belgrade provided a similar intellectual home in Serbia. I thank Božidar Jakšić for the warmth and generosity he has shown every time I visit Belgrade.

I also thank IREX for providing a language-training grant that allowed me to greatly improve my command of what was known until recently as Serbo-Croatian, as well as for several short term travel grants that allowed me to visit the region for shorter periods of time. And I am grateful to the United States Institute of Peace for a research grant that enabled me to take a semester's leave from a heavy teaching schedule. Without that leave this book would not be finished. Thanks also to the Provost's Office at Ithaca College for a Summer Research Grant, and to the Center for Faculty Research and Development at Ithaca College for providing me with course release time for several semesters.

A special thank you goes to the Peace Studies Program at Cornell University, which has been my research home for ten years now. In addition to providing me with a desk and shelves on which to store accumulated books, journals, and newspapers, the PSP has provided me with intellectual stimulation, collegiality, and support, all of which have been crucial to this project. I thank in particular the participants in the PSP Dinner Seminar who gave me some of the first and most useful feedback on my thesis of demobilization. Thanks also to Judith Reppy who makes the PSP such a special place; to the staff of the Program, Elaine Scott and Sandy Kisner, for their assistance over the years; and to Barry Strauss and Matt Evangelista for their support during their tenures as director.

Thanks to my friends in Zagreb, who provided tremendous help and support to a visiting family with a three year old and a six month old. Thanks especially to Dubravko, Tamara, Zoran, Mira, Rajka, and Mladen for their friendship and support, and to Mijo, Peggy, and Nada Mirković for their generosity in providing us with a place to live in Zagreb. Special thanks to Saša Štulhofer, to whom I owe not only an intellectual but also a social debt. Saša was always there to help out our family when we needed it and continues to be incredibly supportive as a friend and colleague.

In Belgrade, I owe a special debt to Seka Ćurčić for providing me a home away from home, friendship, excellent meals, and a rakija whenever I return. Thanks also to Tanja Ćurčić for her patience when I was struggling with her language, and for her continuing friendship. Thanks to the friends who were graduate students during my stay in Belgrade, who made my time there more enjoyable. Thanks especially to Ivana Spasić for her continued support and interest in my project, and for providing me with important sources that I otherwise would not have been aware of. Thanks also to Sanja Rodojković and her family for their wonderful hospitality.

I'd also like to thank all the people I interviewed in Serbia, Croatia, and Bosnia-Herzegovina, most of whom will remain nameless and whom I do not quote. Many of those persons, especially in Croatia and Bosnia, spoke to me at great risk to their own safety, and I am humbled and indebted to them for their trust. Though I do not quote them, the information they provided me has proved crucial as background and as confirmation of information I received from other sources.

I also owe much to many people with whom I have shared my ideas over the past years, who have helped me develop them, and who have provided encouragement and support. Thanks to Dominique Caouette, Peter Katzenstein, Steve Majstorović, Sasha Milićević, John Oakley, Roger Petersen, John Weiss, Liz Wishnick, Tamara Cofman Wittes, and Zillah Eisenstein, all of whom provided extremely helpful feedback at various stages. Thanks to James Lyon, Chris Bennett, Tone Bringa, Obrad Kesić, and Nexhmedin Spahiu for generously sharing their insights with me. Thanks to Martijn van Beek and Stefan Senders for having the patience to explain their fields to a political scientist. Thanks to Georgii Derluguian for intellectual insights as well as friendship over the past ten years. Thanks to Mia Bloom for her comments on early versions of several chapters. Thanks to Paul Cody, Ben Kohl, Beth Harris, Naeem Inayatullah, and Stacia Zabusky for their support and encouragement over the years. Thanks to Barbara M. Kledzik for her support and assistance, to Roger Haydon and the anonymous reviewers for their very helpful suggestions. Thanks to Ana Dević for her insight and support.

Special thanks go, as well, to Aaron Presnall who provided me with suggestions that proved to be a real breakthrough, which is why this book is now finished. Thanks to Val Bunce for detailed feedback on several of the chapters. Very special thanks to Aida Hozić for her extremely helpful input, her active support and her generosity, and for being a great friend.

Finally, thanks to my parents, Barb and Val Gagnon, for their support over the years. And most of all thanks to Lisa, Nellie, and Lucas, for their love and encouragement throughout the long life of this project.

CHIP GAGNON

Ithaca, New York

PREFACE

I first went to Yugoslavia in October 1980, five months after Tito's death. Traveling south from Germany, where I'd been working, I visited a friend outside of Ljubljana and another friend in Zagreb. I also accompanied the students of the Economics Faculty of the University of Zagreb on their school trip to Belgrade, where we laid a wreath on Tito's grave. I returned to Yugoslavia the following year and visited Belgrade, Zagreb, Skopje, Sarajevo, and Ljubljana.

Yugoslavia struck me as a fascinating place. "Yugo-rock," the excellent rock and punk music performed in Slovenian and Serbo-Croatian and popular in all parts of the country, seemed exotically cool. I was also taken by the wry humor of the people I met, including young communists, and their cynical view of the ruling communist party, self-defense forces, and the slogan "brotherhood and unity." Yet this was a cynicism tinged by idealism, and many people seemed at some important level to still believe in the ideals of the Yugoslav experiment.

When I returned home I read more about Yugoslav history and politics. What I discovered, combined with my experiences, led me to pursue the study of this intriguing place. I learned Serbo-Croatian and wrote a doctoral dissertation that looked in-depth at Yugoslav domestic and foreign policies in the 1960s. Just as I was finishing the dissertation, war broke out.

When in the early 1990s I revisited what *had* been Yugoslavia, I returned to a place that had changed in fundamental ways. Deranged men marched menacingly through downtown Zagreb sporting fascist insignia; kiosks and stands sold ustaša relics; foreigners were treated with great suspicion.

Not too far away, an uneasy truce was being enforced by the Croatian army and the armed forces of the secessionist "Krajina Republic," while entire villages had been razed to the ground, their populations killed or expelled. In Sarajevo, where eleven years earlier I'd gone to nightclubs, drunk beer, eaten burek and ćevapi, and admired the Ottoman-era architecture, the city was now besieged by extremist forces shelling the town from the surrounding hills. In the rest of Bosnia paramilitary forces from Serbia were undertaking what came to be known as "ethnic cleansing." What had happened in those eleven years?

In the West there was no shortage of explanations. Journalists who had just discovered the Balkans painted images of primitive Yugoslavs nursing ancient ethnic hatreds, suddenly free to act out their fantasies of bloodlust. Neoprimordialist scholars focused on the historical and cultural inevitability of the wars and on leaders mobilizing the ethnic masses into violent conflict. More rational-choice-oriented academics echoed the arguments of the ethnic cleansers by explaining the violence in terms of conflict between clearly defined "ethnic groups" whose desire for security perversely brought them insecurity.

What was most striking to me at the time was that these views of the wars did not fit in with my understandings of those places, based on personal experiences. Although my direct experiences had been limited to urban areas, these views also did not reflect what I had learned in my academic work on Yugoslav society as a whole. Indeed, the more closely I looked at the data on the state of Yugoslav society before the war, the more puzzling the outbreak and the intensity of the violence became. Also problematic, in this light, were the explanations that had been advanced in the West. As this book demonstrates, indicators on the ground, within specific communities, showed no sign of inevitable violence. Nor did the academic literature on ethnic conflict adequately describe what had occurred—especially the literature that focused on the overwhelming power of ethnic identity to mobilize people to violence. What I found were approaches and explanations that did not fit in with the society, culture, or history I had come to know, nor with the information and reports about the violence that came from the region itself.

This book is an attempt to understand the wars in Yugoslavia in a way that takes into account the social reality of identities and culture, but that also sees them in the broader contexts of everyday life and of the structures of power within which that takes place. My book is not meant to be an exhaustive history of the wars, nor is it an ethnography of everyday life before, during, or after the wars. Rather, it is an attempt to tell the story

of the wars in a way that does justice to social realities and that recognizes
the agency of human beings, while acknowledging the importance of larger
structures of power in constraining individuals' choices and perceptions
of choice, and in shaping outcomes.

I show that the violence of the Yugoslav wars of the 1990s was part of
a broad strategy in which images of threatening enemies and violence
were used by conservative elites in Serbia and Croatia: not in order to
mobilize people, but rather as a way to *demobilize* those who were pushing for changes in the structures of economic and political power that
would negatively affect the values and interests of those elites. The goal
of this strategy was to silence, marginalize, and demobilize challengers
and their supporters in order to create political homogeneity at home. This
in turn enabled conservatives to maintain control of existing structures of
power, as well as to reposition themselves by converting state-owned
property into privately held wealth, the basis of power in a new system
of a liberal economy.

The wars and violence seen in the 1990s were thus not the expression
of grassroots sentiment in the sites of conflict. They were also far from
being the democratic expression of the political and cultural preferences
of the wider population. Rather, the violence was imposed on plural communities from outside of those communities by political and military forces
from Serbia and Croatia as part of a broader strategy of demobilization.

In making this argument, I also need to point out a few caveats. I am
not arguing that ethnicity was meaningless. I am not arguing that Yugoslavia
was a paradise of multicultural coexistence. I am not arguing that history
is irrelevant.

Approaches to ethnic conflict often portray it as an all or nothing propo-
sition: that is, either ethnicity in and of itself is the cause of violence, or
else ethnicity is a construction that has no real meaning. The approach
in this book recognizes ethnic identification as a social fact. That is, many
people in the former Yugoslavia did identify as Serbs, Croats, or Muslims.
But the meaning of that identity was contextual: it was not homogeneous
nor was it unchanging. Along these lines, sociologist Martijn van Beek
describes the tendency of observers of conflicts that are framed and
described as ethnic to focus on that ethnicity in their explanations.[1] He
labels this tendency "identity fetishism," or a fixation on "the imputed
stability and irreducibility of identity and the groupness it supposedly

[1] Martijn van Beek, "Beyond Identity Fetishism: 'Communal' Conflict in Ladakh and
the Limits of Autonomy," *Cultural Anthropology* 15, no. 4 (2002): 528–529.

reflects." Such a focus, van Beek argues, "leads to a 'misrecognition' of social identification, obscures the processes and conditions that give rise to conflict, and reproduces the logic of discrimination that it seeks to resolve." These fallacies are exactly what this study is attempting to avoid.

As van Beek and others suggest, it is much more useful to conceptualize identity as a process of identification rather than as a static attribute. In fact, the Yugoslav cases show quite well how conceptualizing identification as a process, rather than identity as an attribute or thing that people "have," helps us understand much better the interaction between categories of culture and politics.

So while the story I am telling does focus on the goals and strategies of elites, it is *not* a story of pure and simple manipulation, of leaders "playing the ethnic card" or pushing buttons and getting Pavlovian responses from the ethnic masses. Indeed, elites are forced to resort to violence to accomplish their goals precisely because it is not easy to translate ethnic identification into mobilization or violence, given the social realities reflected in processes of ethnic identification. It is the very inability of elites to "play the ethnic card" as a means of mobilizing the population that leads them to use other options, most notably the creation of violent conflict as a strategy of political demobilization.

Historical awareness of the participants is also relevant, in part because of the selective ways in which participants in and observers of conflict draw on history to "prove" the correctness of their positions or the inevitability of particular outcomes. Yet stories that focus on history or historical memories as determining current outcomes miss the point that within each republic both proponents and opponents of the wars drew on the same history in selective ways in order to make their points. Even among those who invoked "nationalist ideologies," there existed differing views of proper goals, of the best way to achieve those goals, and of the lessons to be drawn from history. Indeed, history is one of the main fields in which current politics is contested. Every group has collective memories of injustices and grievances. The relevant question is what meaning is attributed to those memories; which memories are foregrounded and which are ignored or minimized; when do memories become instrumentalized in order to justify violence; who undertakes such instrumentalization, and to what purpose?

If we can learn anything from Balkan history, it is that ethnic identities the meanings attributed to them are fluid. This is a region where coexistence was the norm, where homogeneity has historically not been a prerequisite for peace, and where violence was most often a tool used by outsiders in order to deal with social and/or political realities that they did not like and could not otherwise control. Indeed, in other work I have shown that the dynamics of the wars of the 1990s in many ways are a replay of earlier conflicts that are often cited as "proof" of the existence of ancient ethnic hatreds and the overwhelming power of ethnic identity.[2] Yet looking at it from a social constructivist perspective, what becomes clear is that in those cases too the goals and strategies of elites were of vital importance in determining outcomes. Existing identities, and the meanings of those identities, were in these cases obstacles to elite goals rather than the means by which elites achieved their goals. In response, elites fomented and provoked conflict in ethnic terms in order to change the meanings of ethnic identities and the nature of ethnic groupness, that is, the nature of the relationships among people who identify in common ethnic terms. Violence was thus used to force a change in how people identified and what it meant to identify in particular ways. So rather than being determinative, historical events set the parameter of choices facing various actors, while historical discourse seeks to justify and rationalize current actions.

The discourse of ethnicity, for example, is the result of historical factors related to the institutional framework of the Ottoman Empire, the development of nationally defined states in Western Europe, the approach to the "national question" of the Communist International, and the decision to institute the "ethnic key" in Tito's Yugoslavia. But while these factors may constrain possible choices, none of them determines outcomes, despite the ways in which historical experiences are invoked by political actors.

Of course, at the other extreme is the similarly simplistic view of history, say, of Bosnia as a kind of "multicultural paradise." This view is also not much more than a projection of a Western fantasy about itself. The important question is not whether a society has conflicts—historical and current race relations in the United States are arguably in a worse state than Croat-Serb relations in Croatia before the war—but rather how conflicts are handled. Every society has coping mechanisms, institutions, rituals, or other social forms that serve to channel conflict in ways that ensure basic societal stability at the local level. The violence that we have seen in the Balkans did not come out of these organic coping mechanisms: it was not the result of the social situation "on the ground." Rather, the violence consistently came from outside those communities that became the sites of violence.

***

[2] V. P. Gagnon Jr., "Historical Roots of the Yugoslav Conflict," in *International Organizations and Ethnic Conflict*, ed. Milton Esman and Shibley Telhami (Ithaca: Cornell University Press, 1995), 179–197.

At the macro level, just as throughout both Eastern and Western Europe, so too Yugoslavia was inevitably facing some major restructuring in response to pressures for political and economic liberalization. But in many ways it was better placed than other east European states to undergo those changes. While it is doubtful that Tito's Yugoslavia would emerge intact from the transition process, it is also far from inevitable that it would lead to the violent war we actually did see. Other options were put forward by elites, and those other options tended to be the most supported among the wider population. Yet violence and warfare, the least favored option, came to dominate. An explanation for this cannot be found in the culture of the region or the state of society in the communities that became the sites of violence.

My work seeks to problematize not just the primordialist or essentialist views of the Yugoslav conflict that view it as the result of ethnic passions, but also to question the implicit assumptions of many works that claim to be constructivist but that nevertheless use an essentialized understanding of "ethnic groups" as political actors. I show that elites, because of their control over resources (including economic, military, political, and informational), are able to use violence to try to *create* a particular notion of groupness that did not exist before; that is, the violence seeks to change what it means to identify as Serb or Croat and to impose an equivalence between ethnic identity and political position—in other words, a political homogeneity. The strategy of violence and demobilization is necessary precisely because ethnic identities are not the powerful motivating forces that neoprimordialists and essentialists assume they are. Simply appealing to those identities, therefore, cannot automatically induce (or prevent) specific political behavior.

The term "demobilization" as used in this book refers to a process by which people who had previously been politically mobilized, or who were in the process of being mobilized, become silenced, marginalized, and excluded from the public realm. For example, in Serbia and Croatia, just as in the rest of Eastern Europe, people were mobilizing against the existing structures of power. But unlike in Czechoslovakia or East Germany, where the mobilizations succeeded in changing not only the ruling elites but also the very nature of the political and economic systems, in Serbia and Croatia the regime managed to use a strategy of violence to *demobilize* those people, to silence their voices and the voices of challenger elites, to marginalize them and the issues they were using to challenge the status quo, and to portray them and their concerns as outside the realm of legitimate political discourse.

Demobilization is thus a strategy whose effectiveness is due not to its appeals to ethnicity or identity, but rather to the willingness of its purveyors to use violence and coercion in order to silence people.

Much of this comes as no news to scholars who work in the constructivist paradigm, and there are works on Yugoslavia that take that approach. But unfortunately this approach is very far from representing the "conventional wisdom," especially among political scientists and scholars of international relations, a point I elaborate in the appendix. The challenge for political scientists, in particular, is to take what is common knowledge among many sociologists and anthropologists and apply it seriously to their work. My book is an attempt to do just that.

The focus of this work involves two cases—Serbia and Croatia. These two cases are interesting and important, because they represent cases of what western observers characterize as extremist nationalism leading to violence, and they are often held up as *the* paradigmatic examples of ethnic conflict. Within these cases there is also variation over time in terms of the political strategies used by elites and in terms of which parts of the elite were dominant. By tracing the development of elite strategies over time, the challenges to elite interests, and the discourse of threat and the strategy of conflict, this work seeks to demonstrate that the strategies of conflict had as their goal a political demobilizing of the wider population as a way of preserving control over the structures of power.

The Croatian case is in many ways the more complex one, and chapter 5 covers in more detail than the chapter on Serbia the course of the war in Croatia itself, as well as the dynamics and conflicts not only within the ruling HDZ party, which were much more marked and important than conflicts in Serbia's ruling SPS, but also to some extent within the self-proclaimed "Serbian party" in Croatia, the SDS. The relatively asymmetrical nature of the two book chapters is also due to the relative dearth of information on events in Croatia in the secondary sources available in English. This has led me to undertake a more in-depth look at Croatia, drawing on primary source materials that have not yet been tapped in the West. The tendency in the West to view the wars as "bad Serbs" against "good Croats and Bosnians" has also led many to overlook the dynamics internal to Croatia. I show that these dynamics are absolutely necessary to understand not only the war but also the course of political events in both Croatia and Bosnia-Herzegovina.

Among the evidence that I use are two types of polling data. One type, which I use heavily in chapter 2, is social science polling undertaken by Yugoslav sociologists and political scientists in the late 1980s and early

1990s. These polling data are as relevant and valid as any social science data in the West, and are particularly interesting, because they do show variations across place and region in questions about ethnic relations and political attitudes. My argument does not depend on the polls being a 100-percent-accurate reflection of "reality." Rather, I see them as indicative of relations and of general attitudes; the polls are also just one type of data that are used in the argument. My overall point is that a number of different kinds of evidence (intermarriage rates, election returns, etc.) all lead to similar conclusions.

The second type of polling data I use is newspaper opinion polling, especially in the second half of the chapter on Croatia. This polling is much less reliable than social science polling and is problematic in terms of methodology and in other ways. But I decided to use the polling, again as indicative rather than definitive, for a few reasons. One, it is the only data that is available on these issues and topics; two, in general, the election results have tended to bear out the relative accuracy of the newspaper polling; and finally, in Croatia the polls were themselves a major part of the political discourse of the Tudjman years.

Another form of evidence I use is political discourse, a purposeful activity meant to have specific effects. For political actors, speech acts are intended to influence specific audiences. Some argue that speech acts of authoritarian leaders cannot be taken at face value, because they are either nothing more than rituals whose content is empty, or because they contain hidden meanings within them. Thus when Milošević is portraying himself as a peacemaker, the real message is behind the words; because the audience knows he is not a peacemaker, the rhetoric is empty. I dispute this argument. The rhetoric of politicians is meaningful. It varies over time, and these variations correlate to different outcomes. Thus, for example, political rhetoric was very much modified before elections. There seems no reason for that to be the case if these words were meaningless. The discourse of politicians is a story they are telling about themselves and about how they would like to be perceived by the relevant audiences. When Milošević claimed to be a peacemaker, he was not establishing a truth, but rather was telling a story, creating an image that was meant to influence the behavior of various domestic audiences. In this sense, speech acts are meaningful as evidence regarding the calculations of political actors about the preferences and values of the politically relevant audiences.

Finally, how we think about the causes of ethnic conflict is not just a matter of observation or analysis from a distance, but has direct feedback into the lives of people in the region. In this calculus, scholars are far from being merely neutral analysts, but are integral parts of how these kinds of wars, and this set of wars, in particular, have been and are being constructed in the minds not only of their students and academic colleagues, but also policy makers and the general public. The West's involvement in the crisis and its aftermath meant that the way Western decision makers thought about the conflict has had a tremendous impact on the policies Western states pursued in the region. Exactly because its understanding of the causes and effects of the violence were derived from assumptions and concepts described above, the West's policies in the region have been very often counterproductive.

While it is clear that local actors are the ones who made the choices to pursue policies of massive violence against civilian populations, their choices were structured and facilitated by decisions of Western policy makers. By providing the intellectual justification for seeing these conflicts as the result of irrational passions or of politicians mobilizing populations by appealing to hatreds, scholars bear at least part of the responsibility for the negative consequences of Western policy in the region. This book provides a framework that addresses the above-described puzzles, while recognizing the responsibility and complicity of academics in questions of power.

YUGOSLAVIA IN 1998

CHAPTER 1

THE PUZZLE OF THE YUGOSLAV WARS OF THE 1990s

The wars in Bosnia-Herzegovina and in neighboring Croatia and Kosovo grabbed the attention of the Western world not only because of their ferocity (over 200,000 people killed and more than 3 million displaced or expelled from their homes) and their geographic location (in the heart of Europe), but also because of their timing. Spanning the entire decade of the 1990s, this violence erupted at the exact moment when the confrontation of the Cold War was drawing to a close, when Westerners were claiming their liberal values as triumphant, in a country that had only a few years earlier been seen as very well placed to join the West. In trying to account for this outburst, most Western journalists, academics, and policymakers have resorted to the language of the premodern: tribalism, ethnic hatreds, cultural inadequacy, irrationality; in short, the Balkans as the antithesis of the modern West.

Yet one of the most striking aspects of the wars in Yugoslavia is the extent to which the images purveyed in the Western press and in much of the academic literature are so at odds with evidence from on the ground. Here are three brief stories that illustrate this point:

* * * * *

Ethnic Solidarity as a Mobilizing and Motivating Force

The images were horrific: there were mutilated corpses of women and children, whole villages of burnt-out houses and churches, and evil hordes of men in black masks carrying out the atrocities. Official Serbian television bombarded its viewers with these visuals in 1991 with accompanying discourse to highlight the horrors. Drawing on the atrocities of the Nazi-imposed Ustaša regime during World War II, which had sought to destroy Serbs in its "Independent State of Croatia," Belgrade newsreaders made it clear that Croats were trying to wipe out Serbs once again. The broadcasts were psychologically powerful. Anyone who watched these scenes, hearing a discourse of genocide night after night over a period of years, could easily become convinced that at a minimum the new nationalist government of Croatia was responsible for these horrible atrocities. After all, didn't this government use some of the symbolic imagery of the Ustaša, and didn't some of its members openly admire it?

Given this background, the Serbian government in the summer and fall of 1991 called up reservists to defend the innocent Serb women and children who were being slaughtered by the Ustaša. Yet, despite these heart-wrenching and quite convincing images, the result of this call-up was what may be one of the most massive campaigns of draft resistance in modern history. The vast majority of young men who were called up went into hiding, spending each night in a different place in order to not be caught by the military police sent out to bring in draft evaders. Others, by some estimates over 200,000, left the country rather than fight, fleeing to western Europe, North America, Australia—anywhere to avoid being sent to the front. The figures for Belgrade are more than striking: according to the Center for Peace in Belgrade, *85 percent to 90 percent* of the young men of Belgrade who were called up to fight refused to serve. In Serbia as a whole, that figure was between 50 percent and 80 percent. And even among those who did serve, there were massive desertions from the battlefield.[1]

When war came a year later to Bosnia, Serbia did not rely on reservists, but rather on Serbs originally from Bosnia but then living in Serbia. But again, it relied not on ardent young men seeking to defend Serb lands in Bosnia. Rather, it sought out and forcibly drafted Serbs living in Serbia who had connections to Bosnia, often quite tenuous, hunting them down, packing them into buses, and shipping them off to the Bosnian front against their wills.

[1] Figures from Vesna Pešić, Centar za Antiratnu akciju, Belgrade; see also Paul Shoup and Steven Burg, *The War in Bosnia-Herzegovina: Ethnic Conflict and International Intervention* (Armonk, N.Y.: M. E. Sharpe, 1999), 84. On battlefield desertions, see for example Dragan Todorović, "To nije njihova kolubarska bitka," *Vreme*, October 7, 1991, 24–26; Milan Milošević, "Marš preko Drine," *Vreme*, October 7, 1991, 20–22; Toras, *Danas*, October 1, 1991, 32.

Later that year, in another striking contrast to official imagery, the Serb-American, Milan Panić, ran against Milošević for the presidency of Yugoslavia on an anti-nationalist platform. He called for an immediate end to the war in Bosnia and called on Serbs to look to the future rather than the past. Milošević responded to this challenge by stressing ethnic tolerance and equality of all citizens of Serbia regardless of ethnicity, and by portraying himself as a moderate who wanted peaceful coexistence with other Yugoslav nations and republics. Panić was at a disadvantage: over 200,000 of his natural constituents, young Serbs who had refused to fight in the wars, had fled the country. Official media accused Panić of being a CIA agent, and the regime, feeling very threatened, initially tried to legally block his candidacy. Because of legal challenges by the Milošević government, Panić began actively campaigning only a week before the election. On the day of elections, 5–10 percent of voters were turned away at the polls, mostly younger voters, who favored Panić. Yet in the election itself, according to exit polls, Panić received about half of the vote.[2]

The massive draft-dodging and desertions, the campaign discourse of both candidates, and the electoral behavior of Serbian voters all belie the image of a powerful, emotional attachment to Serb identity that overpowered all other concerns and interests, and that provided a powerful tool for "ethnic entrepreneurs." Indeed, the contrast between Western images of a war driven by nationalist politicians whipping up the masses by playing the nationalist card, and the actual situation on the ground, is striking.

* * * * *

The Strength of Ethnic Solidarity and Sense of Belonging and Togetherness

From 1991 onward in Zagreb, Belgrade, and Sarajevo, refugees, especially from rural areas, flooded the cities. The refugees were, ethnically, "correct": refugees in Zagreb were Croats (from Krajina and Bosnia); in Belgrade they were Serbs (from Krajina, Bosnia, and Kosovo); in Sarajevo

---

[2] Exit polls showed both Milošević and Panić receiving about 47 percent of the vote. Official tallies were somewhat different, reporting that Milošević received over 55 percent, while Panić received only 34 percent. For official results see the website of the Center for Free Elections and Democracy at http://www.cesid.org/rezultati/. Douglas E. Schoen, "How Milosevic Stole the Election," *New York Times Magazine*, February 14, 1993, 40.

they were Bosnian Muslims (from eastern and northern Bosnia). Yet in all of these places the most striking topic of conversation among locals was bitter complaints about the refugees: at Easter Mass in Zagreb, native Zagrebers complained about all of the refugees who were crowding the church; in Belgrade, there was grumbling about the "Croats" and "Bosnians"—that is, Serb refugees from Croatia and Bosnia who speak in the fluid accents of their native regions rather than with the flat, nasal Belgrade pronunciation; in Sarajevo, there were very bitter complaints about all the "hicks": Bosnian Muslims from the rural regions of the country who were seen as "destroying" Sarajevo. This concerned not the physical infrastructure, but the spirit of what locals saw as the cosmopolitan city it had been before the war but which was now, thanks to the Muslim refugees, viewed as just a large rural village.

In all of these cases, instead of the expected ethnic solidarity and bonds of emotional attachment, people behaved in a very different way, expressing resentment and even bitterness toward the newcomers. And in all cases, the main complaints were cultural but not ethnic. Rather, the focus of resentment was on the rural nature of the newcomers who were seen as out of place: as invaders and "others" who threatened the culture of the city dwellers. The feeling of cultural superiority drew on pre-existing prejudices and was powerful in that it contradicted the images and theoretical notions of ethnic solidarity that underlie much of Western scholarship on ethnicity and ethnic conflict.

The assumption that people were sacrificing for the idea of an ethnically homogeneous polity, that the wars were driven by an overwhelming bond of ethnic solidarity, seems hollow when those who suffered the most for the cause—by being the worst victims of the "evil others" who had expelled them—were seen not as heroes by their fellow ethnics but rather as undesirable refugees who were degrading the cities in which they sought refuge.

* * * * *

Violence as Caused by Ethnic Solidarity

From the summer of 1991 onward, forces of Croatia's Serb nationalist party (SDS) together with the Yugoslav Army (JNA) ethnically cleansed "Krajina," the parts of Croatia that were claimed as Serb lands. This included regions that did not have a clear Serb majority before the war. Striking images of innocent civilians being used as human shields, people being forced to sign over all of their property, and whole villages destroyed, were only visual representations of what was a radical restructuring of the ethnic composition of the regions. But the violence and terror did not end with the expulsion of the non-Serbs. Indeed, even after Krajina was cleansed, the violence mounted, as moderate Serbs in the region who criticized the Belgrade-allied Krajina leadership were harassed, threatened, and even killed. Consistently in the four years of the existence of the Krajina Republic, extremists in the ruling political parties used terror and violence against those Serbs who called for a more moderate policy that reflected the values and priorities of the Serb population of Croatia prior to the war.

A strikingly parallel situation was seen in neighboring Bosnia, where the hard-line faction of the Croatian nationalist party, the HDZ (supported by Zagreb), undertook a violent campaign of ethnic cleansing against non-Croats in order to create an ethnically homogeneous Republic of Herceg-Bosna. But here too, the terror did not stop once all the non-Croats were eliminated. Indeed, the atmosphere in HDZ-controlled Mostar was described in terms that were strikingly reminiscent of Stalin's terror, given that anti-regime intellectuals and politicians were made fearful for their lives if they were suspected of speaking out against the regime, daring to express what polling before the war indicated were the preferences of the large majority of Bosnia's Croat population.

* * * * *

Such anecdotes, as well as much of the rest of what happened during the wars, seem very puzzling from the perspective of much of the literature on ethnic conflict and on the Yugoslav wars in particular. Journalistic accounts that dwelt on "ancient ethnic hatreds" tended to ignore stories that contradicted that view. Academics who focused on cultural or economic "backwardness," or who took a neoprimordialist approach focusing on the power of cultural identities or symbols to mobilize people to violence, dismissed such stories as irrelevant to their culturally framed accounts, or else subordinated them to what they assumed to be the more important "cultural" dynamics. Similarly, rational choice approaches ignored factors that did not seem to fit into their neat models of ethnic groups in conflict. Yet these anecdotes are much more typical of the Yugoslav wars than the stories focusing on ethnic hatreds, on ethnic solidarity, and historical or cultural determinism, or on security dilemmas among ethnic groups. The challenge then is to explain the violence and the framing of that violence: to explain the massacres and expulsion of people along ethnic lines while also explaining the kinds of events described above that put into question the importance of ethnic identity.

From a broader perspective, too, the Yugoslav wars of the 1990s are puzzling in a number of ways. Why did such apparently irrational violence break out in the one eastern European country that only a few years before had been seen as the "shining star" of Eastern Europe, the one most open to western ideas, the one whose citizens traveled freely to the West, the one which was mentioned as the prime candidate to join the European Community? As will be shown, explanations that focus on the pre-modern nature of the Balkans, or on the supposed primitiveness of rural culture in the Balkans, completely miss the point that these wars were the creation of modern, urban elites; that they occurred in a relatively open and cosmopolitan society; and that they were a direct response to the very strength of economic and political trends of liberalization in the country.

This in turn leads to another puzzle. During the Cold War the Yugoslav communist party (League of Communists of Yugoslavia—SKJ) was the most politically diverse of the ruling communist parties. Long before the advent of Mikhail Gorbachev in the Soviet Union, the SKJ actively and openly debated such heresies as popular participation in decision making, the legitimacy of minority factions within the party, and multiple candidates in elections. Yet these wars emanated from elites within this same SKJ.

An additional puzzle is that while other regions of post-socialist east-central Europe and the former Soviet Union were just as ethnically heterogeneous as Bosnia and Croatia, in the vast majority of those places there were no sustained, violent ethnic conflicts. Likewise, in Yugoslavia itself, ethnically heterogeneous Macedonia, long described as a potential powder keg because of its ethnic mix, has remained generally peaceful, even when the Macedonian nationalist party was in power. Vojvodina, one of the most ethnically heterogeneous regions in Yugoslavia, also did not experience sustained violence despite its mix of Serbs, Croats, Hungarians, and twenty-five other nationalities. Why have other ethnically mixed regions, many of which have histories of tensions that Bosnia and Croatia do not have, avoided ethnic conflict? And why were Bosnia and Croatia peaceful for so long? How can we account for the predominance of ethnic coexistence prior to the wars?

And, moreover, there is perhaps the "metapuzzle" of why the discourse of ethnic conflict has been so prevalent in the West, unifying political, ideological, and theoretical approaches that seem quite disparate. Why, among people who were so skeptical of the communist parties' claims to be the voice of the working class, is there such a willingness

iccept unquestioningly nationalist parties' claims to be the monolithic
ce of the nation, rather than seeing that as something to be empirically
sted? Why is there the focus on irrationality and emotion, rather than
on the clearly strategic rationales behind the wars themselves?

One clue may be the way in which Western observers in particular often
cite the Yugoslav case as confirming the qualitatively different security
environment of the post-cold war era, portraying it as a resurgence of the
primordial and emotional, as evidence that the new threat to international
security comes from regions where ethnic difference is still the fundamental social cleavage and thus the main cause of violence. From this perspective, the key to peace and security in regions like this lies in removing the
perceived cause of conflict: cultural difference. For some, partition and
transfer of populations is the best way to secure peace. For others, the
spread of universalistic liberal ideas and institutions, along with assimilation or consociational political structures, is the solution. For virtually
all observers in the West, the problem lies in the power of ethnicity to
mobilize people to violence.

This book tells a very different story. Rather than pre-rational sentiments or bonds of ethnicity causing violence, in the Yugoslav cases violence was part of a very modern story. The violence in the former
Yugoslavia was a strategic policy chosen by elites who were confronted
with political pluralism and popular mobilization. A segment of the
Yugoslav elite responded to such challenges by inflicting violence on
diverse, plural communities, with the goal of *demobilizing* key parts of
their population by trying to impose political homogeneity on heterogeneous social spaces. Such a strategy is quite commonly used by elites who
are faced with a serious threat to their interests and values, particularly
in moments of high political mobilization, economic and political liberalization, and democratization. When the very structure of power itself
is threatened, elites can either try to protect the status quo, or they can
accept change and attempt to secure a place in the new order. Whether
they protect or defect[3] depends on a number of factors, including the
degree of threat, the political, military, and other resources they have
available, and their prospects in the new order.

For those elites who decide to protect the status quo, demobilization is a crucial goal, since the most serious immediate threat comes
exactly from that part of the population being mobilized by challenger
elites for fundamental change. One way to demobilize the population is

---

[3] Thanks to Val Bunce for this phrase.

to reconceptualize political space, thereby fundamentally shifting the focus of political discourse away from issues around which challengers are mobilizing the populace, toward the question of who "owns" space; the right to make decisions about this space belongs to these "owners." Violence can play a crucial role in such a reconceptualization, eclipsing demands for change and redirecting the focus of politics toward a purported threat, as well as reshaping demographic realities on the ground in a way that reinforces the sense of threat. Such violence is thus targeted at least as much against the home-state population, those defined as "us," as it is against the direct victims of violence, since the major intended effects of the violence—demobilization and homogenization of political space—are aimed at the home population; the impact on the direct victims may even be only a secondary effect.

Yugoslav elite policies of violence along ethnic lines are exactly this kind of demobilizing strategy. The ethnic conflicts in the former Yugoslavia were an attempt to force a reconceptualization of ethnicity itself for political ends. The violence achieved this end by constructing ethnicity as a hard category, and ethnic groups as clearly bounded, monolithic, unambiguous units whose members are linked through ineffable bonds of blood and history and who thus have a single, objective common interest, which is identified with the status quo elites.

This is a conceptualization of ethnicity that was extremely different from the social realities on the ground, where ethnicity was a fluid and complex relational process of identification, rather than a static attribute or interest. Since identification is the product of social interactions and has meaning only in the context of those interactions, the meaning of ethnicity must be understood within a particular social context. Elites cannot simply "push buttons" or "play cards" to mobilize people. To motivate someone, it is necessary to tap into relationships, into relational senses of identity and self, or into environmental factors that do so. The violence of ethnic conflicts is thus not meant to mobilize people by appealing to ethnicity—that is, it does not tap into these relational processes. Rather, its goal is to fundamentally alter or destroy these social realities. Indeed, given the rootedness of such realities in peoples' everyday lives, the only way to destroy them and to impose homogeneity onto existing, heterogeneous social spaces is through massive violence.[4] In other words, it is the very inability of elites to "play the ethnic card" as a means to mobilize the population that leads them to rely on violence.

[4] Thanks to Tone Bringa for this insight.

The ultimate goal, however, is not so much ethnic homogeneity as it is the construction of homogeneous *political* space as a means to demobilize challengers. The status quo elite relied heavily on terror and violence not only in areas that were ethnically heterogeneous, but also in apparently (ethnically) homogeneous regions, both those that were ethnically "pure" before the conflict, as well as those that had been "cleansed" by the conflict itself. The homogeneity being sought is thus a political homogeneity; the means to such an end is the silencing, marginalizing, and demobilization of those voices that were calling for fundamental shifts in the structures of power. The wars of ethnic cleansing proved in many ways a very effective means of imposing such political homogeneity and thus effectively demobilizing the population.

Given the complexities of social relations, however, any attempt to reconstruct political space in homogeneous terms can never be fully realized. Homogenization projects are always works in progress, always requiring some level of violence, overt or covert, explicit or implicit, to reinforce and reimpose an idealized sameness on the messy realities of society. Strategies of violence do not end with the ethnic cleansing, but rather are an integral part of the very process of thinking about political space in homogeneous ways.

Indeed, the pressure for homogeneous political space is ubiquitous. In some respects it is a requirement of the international state system itself, which divides the world up into geographical units that are, in terms of sovereignty and international law, considered to be internally homogeneous. This pressure is also seen in liberal political systems that display a tension between assumptions of a common community, that is, the equality and equivalence of all citizens, on the one hand, and the realities of social, economic, and cultural heterogeneity, on the other hand. This tension is especially clear in cases where suddenly the entire adult population of a country is included in formal politics. The basic questions of formal politics—who is a member of the community, what are the main goals of the community, what is the basis of legitimacy of the ruling class?—are suddenly not so clear, and indeed may be up for grabs. Perhaps for these reasons the concept of homogeneous political space also has a grip on the minds of many in the West who, as pointed out above, see stability and peace in this region and at home as intimately tied to a homogenization of political space in ethnic or cultural terms.

My book attempts to look at the politics of the wars while taking seriously the social realities and context. While it is not an ethnography, it takes and applies seriously the findings of anthropologists and sociologists on

the fluidity of meaning associated with categories such as ethnicity, diversity, and the Other, the contexts within which political action is examined.
This approach provides the framework within which the wars of the 1990s
are examined and explained.

The framework that informs this study thus recognizes the social reality of processes of identification such as ethnicity and starts from the premise that the meaning of ethnicity and the conceptions of attachment to
an ethnic identity are constructed in everyday life.[5] Cases like Yugoslavia
represent the intersection of these socially constructed meanings of ethnic identification with attempts by what the sociologist Pierre Bourdieu
calls the field of power to reconstruct those meanings, the use of massive
violence playing a key role.

Such an approach recognizes that ethnic identification is the result of
social processes; but it allows for a much more complex and nuanced understanding of the link between ethnicity, politics, and war than the standard
approach focusing on ethnic entrepreneurs mobilizing the masses. The
result of such an approach applied to the Yugoslav cases sheds light on ethnic conflict by seeing it not only as the product of modernity and liberalism, but as the very essence of them; for the conflict is the product not of
primitive, irrational rural peasants, but of educated, urban elites who rely
on violence not to mobilize, but to demobilize populations in response to
the demands of modern, liberal political institutions and concepts.

Thinking about Ethnic Conflict

As a starting point, instead of the question, "why ethnic conflict?" we need
to ask two questions:

1. Why was there sustained violence, especially against civilian targets?
2. Why was the violence being carried out within a discourse of eth-
    nicity? That is, why were the perpetrators describing it as a con-
    flict that is essentially about ethnic difference?

While this set of questions allows for the possibility that "ethnicity"
may be driving the violence, it does not prejudge the answer. Indeed, the
second question is crucial, given that discourse is not just expressive or
reflective, but is itself a behavior that needs to be explained. Discourse can

---

[5] For an ethnographic example of this identity construction in a plural community, see
Tone Bringa, *Being Muslim the Bosnian Way* (Princeton: Princeton University Press, 1995).

also be seen as a constitutive factor. So when perpetrators or participants call a conflict an ethnic one, it does not prove that it really is about
ethnicity; rather, such speech acts are evidence simply that the perpetrators are perceiving or framing the violence as ethnic at some level.

For example, the terror against and killing of Croats by the Croatian
nationalist forces in Bosnia-Herzegovina—or the killing of Serbs by Serb
forces in Krajina or Republika Srpska—is difficult to categorize if we
use the framework of ethnic conflict. Generally such events have been rel-
egated to side notes, minor details that do not concern the "real" story
of Serb vs. Croat, despite the fact that they are a major part of the overall
dynamic of these conflicts. Similar phenomena are seen in other ethnic
conflicts, for example, Hutu Power's victimization of "moderate Hutus"
during the genocide in Rwanda.

Indeed, the perception by participants and victims that violence is essentially caused by ethnicity may be due to the fact that the conflict is being
described, explained and justified in these terms; that is, it is taking place
within a discourse of ethnicity. But to use either of these statements as evidence of what the conflict is "really about" is to use as evidence what has
to be explained and is tautological. While the Bosnian Muslim on the
ground clearly experiences violence against himself as due to the "fact"
of being Muslim, and that in turn may help structure self-perception and
self-identity, the actual purpose of the violence may lie elsewhere.[6]

This highlights another related issue: *what* is in conflict? The discourse
of ethnic conflict leads us to assume that the conflict is between well-
defined groups who are differentiated by ethnicity, with the underlying
premise being that the conflict is about the relationship between these
clear-cut groups, that it was triggered in some way by that inter-group
dynamic. This in turn rules out even considering that the conflict's causes
are to be found elsewhere. In a similar way, the discourse of inter-state
conflict leads analysts to assume that the causes of war between two states
are located in the relationship between states, rather than the possibility
that the war is the result of processes or dynamics within one of the states.

If we ask instead, why is sustained and systematic violence occurring
in this region? it becomes clear that in order to understand the dynamics
of the conflict, we must first problematize the discourse and portrayal of
actors and their motivations. Indeed, violence may be constitutive, that

---

[6] As mentioned earlier, it is strange that political scientists who had no problem separating the discourse of workers and proletariat from the actions of communist parties,
employing that discourse and framing their actions in its terms, suddenly seem rendered
methodologically naive when faced with cases of culturally defined political movements.

is, its goal may be to construct actors or meanings or relationships that did not previously exist. Trying to analyze such a conflict as one between two pre-existing actors would clearly miss the main dynamics of that conflict. As a first step we therefore need to problematize "corporate identities": the issue of who is putatively at war with whom.[7]

The major question thus becomes: who is doing violence to whom? What does it mean to say that Croats are killing Serbs? If we problematize the notion of the group implicit in the term ethnic conflict, then we can say that some people who identify as Croats are victimizing people they have identified as Serbs. But it also unveils other dynamics that are obscured by the discourse of ethnic conflict. The people who are perpetrating violence and who identify as Croats are also victimizing people who similarly identify as Croats. Behind the discourse of Croats against Serbs is a much more complex reality that undermines the simple, straightforward story of ethnic conflict. Problematizing the discourse of ethnic conflict thus also requires problematizing the concept of ethnic groups, focusing on the individuals who are enacting the violence, and investigating the reasons for their violent behavior.

This does not mean rejecting the very concepts of ethnic identification and ethnicity or dismissing them as false consciousness. It merely questions the concepts of *groupness* and solidarity, that is, whether, even if people do identify as Croats, it is in any way meaningful to assume that all such people are *ipso facto* members of an ethnic group with identifiable interests and borders, or that they all share an identical sense of what such an identification as Croat means in their relationships with other Croats and non-Croats. The fact that people identify in a particular common way says nothing about the existence or nature of a sense of "groupness" among those people. It is this sense of groupness, the particular meaning attached to it, that is too often assumed in studies of ethnicity and ethnic conflict. And since groupness itself is often seen as the root cause of violence, one of the major challenges is to link systematic sustained violence to ethnic sentiment and processes of identification on the ground. While the conflicts themselves may not be caused by ethnicity per se, the very fact that they are being framed in a discourse of ethnicity means that somewhere, at some level, the concept is linked to violence. The key challenge is to figure out how and why.

[7] Lars-Erik Cederman, "Nationalism and Ethnicity," in *Handbook of International Relations*, ed. Beth A Simmons, Walter Carlsnaes, and Thomas Risse (London: Sage Publications, 2002). Cederman's project, applying social constructivist or "sociational" analysis to international relations, points out the importance of analyzing, rather than just assuming, the formation of corporate and social identities.

The underlying approach of this book is social constructivist. This approach allows us to problematize corporate identities that are deployed in these conflicts, since constructivism stresses the importance of thinking about identities as processes that are the product of social interactions. If ethnic identity is driving conflict, that must be shown at the level of the social construction of peoples' identities. This approach also emphasizes the importance of thinking about identity as a relational term, that is, as identification rather than as a static attribute or interest of an individual. From the other side of the question, at the level of elites and politicians, one wants to know how they seek to achieve their goals when the wider population is somehow important. By what means do they attempt to influence the population in order to conduce, induce, or compel them to undertake (or not undertake) certain political behaviors? How does ethnicity come into play in this process?

In short, the challenge is how to conceptualize the interaction between the field of power, on the one hand, and social realities in existing communities on the ground, on the other.

Political Space and the Construction of Groupness

Every social space is heterogeneous. Even in societies that are considered to be ethnically or religiously homogeneous, diversity is a fact of life: age, gender, socio-economic status, profession, region, political views or orientation, as well as the meanings attached to those differences. Such diversity is itself an expression and reflection of the lived experiences of the population.

For formal politics, however, such diversity of social space can be problematic, because in many ways formal politics requires a level of homogeneity that diverges from the socially heterogeneous realities. Thus at the most basic level of legitimacy, if the right to rule is derived in theory from "the people," who are the people? What commonality links them as a group, and what links them to the ruler? As Hobsbawm and others have shown, the rise of the modern state brought with it homogenizing projects, that is, the construction and imposition of homogeneous *political* space on top of the heterogeneous social realities.[8]

---

[8] E. J. Hobsbawm, *Nations and Nationalism since 1780: Programme, Myth, Reality* (Cambridge: Cambridge University Press, 1993); Etienne Balibar and Immanuel Wallerstein, *Race, Nation, Class: Ambiguous Identities* (Verso Books, 1992); Ernest Gellner, *Nations and Nationalism* (Ithaca: Cornell University Press, 1983).

Indeed, imaging and imagining spaces is a central part of politics. Formal politics , especially in the modern state, is often geographically bound, taking place within a certain polity: a specific geographic space. But in addition to—and in many ways more important than—that territorially bound space is the image of *political* space, and the "imagined community" which may not, and usually does not, coincide with the social realities within that territory. That community is often not constructed in terms of territorial social realities, because by definition the imagined community is homogeneous: we are all the same in some way and have something in common. The challenge for those who construct political space is to define that commonality, to construct homogenized political space in a geographic and social space that is by nature culturally, ethnically, and politically heterogeneous. How does one get people to imagine that space in a way different from their own social relationships and interactions? In many ways this is the most basic challenge for politics, especially in liberal and liberalizing polities.

The definition of political space is directly linked to the concept of legitimacy; however, what are the bases of legitimacy? Who is the relevant audience? Whose assent is needed? Which audiences must only passively assent? While the natural inclination in answering these questions is to focus on actors within the polity in question, a key audience in all of these questions is external, and this external factor must always be included in discussions of political space. Indeed, the international community and system play a major role in how political space may (or must) be imagined. Thus to understand why political actors in Yugoslavia relied on a discourse of ethnicity, we must look at the environment in which that discourse came about.

The International System and Political Space

From its beginning the modern international state system has been a system of mutual recognition, based on difference. With the Treaty of Westphalia, political spaces of "sovereignty" were constructed as religiously defined, homogeneous spaces. Previously, political space had been constructed in terms of Christendom. With the splintering of the Christian world and the rise of political movements that called for a different kind of political space, not linked to Rome, this construction faced a serious challenge. The resulting wars (often referred to as the wars of religion) ended in the peace of Westphalia, which provided for mutual recognition of homogeneously constructed domestic political spaces: the birth of the modern state system. But as Naeem Inayatullah and David Blaney point out, the Westphalian settlement deferred rather than resolved the question of cultural pluralism and difference by repressing it, since it imposed the image of homogeneous *political* space onto a quite different reality.[9] From then on, new states have come into being not only because of their internal situation, but also in large part because external, powerful states recognize that existence as a legitimate form of geographically bound, homogeneously imagined, political space.

Between the 16th and the 19th centuries, the way in which space in Europe was constructed shifted, from religious and dynastic terms, to the modern nation-state. The literature on nationalism makes quite clear that this shift was not "natural." Ethno-national states therefore did not arise as a reflection of some pre-existing reality on the ground that merely "awoke" after a long period of slumber or repression. While drawing on what Hobsbawm refers to as "proto-national" factors, the phenomenon of space conceived of in ethnically or linguistically homogeneous terms was very much a new one that was constructed purposefully by state-building elites. Because of them, proto-national elements were reshaped and reified, and given new political meanings as a way of trying to create *political* homogeneity.[10] Indeed, given that the territorial spaces in question were neither culturally nor politically homogeneous, one of the major parts of the nation-state project in western Europe was the construction of this homogeneity. As Hobsbawm points out, early to mid-19th century liberals saw this move toward cultural homogeneity—and the disappearance of smaller "peoples"—as positive and progressive. The means by which various state elites fostered or imposed homogeneity differed. There is a range from the use of violence against populations who did not fit into the newly ethnic designation of political space—non-French speakers in France, aboriginal peoples in colonized countries, Jews and Gypsies in Europe—to imposition of a standardized homogeneity through education and linguistic standardization (assimilation and differentiation of regional variants of language and culture by social status). The entire range of strategies has marked the construction and reconstruction of western European nation states right up to the present.

---

[9] Naeem Inayatullah and David Blaney, "The Westphalian Deferral," *International Studies Review* 22 (2000): 29–64; Naeem Inayatullah and David Blaney, *International Relations and the Problem of Difference* (New York: Routledge, 2004).

[10] See E. J. Hobsbawm, *Nations and Nationalism since 1780*; see also Ernest Gellner, *Nations and Nationalism*.

Thus, this new and different kind of political space, defined and imagined in "national" terms, did not reflect social realities. New nation states
were faced with heterogeneity in religious, ethnic, linguistic, regional, and
in class terms, given the increasing rise of the working class over the course
of the 19th century. So how could a common imagined community or political space be constructed from such diversity? As Hobsbawm argues, violence played a key role at home and abroad. Once the "nation-state" form
of political space was established as the norm in western Europe, western Europeans externalized that norm as they spread their power. To be
recognized as a state, a territory had to meet certain standards of political imagining.

Of course, this reconceptualization of political space in western Europe
over the course of the 19th century also had its impact in the Balkans where,
as throughout Europe, it clearly clashed with the demographic and social
realities on the ground. Indeed, the very different, very heterogeneous
societies in the Habsburg realms—and especially in the Ottoman Empire—
came under increasing pressure as the ideas of homogeneous ethnic nations
spread from the West.

In the Ottoman Empire, difference was institutionalized in two ways:
horizontally according to social class and professional activity; and vertically according to legal-religious lines.[11] The ruling class was not an ethnic one and did not identify with cultural groups in the empire; its language,
Osmanli, was incomprehensible to Turkish-speaking peasants. This ruling class was drawn from all ethnic and linguistic elements of the empire,
though non-Muslims had to convert to join.

This institutionalization of difference, in particular, the vertical "millet"
system, was meant to "create a secondary imperial administrative and primary legal structure" for the empire.[12] Movement between millets was
possible (through conversion, except for Muslims) in a way that movement
vertically within a millet was not. The Ottomans were, however, not interested in cultural or religious homogeneity, which accounts for the continued diversity of those parts of the Balkans that they ruled. Rather than
violently erasing difference by imposing their own religion and language
throughout their realm—as the western and central Europeans tended to
do—the Ottomans instead institutionalized difference in religious terms.

[11] Kemal Karpat, *An Inquiry into the Social Foundations of Nationalism in the Ottoman
State: From Social Estates to Classes, from Millets to Nations* (Princeton: Center for International Studies, Research Monograph No. 39, 1973).
[12] Peter F. Sugar, *Southeastern Europe under Ottoman Rule, 1354–1804* (Seattle: University of Washington Press, 1977), 274.

Each person was subject to the legal system of his or her millet, rather than to a common, centralized, empire-wide system. The heads of the millets—the Patriarch of Constantinople for the Orthodox, the Grand Rabbi of Istanbul for Jews, etc.—thus not only had great authority within the millet, but also were very much integral parts of the Ottoman system. But the millets were not territorially based. Millet was in a way a personally located institutionalization of religious difference. Local communities thus enjoyed great autonomy, subject only to taxation if they were Christian, and military service if they were Muslim.

However, as Ottoman power declined and European power increased, this system came under attack as the European states began to pressure the Ottomans to gain access to their closed markets. They forced the Ottomans to recognize European states as "protectors" of various millets beginning in 1774 after the Russian defeat of the Ottomans, when the Porte recognized Russia as the protector of the Orthodox millet. Similarly, the Sultan was forced to accept the "Capitulations" which provided that foreign citizens within the Empire be tried by their native courts and be exempt from Ottoman taxes.

Given the power of the European states, including their hegemony over questions of international recognition of independence and sovereignty, elites who wished to lay claim to a state on the territory of either empire had to frame the claim in western European terms of a territorialized ethnic/linguistic nation, despite the fact that no territory in the region conformed to that demand. Thus the 19th-century disintegration of the Ottoman Empire was in part the result of claims that were advanced for independent western-style nation-states. That is, if you were an elite who wanted to establish a state on the very heterogeneous territory of the Ottoman Empire, you had to be recognized as independent by the West. This in turn required you to show that the geographic space you claimed was "yours," by showing that it was inhabited by "your" people. The claims to such states were based on a mixture of Ottoman political categories, in religious terms (Christians appealing to fellow Christians), alongside the western-defined criteria of language and ethnicity. In fact, the ways in which these territories were portrayed diverged greatly from the complex heterogeneous societies on the ground. The violence that accompanied the disintegration of the Ottoman Empire in Europe was in effect part of the reconstruction of political space, moving away from the complexities of the Ottoman polity in which identities were not spatialized, and toward the Western norm of spatial homogeneity. In many ways it was thus externally directed, a series of attempts to create a particular kind of political space required by the West for recognition.

In addition, the Western powers directly intervened in this region by claiming certain religiously defined populations to be under their "protection," effectively putting certain parts of the Ottoman population under their patronage and recognizing as the local populations' "national leaders" those elites who mobilized a discourse of ethno-religious separatism and boundedness. The Europeans also granted citizenship to Christians living in the Empire; these Ottoman Christians in turn were able to use this citizenship and their connections to western Europe as a tremendous resource.[13] Thus, the western European model of the nation-state

> was imposed on all the Ottoman peoples by their leaders regardless of their historical experience and political culture. Each major ethnic group . . . sharing a kindred language was assembled arbitrarily in a given territory and forced to accept a national identity chosen by the self-appointed 'national' leaders.[14]

The result was the violence and wars in the Balkans over the course of the 19th and early 20th centuries, including the effective "ethnic cleansing" of Ottoman Muslims from the territories of newly independent nation-states.[15] Far from being the result of endemic hatreds or Balkan pathologies, they were the result of a reconceptualization of space along European lines—in effect, the Europeanization of the Balkans.

In the case of Serbia, the elites who were successful in establishing a Serbian state thus used a discourse and an image of a "Serbian people" to construct the territorialized sense of nation. The state-building nationalism that drove these policies was first officially enunciated in 1844 by the

---

[13] As one scholar of the region has noted, these developments played a great role in the fate of the Ottoman Empire. "The rapid rise of nationalism among the non-Turkish population would not have been possible without European patronage. Without the collusion of the Powers, members of the non-Muslim bourgeoisie would have been unable to acquire foreign citizenships, thereby being able to evade Ottoman laws and taxes. Without this privilege such groups might have tried to further their interests via the Ottoman state by supporting its development rather than stunting its growth. . . . [T]he commercial elements among the non-Muslims were not, by and large, nationalists; their interests were better served in a large multi-ethnic empire than in a small nation-state." Feroz Ahmad, "The Late Ottoman Empire," in *The Great Powers and the End of the Ottoman Empire*, ed. Marian Kent (London: George Allen & Unwin, 1984), 22.

[14] Kemal H. Karpat, "*Millets* and Nationality: The Roots of the Incongruity of Nation and State in the Post-Ottoman Era," in *Christians and Jews in the Ottoman Empire: The Functioning of a Plural Society*, ed. Benjamin Braude and Bernard Lewis (New York: Holmes & Meier Publishers, 1982), 1:166.

[15] Justin McCarthy, *Death and Exile: The Ethnic Cleansing of the Ottoman Muslims, 1821–1922* (Princeton: Princeton University Press, 1995).

minister of internal affairs of the Serbian principality, Ilija Garašanin, who argued that "Serbia must place herself in the ranks of other European states." To that end he laid out a basically liberal plan to create a large Serbian-dominated state in what was then the European realms of the Ottoman Empire, as well as in the south Slavic realms of the Habsburg Empire.[16] Although in retrospect many portray Garašanin as the "root of evil" of the "Greater Serbia" project, in fact, his plans were very much in the mainstream of European liberal thinking about the construction of nation states in the mid-19th century.

In this move to assert an independent Serbian policy, the ruling elites of the principality were very strongly supported by Western powers that sought to prevent Russian influence and control over the region. The strategy of the Western powers was to establish west European-style nation states in the region, regardless of the demographic realities on the ground. As a result, just as European states had done earlier, Serbian elites undertook to impose a cultural homogeneity on their new nation-state's territory, in this case, by expelling the Muslim populations from the territories that became incorporated into Serbia.

As Serbian territory expanded, the Europeanization of these territories continued, as Serbian elites sought to ensure the ethnicization of that territory—indeed, this is why the heart of the 19th-century Serbian kingdom, "inner Serbia" (not including Kosovo or Vojvodina), was one of the few ethnically homogeneous parts of the former Yugoslavia. The Balkan wars of 1912–1913 similarly saw fighting over Ottoman territories. Yet despite very diverse populations, the neighboring nation-states laid claim to these Ottoman territories based on ethnic, linguistic, and religious grounds. Given the dissonance between the social and demographic realities and the requirement of ethnic claims to territory, the wars themselves must be seen as attempts by these states to force an ethnic conceptualization onto this diverse space.

The result—ethnic cleansing in the form of massacres and expulsions—was part of this attempt to get the Western powers to accept claims to the territory, as well as an externalization of what apparently had become an internalization of the Western imagining of political space in ethnic terms. Western acceptance, of course, did not mean the West actively condoned

---

[16] For an analysis of Garašanin's "Načertanije," see Dušan T. Bataković, "Ilija Garašanin's 'Načertanije': A Reassessment," *Balkanica* 35, no. 1 (1994): 157–183. This has been available on website of Projekat Rastko, Biblioteka Srpske Kulture na Internetu, at <http://www .rastko.org.yu/istorija/batakovic/batakovic-nacertanije_eng.html> (accessed October 11, 2003).

expulsions; indeed, ironically, the violence was portrayed as the result of ancient Balkan enmities and primitive passions, and the West stepped in to ensure "minority rights" for those who did not fit the new description of the conquered space.[17] But the very notion that people who had lived in territories their whole lives, as had their ancestors, could suddenly become "minorities," along liberal Wilsonian lines, showed that in effect Western liberals, as much as the extremist nationalists, were conceptualizing political space in ethnic terms.

The Versailles Treaty, which ended World War I, formally called for the former multinational empires in the region—the Ottoman and Habsburg—to be broken up into nationally defined states under U.S. President Wilson's slogan of "self-determination of nations." This move furthered the trends of imposing Western conceptualizations of space on regions with very different demographics, effectively ignoring the traditions and social institutions that mediated these demographics. Indeed, as Vojvodina writer Laslo Vegel points out,

> the Versailles Treaty ended the organic development which [. . .] at the least would have offered its own answer to its own questions. The Versailles peace was an attempt to organize eastern Europe in a western model, and in the name of self-determination of peoples created permanent national states. But what was otherwise in principle an acceptable project quickly became absurd for the simple reason that it turned out to be impossible. Wilson's plan failed exactly because on the question of fairness/justice [pravičnost], answers were not sought from the system of institutions rooted in the traditions of this region.[18]

Indeed, what is striking about Yugoslavia is that throughout the 19th and 20th centuries these alternative discourses and social institutions rooted in local traditions survived. For example, in Serbia, when in 1913 the region that is now the Republic of Macedonia was conquered, the opposition Socialist Party argued strenuously that the population there should not be reduced to second-class "minorities" status, calling to give Macedonians full civil and political rights.[19] In terms of on-the-ground

[17] See Carnegie Endowment for International Peace, *The Other Balkans: A 1913 Carnegie Endowment Inquiry in Retrospect* (Washington, D.C.: Carnegie Endowment, 1993).

[18] Laslo Vegel, "Kako je nacionalna država potčinila građansko društvo," *Danas* [Belgrade] (June 2002): 29–30. Thanks to Ivana Spasić for drawing my attention to this article.

[19] See the discussion of the Serbian opposition's strong criticisms of the ruling party's views on how to govern the newly conquered territories in what is now the Republic of Macedonia, in *The Other Balkan Wars: A 1913 Carnegie Endowment Inquiry in Retrospect* (Washington, D.C.: Carnegie Endowment, 1993), 158–186.

lived experiences, the most ethnically diverse parts of what became the state of Yugoslavia maintained those realities up until the wars in 1991 and 1992 (see chapter 2), and some survive even afterwards.[20]

The two conceptualizations of space continued to battle: on the one hand, the imagining of ethnically defined nation-states, with some arguing for ethnic exclusivity and even expulsions to create homogeneous space, while others argued for tolerance and liberal minority rights; and, on the other hand, the social realities of plural, multiethnic communities. It seems contradictory that the West has effectively come down on the side of those who have used violence to achieve the ethnification of territory and the territorialization of ethnicity—which, after all, is a long tradition among liberal states in the West—while, at the same time, portraying the Balkans as a pre-modern irrational field of violence, and demanding that the Balkan natives accept an ethos of multiculturalism.[21]

This way of imagining political space in the international state system continues. Although few states are actually so constructed, especially in the former colonies of the European powers, most striking is that claims for independence, for separate political space, must be framed in nationalist terms, most often defined as a particular, cultural—linguistic or ethnic—kind of difference. In that sense, every polity has a strong incentive from the external side to construct its political space in cultural terms: to imagine itself as a homogeneous community and to thus at a minimum ignore the complex heterogeneous social realities that exist.

Internal Political Space and Legitimacy

Domestically, the way political space is constructed depends on who is included in the politically relevant population. In a system where ruling party members constitute the relevant active audience, and the wider population is effectively a passive audience, political space is constructed and

[20] See Nenad Dimitrijević, ed., *Managing Multiethnic Local Communities in the Countries of the Former Yugoslavia/Upravljanje multietničkim lokalnim zajednicama u zemljama bivše Jugoslavije* (Budapest: Open Society Institute, 2001); <http://lgi.osi.hu/publications/books/mmcpxyu/01.pdf> (accessed October 11, 2003).

[21] On how the West has constructed the Balkans as a site of irrationality, see Maria Todorova, *Imagining the Balkans* (New York: Oxford University Press, 1997); Adam Burgess, *Divided Europe: The New Domination of the East* (Chicago: Pluto Press, 1997); Lene Hansen, *Western Villains or Balkan Barbarism: Representations and Responsibility in the Debate over Bosnia* (Copenhagen: Institute of Political Science, 1998); Dušan I. Bjelić and Obrad Savić, eds., *Balkan as Metaphor: Between Globalization and Fragmentation* (Cambridge, Mass.: MIT Press, 2002).

imagined in a different way than in a system where the wider population actively takes part in elections. In the case of a ruling party, the need for homogeneous political space concerns mainly those within that party, and the homogeneity may be an ideological one. But in a liberal democracy, where the wider population is by definition part of that political space, the very social diversity that is inherent in society becomes a major challenge. There is no homogeneity among the wider population, and unlike within political parties, it may be much more difficult to remove or purge those who are different. Thus liberal democracy sets up very specific dynamics in terms of political space, dynamics which, combined with pressures of international norms, can be tragic precisely because of the contradictions between liberal political theories and practices, in particular, the assumption and requirement of a common political community versus the complex heterogeneous realities on the ground. Liberal systems require the active construction of a non-existent homogeneity that constructs and binds the population of a territory into a "community." It is no coincidence that the first Serbian state was a liberal democracy; the political relevance of the entire male population in the territory of Serbia, combined with international norms, was a key factor in the moves by parts of that state's elite to ethnically cleanse that territory as a means of maintaining its political hegemony.

Although liberalism claims to be tolerant and open to diversity, the extreme difficulty it has in dealing with cultural difference is strikingly and most manifestly demonstrated not only in the politics of cultural difference within liberal countries, but in the work of liberal theorists who are trying to grapple with the question of culture in a liberal society. One of the central tensions is that between liberalism's assumption of individualism, on the one hand, and justificatory discourses of ethnic or cultural groupness or solidarity that override individual interest, on the other hand. Indeed, there is an acceptance of the need to create the borders of a community within which liberal politics will take place. The borders and the community are, however, usually assumed to already exist. As Margaret Canovan, a liberal theorist of nationalism, points out, liberal theory does not concern itself with the formation of these communities.[22]

In fact, though, the assumption is that the borders are constructed in terms of a culturally defined group, which in turn is assumed to have special kinds of affective bonds that tie the community together. Once the

[22] Margaret Canovan, *Nationhood and Political Theory* (Cheltenham, UK: Edward Elgar, 1996).

nation is constructed, it somehow becomes a natural community that automatically commands the affections and loyalties of those who are members. That is, the community is considered natural rather than the result
of the repression of differences and the enforcement of an image of solidarity. Ethnic politics is thus portrayed as something outside of and beyond
liberal democracy, something that must be dealt with—through creating
ethnically homogeneous political space—before "normal" liberal politics
can take place. It is this underlying logic and these assumptions that explain
why liberals are among the biggest proponents of the homogenizing project, despite their proclaimed devotion to tolerance and diversity. The tolerance and diversity of which they speak only goes so far and can be seen
as a superficial diversity.[23]

While the international system and liberalism both are factors that may
foster the construction of homogeneous political space, the methods by
which national elites actually construct homogeneity can vary from benign
to horrific. So while social space always diverges from political space, the
lack of congruence can be dealt with in a variety of ways. The question
here is, why in certain cases do elites rely on violence and atrocities in
order to construct homogeneous political spaces?

First, as Hobsbawm, Balibar, and others have pointed out, violence and
atrocities have been part and parcel of the construction of every liberal
polity. Beyond that, currently in most cases the "benign" strategy has had
to do with constructing others, internal and/or external, as enemies. This
in itself is a form of violence, but it is endemic to liberal political systems.
For example, in both the United States and western Europe, both benign
and malign versions of political space are represented. The Jean-Marie Le
Pens, Jörg Haiders, Pat Buchanans, David Dukes, all have projects that
rely to one degree or another on overt violence in order to "take back" an

[23] For example, the work of liberal theorists who explicitly address questions of cultural communities is extremely revealing. Thus Yael Tamir argues that liberal democracy
requires the existence of a public sphere defined in terms of a common culture where people can feel "comfortable." Yet her idea of "common culture" is in fact a homogenized one
with hard and clear borders that she defines as "the nation." Yael Tamir, *Liberal Nationalism* (Princeton: Princeton University Press, 1993). Jeff Spinner in his work focuses on the
supposed contradiction between liberal politics and the existence within a polity of culturally distinct groups; although he is very slippery about this, and he seems not to want
to admit it, a major point seems to be that in liberal societies true diversity is not in fact
possible, that assimilation is part and parcel of liberalism. Jeff Spinner, *The Boundaries of
Citizenship: Race, Ethnicity, and Nationality in the Liberal State* (Baltimore: Johns Hopkins
University Press, 1994). See also Will Kymlicka, *Politics in the Vernacular: Nationalism, Multiculturalism, and Citizenship* (New York: Oxford University Press, 2001). For a trenchant
critique of Kymlicka, see Thomas König, "The Hegemony of Multiculturalism," *Croatian
Political Science Review* 38, no. 5 (2002): 48–61.

idealized homogeneous political space. The liberal response is to affirm the importance of the rights of minorities, to "celebrate" multicultural-ism, and to denounce the overt violence of these projects. But the differ-ence may be only superficial.

Thus liberals perhaps more than non-liberals tend to accept the homog-enizing project; that is, they construct political space in homogeneous terms often defined culturally, while calling for rights to be extended to "minorities."[24] This in turn explains the pressure from international actors, many of whom are domestically liberal states, to construct political space in post-war former Yugoslavia in cultural terms. Again, although lip serv-ice is paid to diversity and multi-ethnic communities, the internationals have had no problem accepting and imposing the logic of a territorial homogenization project in their own policies and in the institutions that they are imposing on the region. This was especially clear in the various peace plans put forth for Bosnia beginning in 1992; from the way in which the West accepted the heads of the nationalist parties in Bosnia as the legit-imate representatives of "their ethnic groups"; and from the way in which the conflict was discussed by journalists, scholars, and policy makers (as a fight between Serbs and Croats and Muslims).

But while the international system and liberalism itself are facilitat-ing factors for violence as a way of constructing a very particular kind of homogeneous space, there is a question of why some elites take the more benign way rather than overt, systematic violence. Just as in the United States and western Europe, in Yugoslavia too there were propo-nents of both options in each of the various republics. The option of vio-lence was never the single, monolithically supported option of the elites, and certainly not of the general population, as indicated in the anec-dotes above. Indeed, it was opposed by a large majority. But regardless of the reasons for the violence option—in fact, the dynamics are very simi-lar to those in the United States and western Europe—the fact remains that the international community's way of thinking about political space,

---

[24] An example of this privileging of the ethnic majority by those who see and por-tray themselves as the "owners" and "managers" of national space within the United States is pointed out by African American scholar Cornel West, who notes that "[F]or liberals, black people are to be 'included' and 'integrated' in 'our' society and culture . . . [but they] fail to see that the presence and predicaments of black people are neither additions to nor defections from American life, but rather *constitute elements of that life*." Cornel West, *Race Matters* (New York: Vintage Books, 1994), 6. On this point, see Ghassan Hage, *White Nation: Fantasies of White Supremacy in a Multicultural Society* (New York: Routledge, 2000), who demonstrates how liberal multiculturalism often replicates and reinforces the logic of ter-ritorialized ethnic or racial supremacy.

and the pressures of liberalism, were not only facilitating factors, but were in fact conducive; that is, they strengthened the positions of those who would use violence to construct political space.

Violence and the Construction of Political Space

As mentioned above, the notion of community is crucial to liberal theory, despite its focus on individualism. But where, why, and how are borders of political communities determined? The hegemonic answer seems to be: along "natural" ethnic or national lines, though it is clear that such lines do not exist. Accepting them as natural, however, has disastrous consequences.

As countries democratize, they are suddenly faced more than ever with the divergence between the complex heterogeneities of social space and the requirement of homogeneity of political space. The literature on democratization does indeed portray ethnically defined conflicts as pre-democratic phases. The case of Yugoslavia, for example, is not included in discussions of democratization in eastern Europe, because it is portrayed as an exception: ethnic heterogeneity "naturally" led to conflict which has prevented the institutionalization of real democracy. Ethnic conflict from this perspective is the result of democratization. If violent conflict broke out along ethnic lines during democratization, this is assumed to have been a reflection of sentiments and/or interests that had previously been repressed but that the coming of political freedom allowed to finally be openly expressed. This in turn is said to "prove" that the "real" or "natural" fault lines in society were ethnic all along, and that the overriding concern of the population is the ethnic question. According to this perspective, until these ethnic issues are dealt with, democracy is impossible.

Although this vision of natural fault lines and passions has become naturalized in the eyes of many Westerners, what is missing is the impact of structural power: the ability, in even liberal democratic states, of elites who control or have access to resources of power (including information) to construct environments that severely limit individuals' free expression of self-perceived interests; to construct images that affect how individuals perceive their interests; and to use discourse as a justificatory tool that apparently reconciles politics and elite behavior with the putative interests of non-elites. In short, resources of power enable elites to deal with tensions inherent in the non-congruence of social and political spaces.

Agenda setting has long been recognized as a fundamental power strategy.[25] If you are able to set the terms of debate, you have won over half the battle; you have excluded certain options, silencing some people and empowering others. If this situation is "naturalized," one has even more power and control. Politics takes place at this level of discourse in the form of contention over the construction of political space at the conceptual level in which such space is imagined: who is and is not a member of the community, what the main challenge or problem of the community is, how that challenge should be met. In the case of violent conflicts, the political discourse and the justificatory rhetoric used to explain and describe the causes of conflict must be separated conceptually from the root causes of the conflict itself. These two may or may not coincide. But to accept at face value the discourse of security and external threats is to ignore that that discourse is itself an extremely effective power strategy.

The key here is to focus on the ability of those who control power resources—not only resources owned by the state but also privately held resources—to shape and construct images of interest; the way in which those with power can structure situations such that some interests can or cannot be expressed; the ability of power elites to set the political agenda and limit options; the fact that discourse is not just "expressive" or "reflective" but is itself an exercise of power. As a consequence, behavior of the wider population may be a reflection not of some objective "interest" but rather a reaction to an environment that has been constructed, and in which choice is very limited or nonexistent. The ability of those with power to construct interest by constructing perceived possibilities or options is a crucial factor here.

In applying this to identity and ethnicity, one does not have to argue that elites are constructing or manipulating people's identities, or that such identities are a kind of "false consciousness," in order to problematize the image of ethnic groups as reflections of social fact. As discussed, people identify in multiple, overlapping, porous, and contextually dependent ways that are not reducible to the narrow term "ethnic." These identifications are constructed socially in day-to-day interactions and social environments. The key in politics is to make certain identities more relevant than others, and others irrelevant to politics; and to impute very particular meanings to the relevant ones, meanings that seem to lead "naturally" to particular policies or outcomes.

[25] Peter Bachrach and Morton Baratz, "The Two Faces of Power," *American Political Science Review* 56 (1962): 957–962.

This doesn't necessarily require changing people's self-perceived identifications. Rather, it means forcing them in particular contexts to act—
or not act—within the narrow range of one "identity" defined in a very
specific and particular way. It may also mean constructing identities or
meanings of identities that did not formerly exist. For example, the violence in the Bosnian war had a number of constructive effects. In terms of
Bosnian Muslims, many of whom had not strongly identified in national
or ethnic terms before the war, genocidal violence radically altered the
meaning and relevance of identifying as a "Bosnian Muslim." But another,
more important, construction here involved "Serbs." This took the form
of violence perpetrated in the name of Serbs against non-Serbs, and was
the construction of a particular kind of Serb identity and the meaning and
relevance of that identity. Here identity was not the cause of violence, but
rather the goal and result of violence. Power elites in Serbia and their allies
in Bosnia used their control over resources—the means of violence and
information—in order to fundamentally alter the environment in which
Bosnian Serbs found themselves, hence affecting how and with whom
they could identify themselves. They no longer had the choice to live and
identify in the ways they had before. Their resulting behavior was not
so much the result of "free choice" but rather had been structured by the
actions of elites. Their particular sense of community was not the result
of bonds predicated on ethnic sentiment, but was determined by violence
that structured political space. Hence most people, such as the Serbs within
the "Republika Srpska" part of Bosnia, but also the Croats in the Croatian "Herceg-Bosna," had very limited choices, the least evil of which was
often silence.

Violence

Given the problematic nature of the concept of community, especially the
notion of "ethnic groups," violence plays a key role in creating the image
of such common bonds. Violence and images of threat to a group creates
the image or perception of such a group as having "real" and "hard" borders. Moreover, it constructs an image of common culture as a single, objective, identifiable common interest. If the threat is to the very existence or
survival of people only because of their culture, other aspects of identification and interest can be portrayed as secondary. Inflicting violence on
plural societies constructs the ethnic group in "hard" terms, and creates
the image of solidarity in a way that did not (and does not) necessarily

exist: an (enforced) solidarity based on a negative of fear and threats rather than on a positive (or organic) one of commonality and sharing. Indeed, this constructed group exists only if its borders are constantly enforced or reinforced. Violence also has implications for the contested nature of community and identity: it silences contention in the interest of survival. Those who can credibly appeal to existential threats can shut down opposition and contention. The strategy of violence is thus a way to impose a very specific meaning and interest on ethnic identity.

What is also very significant is that violence is necessary in order to construct this notion, because it must first destroy other existing notions of group and community. So it was no coincidence that the worst violence in the Yugoslav wars occurred in the most ethnically mixed and tolerant regions of the country, places where such notions had a strength and reality that came from a shared sense of community. Exactly because of the strength of those bonds, horrible levels of violence and atrocities were the only way to construct and impose new "clear" borders of ethnicity.[26] The ruling parties in Belgrade and Zagreb directly or indirectly sponsored violence that was carried out by paramilitaries, special police units, and other groups who were sent into ethnically plural communities as part of a strategic plan to destroy those communities. Rather than appealing to ethnic interest or solidarity, such violence determines a particular notion of groupness and solidarity by means of force. Those who disagree or dissent, or who seek to promote other forms of community, are at best excluded from political discourse and at worst physically eliminated. Such measures are necessary, because appeals to these other forms of community have a power rooted in previously existing social realities. Those who appeal to older forms of community pose a serious threat; such notions are inherently more attractive than the sterile, homogeneous "community" of fear that is imposed by the purveyors of violence.

Political Space

The overall goal of the strategy of violence is thus to redefine and reconstruct political space at two levels. First, in the short term, images of threat and violence serve to silence and marginalize those who disagree with those in power; it demobilizes people who may in other circumstances have mobilized against the regime and effectively prevents their political

---

[26] Thanks to Tone Bringa for this insight.

participation. At the same time it seeks to reconfigure the borders of "our" political community, to redefine them based on a "hard" notion of culture or ethnicity, again based on fear, and to delegitimize other notions of political community. To do this, elites construct a threat defined in particular ways: "us" versus "them." This constructed threat is not a reflection of some natural relationship, but rather is the product of fear, an image that is imposed and enforced.

At another level, and with a longer-term view, the actual policies of violence and "ethnic cleansing"—harassment, rape, expulsion, murder, genocide—are meant to alter the existing demographic facts on the ground in order to turn these new notions of group borders and political community into a territorial reality. Previously existing communities and bonds, which deny the reality or hardness of newly constructed, culturally defined political community (for example, ethnically mixed families, homes, neighborhoods, regions, political parties) are, in particular, targeted for destruction. Only violence and atrocities are sufficient to destroy these realities and to make "real" the new hard borders of the ethnic group.

The goal of this strategy is to prevent or delay fundamental shifts in the structure of power within the domestic arena, shifts that reflect trends and pressures from within society, but also and often more importantly those coming from outside, which threaten to provide challenger elites with powerful external allies and/or resources. These are shifts that threaten core interests of elites who benefit from the status quo, elites at all levels of society, from local to center. The threat often comes in the form of challenger elites who are able to mobilize the wider politically relevant population on issues that would bring about these shifts.

The degree of violence involved in the elite strategy depends on what is at stake for them. Elites who are highly dependent on the existing structures of power, and for whom change would mean a total loss of access to and control over resources, will be much more willing to pursue strategies that are extremely destructive to society overall. If looked at from the perspective of the interest of the state or of the wider society, such strategies seem irrational and counterproductive. But from the narrower perspective of the threatened elites, the benefits in terms of their own personal agendas far outweigh the costs they have imposed onto their own societies as well as onto others. In short, the higher the degree of threat to elites, and the more limited their fallback positions, the more willing they will be to undertake strategies that impose very high costs on society as a whole. Thus in the case of Serbia and Croatia, those elites threatened by fundamental shifts in the power structures had very large incentives to try to prevent or delay those shifts, since they tended to be the parts of the elite which faced enormous losses in a newly structured system. While the strategies of violence that they pursued proved extremely costly to their societies, they also proved extremely successful in achieving their main personal goals: the maintenance of control over and access to resources and structures of power in Serbia and in Croatia.[27]

The remainder of this book looks in detail at the case of the Yugoslav wars of the 1990s, focusing, in particular, on Croatia and Serbia, because the wars were very much the product of the elites of those two countries. The next chapter looks at the state of society in Croatia and Bosnia, the site of the wars, as well as in Serbia. The focus is on Yugoslav sociological and political science studies of inter-ethnic relations as well as on surveys of the priorities of the populations in the years leading up to the outbreak of war. Chapter 3 looks at political developments in Croatia and Serbia from the 1960s to the late 1980s, tracing the political cleavages within the ruling parties of those republics, and the ways in which certain factions attempted to achieve their goals by focusing on political space defined in homogeneous terms. Chapter 4 looks in detail at the case of Serbia, explaining why and how the Serbian government prosecuted wars in the 1990s. Chapter 5 does the same for Croatia. Chapter 6 concludes with lessons learned from the Yugoslav wars of the 1990s.

---

[27] For more on the strategy of conflict see Gagnon, "Ethnic Nationalism and International Conflict: The Case of Serbia," *International Security* 19, no. 3 (winter 1994/95): 130–166.

CHAPTER 2

IMAGE VERSUS REALITY

WESTERN MISIDENTIFICATIONS OF THE CAUSES OF VIOLENCE

Much of the literature on ethnic conflict and on the violence in the former Yugoslavia has focused on ethnicity and ethnic solidarity, seeing people's emotional or affective attachments to ethnic identities and the ability of politicians to mobilize those identities as the main cause of the Yugoslav wars of the 1990s. In this chapter I draw on Yugoslav sociological and political science surveys to show the state of Yugoslav society at the end of the 1980s: the main issues about which people in Croatia, Bosnia-Herzegovina, and Serbia were concerned, and their attitudes toward issues related to ethnic identity and interethnic relations.

Before addressing relations in the 1980s, though, it is also important to note that arguments often seen in journalistic accounts (and even in some academic accounts) that focus on "ancient ethnic hatreds" are also inaccurate. Yugoslavia never saw the kind of religious wars seen in Western and Central Europe.[1] In addition, Serbs and Croats never fought before the beginning of the 1900s. Indeed, under Hungarian rule, Croatian and Serbian political parties often cooperated and even formed coalitions—though to be sure, there were also some political conflicts between representatives of the two within the empire.[2] During World War II, the ruling

[1] Ivo Banac, *The National Question in Yugoslavia; Origins, History, Politics* (Ithaca: Cornell University Press, 1984), 410.
[2] Wolfgang Kessler, *Politik, Kultur und Gesellschaft in Kroatien und Slawonien in der ersten Hälfte des 19. Jahrhunderts* (Munich: R. Oldenbourg, 1981); Sergei A. Romanenko, "National Autonomy in Russia and Austria-Hungary: A Comparative Analysis of Finland and Croatia-Slavonia," in *Nationalism and Empire* (New York: St. Martin's Press, 1992). On cooperation

Ustaša forces in the puppet Independent State of Croatia did perpetrate massive atrocities against Serbs and others; but they were a marginal party imposed by the Germans and Italians after the highly popular Croatian Peasant Party refused to collaborate. The Ustaša policy of genocide against Serbs, its use of Muslims to carry out this policy in Bosnia, combined with its authoritarian repression of Croat and Muslim dissent, rapidly alienated most of the state's population.[3] And while the Serbian nationalist Četnik forces perpetrated atrocities against Muslims in Bosnia, most Serbs in Croatia and Bosnia joined the multi-ethnic communist led partisan forces, rather than the purely nationalistic Četniks. Thus the image of "ethnic groups" in conflict even during World War II must be seen as part of a selective, ideological construct in which "ethnic groups" are portrayed as actors by nationalist politicians and historians. And while there certainly was conflict defined as ethnic in the twentieth century, it was relatively new and had roots beyond attachment to ethnic identities.

The remainder of this chapter will examine the state of Yugoslav society in the 1980s. The data used in this chapter comes from social science polling undertaken by Yugoslav sociologists and political scientists in the late 1980s and early 1990s. In terms of methodology, this polling data is as relevant and valid as any social science data in the West. Some critics claim that polling in Yugoslavia cannot be considered valid because people were not willing to express their true opinions, giving instead the answers that were officially acceptable. What is interesting about the results reported in these polls, however, is that they show considerable variation across place and region in questions about ethnic relations and political attitudes. People were fully willing to express their views that ethnic relations were not perfect when they had those perceptions, and the responses were different in different parts of the country, reflecting different experiences. The results, including the variations, were also consistent across time and are backed up by such data as intermarriage rates. Anecdotally too, the polling results reflect social realities at this point in time. So while these polls have the drawbacks associated with any social science polling, they are at a minimum indicative of the state of Yugoslav society at the time they were conducted.

---

in the first Yugoslavia between Serb and Croat parties in Croatia against the central government in Belgrade, see Ljubo Boban, *Svetozar Pribićević u opoziciji (1928–1936)* (Zagreb: Institut za hrvatsku povijest, 1973); Drago Roksandić, *Srbi u Hrvatskoj od 15. Stoljeća do naših dana* (Zagreb: Vjesnik, 1991).

   [3] Fikreta Jelić-Butić, *Ustaše i Nezavisna Država Hrvatska* (Zagreb: Sveučilišna Naklada Liber, 1978).

What becomes clear from this data is that the image of ethnic hatreds seething below the surface is an inaccurate one. In fact, ethnic relations in the most ethnically mixed regions of the country tended to be very good. Indeed, the main priority for the vast majority of the population throughout the country was not issues related to ethnicity, but rather the desire for changes in the political and economic system that would bring about increases in the standard of living and in basic economic security in everyday life. As pointed out, I am not arguing that this kind of data shows Yugoslavia to have been a "multicultural paradise." Clearly there were conflicts and issues that were contentious and would have to be resolved. In addition, the polls show a minority of people who were mainly concerned with "ethnic" issues and who did perceive the situation to be negative. What this data indicates is that the large majority of people had very different perceptions and priorities and that the violence that was seen in Croatia and Bosnia in the 1990s was not the reflection of the sentiments or preferences of the wider population.

This chapter documents those concerns and priorities. It looks at appeals made by nationalist parties that won the 1990 elections in order to show problems with narratives that portrayed the wars as the result of nationalist hatreds and mobilizations.

The general story told in the West about the wars is that, as the repression of the communist era lifted, people throughout eastern Europe could finally express their true interests, sentiments, and values. When democratic elections were held in the various Yugoslav republics, nationalists were elected to power; the nationalists proceeded to go to war to create ethnically homogeneous states. These wars were therefore expressions of the wider population's sentiments, policies that reflected the goals of the various ethnic groups that lived in these territories. Variants of this story focus either on ancient ethnic hatreds as the driving force behind the violence, or on evil leaders who push buttons and manipulate people in order to mobilize their support. The population is seen as having deeply ingrained and easily manipulated sentiments of hatred and desire for ethnic purity. This unproblematic focus on ethnic groups and their purported interests dominates the accounts of even those who were calling for the continued existence of a multiethnic Bosnia.[4]

A key theme of this narrative is that much of the violence was due either to the hatreds Serbs, Croats, Muslims, etc. had for others (because of historical memories and experiences, for example) or else it was the result of

---

[4] Richard Holbrooke, *To End a War* (New York: Modern Library, 1998), 365–366.

manipulation by extremist politicians in Serbia, Croatia, and Bosnia. Here, the existence of Serb populations in Croatia, Bosnia, and Kosovo (and Croats in Bosnia and Serbia) is seen as having provided the opportunity for these politicians to instrumentalize them, to mobilize them into violent conflict. Serbia's ruling class is thus portrayed as having tapped into preexisting sentiments, resentments, and fears as a way to mobilize Serbs in Serbia, Croatia, Bosnia, and Kosovo to destroy Croatia and Bosnia and to maintain control over Kosovo, and thereby to construct an enlarged Serbian state; a very similar story is told about Croatia. Such stories usually assume that these destabilizing effects were a natural consequence of the existence of what are portrayed as "minorities" throughout the former Yugoslavia and especially in Croatia, Bosnia-Herzegovina, and Kosovo. In other words, if there had not been Serbs (or Croats, or Albanians) in those places, there would not have been violent conflict.

Comparing these narratives to actual events on the ground provides a striking contrast, however. In both Croatia and Bosnia, survey data from the late 1980s show very high levels of positive coexistence, little evidence of resentments or suppressed violence, and the growing attractiveness, especially among young people in Bosnia, of a Yugoslav identity. Serbs in both places were among the strongest proponents of peaceful coexistence. In short, there is very little evidence from the ethnically diverse communities of these republics that would indicate that within the next few years massive violence undertaken in the name of Serbs or Croats would wrack the region and tear apart the most ethnically heterogeneous communities.

This does not deny that some people did identify as Croats, Serbs, or Muslims, nor does it deny that the level of such identification ranged from strong to weak. What this evidence does do is problematize the *meanings* that have been attributed to these identifications by elites claiming to act in the name of various groups, by Western scholars and policy makers who focus on ethnic groups and their interrelationships as the cause of the wars.

Croatia

The nationalist policies of the Croatian government between 1990 and 1999, the wars in Croatia in 1991 and 1995, and the 1993–94 war in the Croat-inhabited parts of Bosnia-Herzegovina have been characterized in Western media coverage and in much of the scholarly work on the conflicts as the result of ethnic hatreds, either ancient ones or ones more recently constructed and mobilized. The main focus has been on Croatia as a land awash in nationalism and ethnic resentments between Croats and Serbs. From this perspective, Croatia was just waiting to explode into nationalist bloodshed and provided fertile ground for ethnic entrepreneurs who mobilized Croats and Serbs (and in Bosnia, Croats and Muslims) into bloody warfare.[5]

Yet empirical survey data from the late 1980s and early 1990 do not support such a view. Indeed, in the case of Croatia, by the late 1980s the focus of the wider population was on the desire for a shift to a liberal democratic political system and economic reforms. By 1989 Croatia was one of the most liberal and open places in Yugoslavia. Croatia's voters showed "a comparatively high level of democratic attitudes,"[6] and it was well placed for the kinds of fundamental changes seen in neighboring Hungary. Yugoslav Prime Minister Ante Marković, who was calling for fundamental political and economic reforms, was popular in Croatia as in the rest of Yugoslavia, reflecting that population's main concerns with those issues.[7] The policies of the ruling League of Communists of Croatia (SKH) regarding Serbs were clearly focused on positive relations; in the 1990 elections about one-half of Croatia's Serbs did vote for the reformed SKH, while only 13.5 percent voted for the Serb nationalist party. Nor was there any evidence that ethnic hatreds or tensions were seething just below the surface, just waiting to be mobilized by Croat and Serb nationalists. The ethnically mixed regions of the republic were among those with the highest levels of positive coexistence and very low levels of intolerance.[8] These

[5] *New York Times* coverage of the war in Croatia, January–December 1991, strongly emphasized "ancient hatreds" and the "traditional enmities" between Serbs and Croats. See also Misha Glenny, *The Fall of Yugoslavia: The Third Balkan War* (New York: Penguin, 1992); Robert Kaplan, *Balkan Ghosts: A Journey through History* (New York: Random House, 1994). For devastating critiques of Kaplan's book, see Henry R. Cooper's review in *Slavic Review* (Fall 1993): 592–593; and Brian Hall, "Rebecca West's War," *New Yorker*, April 15, 1996, 74–83.

[6] Mirjana Kasapović, *Izborni i stranački sustav Republike Hrvatske*. See results of empirical research survey "Izbori '92" undertaken in July 1992 before the 1992 parliamentary elections by political scientists from the University of Zagreb's Faculty of Political Science, using questions and methodologies of Western political scientists. Their sample of 2,369 in 20 electoral districts included 36 municipalities (113–119). The results showed a very striking set of attitudes that are fully in line with liberal democratic values and expectations.

[7] On the popularity of Marković and of his policies as prime minister, see Mihajlovski and Bahtijarević and Milas in *Jugoslavija na kriznoj prekretnici*, ed. Bačević et al. (Belgrade, 1991), 59, 65 respectively.

[8] Randy Hodson, Garth Massey, and Duško Sekulić, "National Tolerance in the Former Yugoslavia," in *Global Forum Series Occasional Papers*, Center for International Studies, no. 93–1.5 (Durham, N.C.: Duke University, December 1993).

regions had high levels of intermarriage,[9] and people in the republic as a whole, both Croats and Serbs, indicated a very positive assessment of inter-ethnic relations in their own communities, as well as a striking lack of perception that the rights of their own groups were threatened. For example, in a survey carried out in Croatia at the end of 1989, 66 percent of Croat respondents characterized relations in their own community as very good or mainly good; 25.5 percent as average; and only 8.7 percent as mainly bad or very bad. Among Serbs the numbers were even more positive: 72.1 percent as very good or mainly good; 23.4 percent as average; and 3.5 percent as mainly bad or very bad. When asked about perceptions of threats to national rights of their own groups, Croats responded 82.7 percent no; Serbs 87.3 percent no; when asked about whether mixed nationality marriages were more unstable than others, 72 percent of Croats disagreed totally or partially (those disagreeing totally rose from 45 percent in 1984 to 62.6 percent in 1989); among Serbs, 86.6 percent (disagreeing totally rising from 60.2 percent in 1984 to 77.6 percent in 1989). As the researchers pointed out, based on this survey, "At the end of 1989 signs of tensions between nationalities in Croatia were hardly discernible. . . . Croats, Serbs, and Yugoslavs were convinced of the possibility of a life together unburdened by considerations of national similarities or differences."[10] Indeed, by late 1989, despite the attempts by Belgrade to purvey an image of ethnic hatreds and to use the issue of Kosovo to undermine local communist party leaderships over the previous several years, the large majority of people in Croatia perceived relations *within their own communities* as very positive.[11] They did, however, perceive that relations between nationalities at the level of *Yugoslavia* were mostly bad (77.6 percent as very bad or mostly bad).

[9] For example, throughout the 1980s 29 percent of Serbs living in Croatia took Croat spouses. See the annual *Demografska statistika* (Belgrade: Savezni zavod za statistiku), 1979–1989, Table 5–3. Given the distribution of the Serb population, it is likely that in the most heterogeneous regions of the republic that figure was closer to 50 percent.

[10] Nikola Dugandžija, "Domet Nacionalne Zaokuplenosti," in *Položaj Naroda i Medunacionalni odnosi u Hrvatskoj*, ed. Štefica Bahtijarević and Mladen Lazić (Zagreb: Institute for Social Research, 1991), 101–114; an English translation of a more detailed version of this paper is found in "The Level of National Absorption," in *Croatian Society on the Eve of Transition*, ed. Katarina Prpić, Blaženka Despot, and Nikola Dugandžija (Zagreb: Institute for Social Research, 1993), 135–152. Compared to similar questions about "ethnic distance" conducted in western Europe, Croatia was an island of peaceful coexistence. See Ana Dević, "Nationalism and Powerlessness of Everyday Life: A Sociology of Discontents in Yugoslavia Before the Breakup." The paper was presented at "Living with the Beast: Everyday Life in Authoritarian Serbia," Clark University, Worcester, Mass., April 2000.

[11] Dugandžija, 138, 136.

This marked disparity in perceptions about interethnic relations is a vivid illustration of the fact that while political elites can attempt to construct peoples' views about ethnicity from above, such attempts have their effect mostly in perceptions about such relations *outside of* their own lived experiences. The impact on their perceptions of their own communities is minimal. As will be seen, this also explains why these elites had to resort to violence; it was the only way to directly impinge on the everyday lived experiences of these communities in a way that had the potential to change such perceptions.

Likewise, in a question about perceptions of equality and inequality of treatment of Serbs and Croats, what is striking is that despite the fact that this was a major element in the political propaganda of the various sides (this included the 1990 electoral campaign), two-thirds of Croats and three-fifths of Serbs in Croatia believed that Croats and Serbs were treated equally or disadvantaged equally. Another poll showed that 80 percent of Serbs and Croats did not agree that members of the other group were privileged. For example, even among HDZ sympathizers, 43 percent believed Croats and Serbs were treated equally (31 percent believed that they were treated equally, 12 percent believed they were equally disadvantaged), while 56 percent believed Serbs were privileged. In the other, moderately nationalist party, KNS, 43 percent saw equal treatment, 25 percent saw equally held back (total 68 percent equally treated), and 30 percent saw Serbs as privileged. Among sympathizers of the SKH-SDP, 79 percent saw equal treatment, 9 percent that both were held back. SDS members were most likely to perceive privilege: 71 percent saw Croats as privileged, only 15 percent as equal, 11 percent as equally held back. Overall, by ethnicity, 65 percent of Croats saw relations as equal or equally held back, and 60 percent of Serbs held the same views. Clearly, among the 34 percent of Croats and 39 percent of Serbs who saw the other group as privileged there was a constituency for a politics of resentment. But even here there is no indication that such resentment would naturally and logically lead to violent conflict.[12] Statistically there was no difference in the socio-professional situation of Serbs and Croats in Croatia, and indeed, one researcher noted

---

[12] Findings from survey research carried out prior to the 1990 elections by members of the Faculty of Political Science, University of Zagreb, sited in Šiber, "Nacionalna," 108–109.

In a similar survey taken at about the same time by the Institute for Social Research of Zagreb University, 79.3 percent of Croats did not perceive Serbs as having a privileged status in Croatia, while 20.7 percent did perceive that; among Serbs, 79.4 percent did not see Croats as privileged, while 20.6 percent did; among Yugoslavs, the figures were 92.2 percent no for Croats, 98.4 percent no for Serbs. Dugandžija (1991), 106; (1993), 141.

that "it can be concluded that the socio-demographic and spatial charac-
teristics contribute little to the differentiation of Croats and Serbs as specific population groups in Croatia."[13] Only 17.3 percent of Croats and 12.7
percent of Serbs felt a sense of threat to their own national rights, and
for Croats it is likely that most of them saw the threat coming from Belgrade, not from local Serbs.[14] When asked in May–June 1990 where they
most markedly felt inequality in Yugoslavia, 16 percent of respondents in
Croatia responded "in relations between different nationalities," equal to
the percentage who listed "in relations between republics," and behind
those who gave "in relations between those with political power and regular citizens" (21 percent), and "in relations between rich and poor" (19
percent).[15] This is especially striking, because, as will be seen in subsequent chapters, by this time Milošević and his allies had been provoking
conflict and violence in Croatia for the previous several years.

On the question of whether there should be separate schools or separate
curriculums or partly separate curriculums for Serb and Croat children, 86.5
percent of Croats and 94.2 percent of Serbs responded that "any differences
are undesirable"—that is, they favored common schools and a single, uni-
form curriculum.[16] And while for HDZ sympathizers the position of Croatia in Yugoslavia was the most significant policy issue (84 percent), for
sympathizers of all other major parties, this issue, though important, was
seen as less pressing than the deteriorating economic situation, which
was the priority concern for supporters of SKH, KNS, and Socialist Alliance.[17]
This is not to say that these issues were not important; rather, it merely indi-

---

[13] Maria Oliveira-Roca, "Demografski profil hrvata, srba i jugoslavena u Hrvatskoj:
Razlike u prostornom razmještaju i socio-demografskoj strukturi ekonomski aktivnih
hrvata, srba i jugoslavena u Hrvatskoj u 1989," in *Položaj Naroda i Međunacionalni odnosi
u Hrvatskoj*, ed. Štefica Bahtijarević and Mladen Lazić (Zagreb: Institute for Social Research,
1991), 253, 263. Research done in late 1989 by Institute for Social Research, Zagreb University. Error significance 1 percent.

[14] Dugandžija (1991), 105; (1993), 140.

[15] Bahtijarević and Milas, "Reakcija javnosti na mjere SIV-a," 99.

[16] Only 1.3 percent of Croats and 0.0 percent of Serbs called for separate schools and separate curriculums; 5.9 percent of Croats and 2.2 percent of Serbs called for joint schools and
only partially different curriculum. Research carried out in November 1989 by the Institute
for Social Research of the Univ. of Zagreb. Milorad Pupovac, "Stavovi govornika hrvatskog
ili srpskog prema jeziku i pismu," in *Položaj Naroda i Međunacionalni odnosi u Hrvatskoj*, ed.
Štefica Bahtijarević and Mladen Lazić (Zagreb: Institute for Social Research, 1991), 178–179.

[17] For SDS sympathizers, Kosovo was the priority issue for 66 percent; for Greens, the
environment was the priority issue, at 96 percent. Šiber, 144.

In another survey, in which respondents were asked in the ten days prior to the 1990 elections to name the top three problems of Croatian politics, the top choices were "peace and
security" (55.5 percent); social justice and security (42.5 percent); integration of Croatia into
to the EU (42.5 percent); "national equality" (34.1 percent). "Croatian independence" was

cates that despite the sense of threat from Milošević's policies, and the attempts to polarize the situation, most peoples' understanding of these issues were very much influenced by their own personal experiences, their interactions in their everyday lives, rather than by attempts from above to construct a quite different sense of ethnic groups and ethnicity.

What is particularly significant about these findings on the state of Croatian society is that they represent opinion at a time when Milošević had been actively putting pressure on Croatia: attempting to divide Serbs and Croats by filling the airwaves and Serbia-based newspapers with provocative and negative images meant to undermine coexistence, and using various allies to undermine and destabilize the SKH leadership and Croatia itself. This was an atmosphere that had been created *prior* to the coming to power of the nationalist HDZ. Nevertheless, the social realities in ethnically heterogeneous communities remained the dominant basis of most people's views of interethnic relations. And this reality was a far cry from the images of ethnic hatreds and violence that have dominated Western analyses.

What is also striking is the amount of support expressed for the reform program of Yugoslav federal prime minister Ante Marković and his government (the Federal Executive Council, SIV), especially given Marković's basically anti-nationalist, liberal, and forward looking position. In a survey undertaken in May and June 1990 (at the time when the nationalist HDZ had just won elections in the republic), 70 percent of respondents in Croatia saw the SIV's reforms as the "correct solution for the country to get out of the crisis,"[18] 51 percent fully agreed with Marković's attitudes, while 38 percent partly agreed.[19] On a scale from 1 to 5, respondents in Croatia rated the SIV at 4.21; 83 percent said they had full confidence in Marković and the SIV.[20]

Bosnia-Herzegovina

The population structure in Bosnia-Herzegovina was even more heterogeneous than in Croatia. Only 18 of the 106 municipalities of the republic

---

among the top three for only 29.3 percent of respondents. Anketa istraživanja IZBORI 1990, 1992, 1995, projekt "Izbori, stranke i parlament 1990–2000" (Polling research project Elections 1990, 1992, 1995), Faculty of Political Science, Zagreb University, on web site "Rezultati longitudinalnog istraživanja političkih stavova birača 1990–1995.," at <http://media.fpzg.hr/hip/stavovi.htm>.

[18] Mihajlovski, "Reakcija javnosti na mjere SIV-a" (65).

[19] Ibid., 59.

[20] Ibid., 62.

had populations that were 80 percent or more of a single group, and the combined population of these 18 municipalities amounted to less than 10 percent of Bosnia-Herzegovina's total population.[21] So it is not surprising that as in Croatia, so too in Bosnia-Herzegovina similar figures prevailed in terms of attitudes toward ethnicity and political priorities.

In surveys of "ethnic distance," Bosnia had one of the lowest levels in all of Yugoslavia (the only place with lower levels was multiethnic Vojvodina), and in the words of one study from that period, "Serbs from Bosnia-Herzegovina and Croatia tend to distance themselves from other ethnic groups much less than their co-ethnics in Serbia proper."[22] In other words, the experience of living with others led Serbs in Bosnia to have a very different and more positive view of ethnic pluralism than Serbs in homogeneous Serbia.

In a 1989 survey of young people in Bosnia, the large majority of youth, 77 percent, disagreed with the statement that "one always needs to be cautious" toward others of different nationality. Similarly, 75.1 percent agreed either fully or mostly with the assertion that "division into nations is harmful or pointless."[23] Social science polling also showed that members of the Bosnian League of Communists were much more likely to have nationalist feelings than the wider population: 29 percent versus 8 percent.[24] In the same survey, undertaken in November 1989, 80 percent of the wider population surveyed considered interethnic relations in the places where they lived to be positive, and 66 percent saw interethnic relations in Bosnia-Herzegovina as the most stable in Yugoslavia. When asked whether ethnicity should be taken into account when choosing marriage partners, 80 percent of Serbs, 77 percent of Muslims, 93.4 percent of Yugoslavs, and 66 percent of Croats replied negatively.[25]

[21] These included Serb-majority municipalities of Bosansko Grahovo, Titovo Drvar, Šekovići, Bileća, Čelinac, Laktaši, Ljubinje, and Srbac; Croat-majority Grude, Lištica, Ljubuški, Posušje, Čitluk, Duvno, and Neum; and Muslim-majority Velika Kladuša, Cazin, and Živinice. The combined population of these municipalities amounted to 9.8 percent of the total population of Bosnia-Herzegovina. (Based on 1981 and 1991 census returns.)

[22] Hodson et al., "National Tolerance." See also Dević, "Nationalism and Powerlessness of Everyday Life."

[23] Ibrahim Bakić, "Stavovi mladih Bosne i Hercegovine prema naciji i religiji," *Sveske* 24–25 (1989).

[24] Report on survey undertaken by Ibrahim Bakić and Ratko Dunđerović, Institute for the Study of National Relations in Bosnia-Herzegovina, "Građani Bosne i Hercegovine o međunacionalnim odnosima," *Oslobođenje*, March 22, 1990, 2.

[25] Ibid. Although a regional breakdown is not given, it seems likely that the negative responses would tend to come from people in the most ethnically homogeneous regions. Thus the fact that one third of Croats in Bosnia lived in areas where Croats formed the overwhelming majority of the population may be reflected in the higher negative figure among Croats than among others in Bosnia.

In another social science poll undertaken in May and June 1990, when asked to evaluate interethnic relations in their own republics, in Bosnia 24 percent responded good, 56 percent satisfactory, and 16 percent bad.[26] But in a different poll, when asked to evaluate these relations in the community where they live, 90 percent responded "good" (42.8 percent very good, 48.1 percent good), while only 4 percent responded "bad." When asked the same question about their workplaces, 80.7 percent responded positively (41.0 percent very good, 39.7 percent good), and only 4 percent negatively.[27] Again, this is a reflection of the difference between lived experience and representations being purveyed by elites.

At least some of this Yugoslav sentiment was due to the fact that in 1981 15.8 percent of children listed in the census of Bosnia-Herzegovina

Also of interest is a poll undertaken in January 1990, in which 25 percent of respondents in Bosnia-Herzegovina gave their nationality as "Yugoslav."[28] Even more striking is that, in a different poll, 33 percent of young people in Bosnia-Herzegovina declared themselves Yugoslav, representing an equal proportion from each of the three main national groupings in the republic, while 81.6 percent agreed with the statement that "I am Yugoslav and cannot give priority to feeling of some other belonging." This is in line with other findings that document the rise of a pan-Yugoslav sensibility and identification among younger people throughout Yugoslavia in the 1980s, as manifested in part through such cultural phenomena as Yugoslav rock music.[29] Indeed, especially instructive in this regard is the fact that the various republic-level communist parties condemned this growing attachment to a Yugoslav identity, while "several younger authors expressed their outrage at the increasingly hostile attitudes of the Party toward growing expressions of 'Yugoslavism.'"[30]

At least some of this Yugoslav sentiment was due to the fact that in 1981 15.8 percent of children listed in the census of Bosnia-Herzegovina

---

[26] Miljević and Poplašen, "Dehomogenizacija političke kulture," 149.

[27] Ibrahim Bakić and Ratko Dunđerović, *Gradani Bosne i Hercegovine o medunacionalnim odnosima* (Sarajevo: Institut za proučavanje nacionalnih odnosa, 1990), 25, cited in Miljević and Poplašen, 149.

[28] Report on survey undertaken by Kasim Trnka, Džemal Sokolović and Ratko Dunđerović, Institute of the CKSKBH for study of nationalities relations, in *Oslobodenje*, March 10, 1990, 2.

[29] Indeed, it was exactly for that reason that the "nationalist" regimes targeted the Yugoslav rock scene. For the case of the SPS in Serbia, and for a description of the Yugoslav rock scene, see Eric Gordy, *The Culture of Power in Serbia: Nationalism and the Destruction of Alternatives* (University Park: Pennsylvania State University Press, 1999); see also chapter 7 of Sabrina Ramet, *Balkan Babel: The Disintegration of Yugoslavia from the Death of Tito to the War for Kosovo* (Boulder, Colo.: Westview, 1999).

[30] Dević, "Nationalism and the Powerlessness of Everyday Life."

had parents of different nationalities.[31] That same year 16.8 percent of all marriages in the republic were mixed marriages; one demographer notes that this means that, given the average household size in the republic, "at least one half of the population of Bosnia-Herzegovina has interethnic family relations."[32]

That ethnic national issues were not the overwhelming concern of most people is also seen in the very strong support for federal prime minister Ante Marković. Indeed, a social science survey undertaken in mid-1990 showed Marković and his policies had the strongest support exactly in Bosnia-Herzegovina.[33] When asked whether they agreed or disagreed with the positions of Ante Marković, 72 percent of respondents in Bosnia agreed fully, 22 percent agreed partially. Ninety-three percent of Bosnian respondents expressed confidence in him; this result was repeated in a newspaper poll in which respondents were asked, "who is doing the most to move Yugoslavia forward?" In Bosnia-Herzegovina 92 percent responded Ante Marković (only 10 percent gave Milošević).[34]

This support extended to Marković's policies: the social science polling found that 79 percent of Bosnia respondents agreed that "the reforms which are being implemented and proposed by the SIV are the correct resolution to get the country out of crisis" (4 percent disagreed and 17 percent responded "don't know"). Bosnia also, along with Croatia, had the strongest support for market orientation: when asked, "do you accept a market orientation?" 66 percent responded "fully," 10 percent responded "partly, without market in labor," 18 percent responded "don't know." Fully 72 percent of Bosnian respondents also supported giving the federal government (SIV) greater legal powers (72 percent supported, 16 percent opposed), while 65 percent supported the idea of the SIV setting up its own political party (20 percent opposed), much higher than any other republic.[35] When asked where they perceive social inequality, 13 percent of Bosnian respondents listed "relations between various nationalities," the same percentage as for "in relations between rich and poor," and behind "in relations between republics" (23 percent), in relations between

---

[31] Srđan Bogosavljević, "Bosna i Hercegovina u ogledalu statistike," in *Bosna i Hercegovina između rata i mira*, ed. Bogosavljević et al. (Belgrade: Institut društvenih nauka, 1992), 40.

[32] Ibid.

[33] Reported in *Jugoslavija na kriznoj prekretnici* (Belgrade: Centar za politikološka istraživanja i javno mnenje, Institut društvenih nauka, Univerzitet u Beogradu, 1991).

[34] Reported in *Borba*, May 22, 1990, 11.

[35] Bahtijarević, "Reakcije javnosti . . . ," 76.

people with political power (*moćnika*) and regular citizens (18 percent), and in relations between employed and unemployed (14 percent).[36]

These results are quite informative because Marković's priority was very much political and economic reform, and he was anti-nationalist in orientation—"ethnic" issues had virtually no place in his program—with the result that he was actually the target of vicious attacks on the part of "nationalists" in Croatia, Bosnia, and Serbia. Yet Marković's popularity in Bosnia, in particular, was enormous. This result is reinforced by another poll taken in the spring of 1990 in which 74 percent of respondents supported the decision by Bosnian leadership to forbid the formation of "nationally oriented parties."[37] Along the same lines, in a different poll taken in 14 places in Bosnia-Herzegovina, 71 percent of respondents opposed the formation of "national institutions and national parties in B-H," and 94 percent favored "a sovereign Bosnia-Herzegovina with existing external and internal borders, within the framework of Yugoslavia."[38] In another poll taken in May 1990 in Banja Luka, Mostar, and Sarajevo, the vast majority of respondents favored Bosnia-Herzegovina remaining within the Yugoslav Federation. This included 91 percent in the municipality of Banja Luka (whose population was 55 percent Serb, 15 percent Muslim, 15 percent Croat, and 12 percent Yugoslav); 86 percent in Sarajevo (49 percent Muslim, 30 percent Serb, 11 percent Yugoslav, 7 percent Croat); and 83 percent in Mostar (34 percent Croat, 35 percent Muslim, 19 percent Serb, 10 percent Yugoslav). Only 2.4 percent of respondents in Banja Luka and Sarajevo and 1 percent in Mostar were in favor of Bosnia separating from Yugoslavia.[39] In a poll of Bosnian students taken in November 1991 (that is, when war was raging in Croatia and nationalist parties were already moving toward a de facto division of Bosnia), 67.7 percent opposed the idea of regionalization of the republic along ethnic lines—95.5 percent of Muslims, 72.4 percent of Croats, and 67.0 percent of Serbs.[40]

---

[36] Bahtijarević and Milas, "Reakcija javnosti na mjere SIV-a," 99.

[37] The poll was taken in the three largest cities in Bosnia, but the results were still striking: in Banja Luka, 81 percent of respondents agreed; in Sarajevo, 72 percent; in Mostar, 68 percent. Poll in *Danas*, May 22, 1990, cited in Vladimir Goati, "Politički život Bosne i Hercegovine 1989–1992," in *Bosna i Hercegovina izemedu rata i mira*, 53.

[38] *Nedjelja*, May 20, 1990, 25, 26, cited in Dušan Janjić, "Građanski rat i mogućnosti mira u Bosni i Hercegovini," in *Bosna i Hercegovina izemedu rata i mira*, 112. Again, on the latter question support was found throughout the country in places with Serb, Muslim, and Croat majorities: eastern Bosnia and Semberija, 83 percent; in central Bosnia, 73 percent; in Herzegovina, 67 percent.

[39] "Strah od vlastitih nacija," *Danas*, May 22, 1990, 24, 25. Cited in Janjić.

[40] Ibrahim Bakić and Ratko Dunđerović, *Stavovi studentske omladine u BiH o medunacionalnim odnosima i društvenim promjenama* (Sarajevo: Institut za pružanje nacionalnih odnosa, 1991). Cited in Janjić, "Građanski rat," 114.

Serbia

We have seen that in the two republics that were to be the sites of the most violent conflicts and ethnic cleansing, there is little if any indication in the years prior to the war that such violence would take place. This is especially important given the ethnic heterogeneity of the regions that were struck by violence. As will be seen in subsequent chapters, this apparent puzzle is explained by the fact that the violence was imposed on those mixed communities from outside, through the policies of a minority of political elites in Zagreb and in Belgrade. But was the war the result or reflection of hatreds or sentiments of Serbs in Serbia against non-Serbs?

The situation in Serbia differed from other republics in a number of ways. First, the only sustained violence that took place in Serbia occurred in the province of Kosovo, and even then, not until the late 1990s; "Inner Serbia" itself (Serbia without its provinces of Kosovo and Vojvodina), as well as Vojvodina, were spared the kind of violence seen in Croatia and Bosnia. In addition, Inner Serbia was one of the most ethnically homogeneous parts of Yugoslavia, with 87.8 percent Serbs according to the 1991 census. The question to be asked here is not the degree to which ethnic relations on the ground in Inner Serbia or Vojvodina caused the violence. Indeed, there was relatively little interaction between Serbs and others in Inner Serbia, while Vojvodina, which is much more diverse (56.8 percent Serbs, 16.9 percent Hungarians, 8.7 percent Yugoslavs, 3.7 percent Croats, and others) was one of the most peacefully coexistent places in the former Yugoslavia. Rather, we are faced with the image of Serbs in Serbia as driving the wars in Croatia and Bosnia; here, rather than hatreds waiting to explode in the ethnically heterogeneous regions in Croatia and Bosnia-Herzegovina, the violence is portrayed as an expression of the nationalism of Serbs in Serbia itself. Yet once again, there is little evidence to support the contention that violence, ethnic cleansing, and a nationalist state were the top priorities for people in Serbia.

Thus the fact that 20 percent of respondents in Inner Serbia found interethnic relations in their own republic good, 20 percent as satisfactory, and 55 percent as bad or very bad probably reflects the fact that most considered Kosovo to be part of Serbia, and the media had portrayed these relations as quite negative by 1990; asked about relations at the Yugoslavia level, 56 percent of inner Serbian respondents responded "very bad." In Vojvodina the response was 41 percent good, 36 percent satisfactory, 15 percent bad or very bad.[41] Again, as elsewhere, the impressions of relations at levels

[41] Miljević and Poplašen, "Dehomogenizacija političke kulture," 153.

higher than those experienced in everyday life are very heavily influenced by media coverage, which in this period was very much emphasizing the negative.

On Ante Marković, 44 percent in inner Serbia, 54 percent in Vojvodina "fully agree" with Marković's policies; 41 percent and 35 percent partially agreed.[42] When asked if their opinions of Marković had improved or gotten worse, 56 percent responded improved, 3 percent gotten worse, 26 percent unchanged; in Vojvodina: 53 percent improved, 2 percent worsened, 34 percent remained the same. Inner Serbian respondents also gave the SIV the highest rating of any republic, 5.26 on a scale of 1 to 5 (respondents were given the option of giving higher ratings than 5), while respondents in Vojvodina gave 4.78. In inner Serbia, fully 19 percent gave the SIV a rating of 8.[43] When asked if they would give the SIV and Marković their vote of confidence, 81 percent of respondents in inner Serbia replied positively; the figure was 87 percent in Vojvodina. Sixty-four percent in Inner Serbia saw the SIV/Marković reforms as the right solution to get out of the crisis, 32 percent responded "don't know" (in Vojvodina: 74 percent "yes," 24 percent "don't know").[44] Respondents also overwhelmingly (74 percent in Serbia, 81 percent in Vojvodina) identified "interethnic and inter-republic conflicts" as the biggest threat to the success of the Marković reforms. (The next most popular answer was social conflicts, at 8 percent and 5 percent). Fifty-eight percent believed that giving the SIV more power would enable faster and more effective implementation of economic reform (75 percent in Vojvodina), 21 percent said no, 20 percent don't know—about the same level as Croatia (in Vojvodina, 13 percent no, 15 percent don't know—about the same level as Bosnia).[45] When asked to give their perception of "where do you most markedly feel inequality in Yugoslavia," respondents in inner Serbia put "in relations of various nationalities" in fifth place (13 percent), after "in relations between individual republics" (21 percent), "in relations between people with political power (*moćnika*) and regular citizens" (21 percent), "in relations between rich and poor" (15 percent), and "in relations between employed and unemployed" (14 percent).[46] At this point a plurality of respondents in Serbia saw the conflict between republics and the powerful in the country as the main cause of inequality, rather than ethnic relations per se.

---

[42] Mihajlovski, "Predstave javnosti o SIV-u," 59.
[43] Ibid., 61.
[44] Bahtijarević, "Reakcija javnosti na mjere SIV-a," 65.
[45] Ibid., 75.
[46] Ibid., 99.

In terms of interethnic relations, in Vojvodina 47 percent said relations in their own workplace were "good," only 1 percent as "bad."[47] No respondents in inner Serbia or Vojvodina gave "very bad" as a response.

Elections and the "Nationalist Parties"

Despite these figures on the state of Croatian, Bosnian and Serbian societies at the end of the 1980s, however, many would point to the victory of nationalist parties in the 1990 elections in these republics as evidence that the wider population nonetheless was motivated mainly by ethnic grievances and sentiments. While the first multi-party elections in Yugoslav republics were indeed won by parties that positioned themselves as nationalist, what is revealing is the kind of appeals that the successful parties made in these elections, and the levels of support they actually received.

In Serbia, in election campaigns from 1990 onward, the ruling communist party (renamed the Socialist Party of Serbia, SPS) under Slobodan Milošević stressed the importance of peace and prosperity and condemned opposition nationalist parties in Serbia as being primitives who sought to drag Serbia into war. This kind of shift was also seen in subsequent election campaigns in Serbia. Rather than ethnic outbidding—a process whereby competing political parties try to outdo each other in nationalist rhetoric and policies in order to appeal to and thus receive the support of the ethnic voters, which spirals to more extreme positions—in these cases we saw a process of ethnic *underbidding*, of parties trying to seem more moderate and less nationalistic, and of the SPS's strategy of ethnic underbidding consistently succeeding.[48] Those parties that were extremist (most notably the Serbian Radical Party, SRS) received a

---

[47] Miljević and Poplašen, "Dehomogenizacija političke kulture," 147–148.

[48] The exception is the 1992 presidential race. Milošević as usual portrayed himself as a peacemaker and concentrated on social and economic issues as well as ethnic ones and was underbid by Milan Panić whose campaign was explicitly anti-nationalist. The regime denied Panić access to television for political advertising—curious from the ethnic outbidding perspective, since the anti-nationalist stance should have served to discredit Panić. In the end, despite enormous disadvantages, including a campaign limited to two weeks and being labeled a CIA agent, Panić received about one half the vote according to exit polls, although the regime's "official" figures, very clearly doctored, gave him only 35 percent. On the details of this strategy of ethnic underbidding, see V. P. Gagnon Jr., "Ethnic Conflict as Demobilizer: The Case of Serbia," *Institute for European Studies Working Paper*, 96.1 (Ithaca: Institute for European Studies, Cornell University, May 1996). See also chapter 4.

small percentage of the vote.[49] The regime, using its complete control of the mass media, also consistently portrayed the wars as defensive and vehemently denied atrocities; information about the violence against civilians by Serb forces was consistently hidden from the Serbian public. And at a time in 1991 when the Serbian media was filled with images of innocent Serb women and children being slaughtered by fascist Croat Ustaša, between 50 and 80 percent of the young men called up to fight in the war in Croatia avoided serving by going underground or leaving the country. These facts indicate that policies of violence can hardly be qualified as responding to or being driven by the demands of major segments of the Serbian electorate.

Similarly in Croatia, the extremist nationalist party (HSP) consistently received small amounts of votes in elections and support in opinion polls,[50] while the most extremist and nationalistic members of the ruling HDZ were consistently the least popular politicians in the polls. In Croatia, as in Serbia, election campaigns brought about a marked shift to moderation and nonethnic themes on the part of the ruling nationalist party. In 1990, though the HDZ was clearly for reformulating Yugoslavia and distancing from Belgrade, the main spokespeople were mostly moderates (for example Stipe Mesić, one of the founding members of the HDZ and the first HDZ prime minister of Croatia), while the more extremist emigré elements linked to the World War II Ustaša regime were notable by their absence from public forums. The victory of the HDZ in the 1990 elections, though usually interpreted as proof of the overwhelming importance of ethnic solidarity among the Croatian population, in fact indicates a quite different dynamic when looked at closely. Indeed, the HDZ portrayed itself as wanting democracy and peace, and as a moderate nationalist party. In addition, it was the best financed and organized opposition party.

There were two key reasons for the HDZ's success. The first was its campaign strategy, which focused on the threats from Belgrade and on the need for a change in governing parties after 50 years of communist

[49] For example the SRS received 2 percent of the vote in 1990. The notable exception is in the election of 1992, when the SRS received the votes of 19 percent of the electorate; but significantly Belgrade television (controlled by the SPS) was at this time presenting the SRS as a moderate, respectable party. When the regime shifted back to portraying the SRS in its true colors in the 1993 elections, SRS support dropped to 10 percent of the vote.

[50] In 1992, at a time when 25 percent of Croatia's territory was held by Belgrade-backed forces, and after six months of warfare that the ruling party had blamed on "Serbs," the HSP received only 7.3 percent of votes cast; consistently in public opinion polls the HSP's support has ranged between 5 and 10 percentage points.

rule.[51] Indeed, the HDZ in 1990 benefited from the general sentiment throughout the former socialist world that the ruling communist parties should be removed from power after a 50 year monopoly, even if they were now reformist and democratically oriented.[52] Among those who voted for the HDZ in 1990 only 14 percent said they did so because "the SKH does not sufficiently represent the interests of my nation [*narod*]."

Second, the HDZ's victories in 1990 and afterward were based on the winner-take-all electoral rules drawn up by the SKH, and then modified before every election to ensure the HDZ the greatest possible advantage. Thus in the 1990 elections the HDZ won 67.5 percent of the seats in parliament with only 41.8 percent of the votes (31 percent of the eligible voters; 53.5 percent of the votes of Croats who voted, and 45 percent of eligible Croat voters). More strikingly, the SDS, which presented itself as the party of Croatia's Serb population, received the votes of only 13.5 percent of Serb voters; and of these SDS voters, only 27 percent said they voted for the Serb nationalist party, "because the SKH does not sufficiently represent the interests of my nation [*narod*]."

During the Serbian war in Croatia in 1991, the Croatian regime denied the atrocities undertaken by extremist Croat forces linked to the ruling party and portrayed Croats only as innocent victims who were defending themselves against Serbian attacks. During the Croatian war against the Bosnian Muslims in 1993, Croatia's state-controlled media seriously distorted the actions of Croat forces, presented the violence as a defensive war, and denied that Croat forces were carrying out atrocities. And when atrocities of Croatian forces against Muslim civilians became public through

---

[51] Thus SKH leader Ivica Račan noted after the election that "Milošević's aggressive policy was the strongest propaganda for Tudjman." Quoted in Silber and Little, *Yugoslavia: Death of a Nation* (84). For a similar argument see the interview with conservative former head of SKH Stipe Šuvar, "Jugoslavija nije razbijena i neće biti," *Nedeljna Borba,* May 5–6, 1990, 12. In addition, one political analyst noted that the HDZ's "criticism of the [SKH] was more specific and more radical than the other opposition parties." Indeed, even among HDZ voters, when asked why they voted against the SKH, 65 percent responded "the responsibility of the SKH for the crisis and to give the opportunity [to govern] to others," while only 14 percent responded "the SKH does not sufficiently represent the interests of my nation [narod]." Dražen Lalić, "Pohod na Glasače: Analiza sadržaja poruka predizbornih kampanja stranaka u Hrvatskoj 1990, 1992, i 1993 godine," in *Pohod na Glasače: Izbori u Hrvatskoj 1990–1993,* edited by Srdan Vrcan et al. (Split: Puls, 1995), 247–248.

[52] Similarly, in the final days of the 1994 parliamentary campaign, Tudjman struck a very conciliatory and moderate tone. He said that with the war over Croatia could now move to real democracy and stressed the importance of peaceful coexistence with Croatia's Serbs. Regime propaganda also portrayed Croatian forces in terms of merely protecting innocent Croatian civilians from the attacks and atrocities of the extremist Serb leaders in Krajina, and often portrayed Serb civilians there as victims of the extremists.

independent media, HDZ support plummeted until Tudjman became a "peacemaker" and signed the February 1994 Washington Accords ending the war and setting up the Federation of Bosnia and Herzegovina. Similarly, during the invasions of Krajina in May and August 1995, the state-controlled media vehemently denied that Croatian forces had undertaken any atrocities, and constantly repeated that the rights of all Serbs from the region would be fully respected.[53] Once again, rather than a means to appeal to or mobilize the population, policies of provoking violence were hidden from public view and denied. And while the HDZ expected that the Krajina victory would produce an overwhelming electoral victory for it, in fact the results were strikingly disappointing, since the party won only 45 percent of the votes (this included "diaspora voters" in the HDZ-controlled areas of Bosnia-Herzegovina who voted about 95 percent for the HDZ) and lost control of every city in Croatia, including Zagreb, for the first time.

In Bosnia too nationalist parties won the elections of 1990. But prior to the elections, in the spring of 1990, polling indicated that 74 percent of the population supported the decision of the Bosnian leadership to forbid the formation of nationalist parties.[54] Once they were allowed, the platforms of the three main nationalist parties were focused on assuring the rights of each group to its own culture; the emphasis was on cooperation of the three nationalist parties. For example Alija Izetbegović, president of the Bosnian Muslim party (SDA) attended the founding congress of the Bosnian Serb nationalist party (SDS); and Radovan Karadžić, head of the SDS, often publicly referred to Bosnian Muslims as brothers of Bosnia's Serbs. During the election campaign none of the main nationalist parties called for dividing Bosnia or for war, even though by this time violence and extremist Serb and Croat forces in Croatia were pushing Serb refugees into Bosnia.

The 1990 election results themselves were far from clear. A strikingly large number of votes cast—25 percent—were declared invalid. The winner-take-all nature of the election also effectively minimized the seats won

---

[53] Although the occasional extremist newspaper columnist would call for all Serbs to "go home" to Serbia, the overall tone in the television coverage was that Croatian forces were behaving very properly. Atrocities that international investigations said took place against civilians were denied.

[54] *Danas*, 22 May 1990, cited in Vladimir Goati, "Politički život Bosne i Hercegovine 1989–1992," in *Bosna i Hercegovina između rata i mira*, 53. This position was supported in all areas of the country, and is at a minimum an indication that the wider population was not at this point being driven in its political preferences by ethnic considerations; indeed, given the level of support for this anti-nationalist decision, as well as the polling results listed above, a strong case can be made that the major grievances and concerns of the wider population were about nonethnic issues.

by non-nationalist parties (the reform communist party, SK-SDP, and the party of prime minister Ante Marković, the SRSJ); for example, the combined vote for these two parties was over 30 percent in over 20 electoral districts in which neither party won a single seat.[55] As in Croatia, the electoral system gave the nationalist parties a much greater proportion of the seats in Parliament than their share of the vote, and thus disproportionate influence on the subsequent course of events.

And indeed, only *after* the 1990 election did extremists and extremist lines come to the fore in Bosnia itself. For example, moderates who'd won election to local and regional bodies on the SDS line in Bosanska Krajina in northwestern Bosnia were pressured after the election to shift to the extremist line by the SDS leadership, which had very close ties to Belgrade. Those who refused were replaced in elected institutions by extremists. The violence itself began with the work of Serbian paramilitaries sent into Bosnia by the Belgrade regime, as well as the Yugoslav army.[56]

Similarly, the moderate leadership of the Bosnian Croat party (HDZ-BH) called for negotiations and a tolerant approach to national questions. Reflecting the moderate and tolerant position of the large majority of Bosnia's Croats, especially those who lived in ethnically heterogeneous regions outside of Western Herzegovina, the HDZ-BH advocated a single (decentralized) Bosnian state and opposed partition. This moderate leadership, reflecting the preferences of the large majority of Bosnia's Croats, was ousted in autumn of 1992 on order of the HDZ in Croatia, which imposed nationalist extremists from Western Herzegovina upon the HDZ-BH. They also worked to oust non-HDZ Croat leaderships, as well as elected HDZ officials who were seen as too moderate in such places as Vareš, in Central Bosnia. These extremists, working on Zagreb's orders, proceeded to open war in Central Bosnia and perpetrate atrocities against Muslim civilians.[57] Again, the image they constructed was one of innocent Croats

---

[55] Figures cited in Steven L. Burg and Paul S. Shoup, *The War in Bosnia-Herzegovina: Ethnic Conflict and International Intervention* (Armonk, N.Y.: M. E. Sharpe, 1999), 50–51.

[56] See statements by Vojislav Šešelj, head of one of the most notorious such groups; and see similar information on other paramilitary groups (including the Tigers and White Eagles) in Laura Silber and Allen Little, *Yugoslavia: Death of a Nation* (New York: TV Books, 1995).

[57] On the fact that this war was directed from Zagreb, used extremists from Herzegovina imposed on the HDZ-BH, and purposely sought to destroy the multiethnic nature of most of Central Bosnia: personal interview with Josip Manolić, a founder of the HDZ and one of the top leaders at the time of this conflict, July 8, 1996, Zagreb; see also interview with Manolić in *Nacional* (Zagreb), July 5, 1996, 8–9. On atrocities, see Helsinki Watch, *War Crimes in Bosnia-Herzegovina*, vol. 2 (New York: Human Rights Watch, 1994).

as victims of Muslims who began the war, and they consistently and vehemently denied that Croat forces had undertaken any atrocities.

The data presented in this chapter demonstrate that the wars in Croatia and in Bosnia-Herzegovina were not the expression of grassroots political sentiment of the Croatian and Bosnian population. They were also far from being the democratic expression of political and cultural preferences of the wider population in Croatia, Bosnia, or Serbia. This is not to say that relations were totally harmonious, or that Yugoslavia was a paradise of multicultural coexistence. As mentioned earlier, there were issues and conflicts that had to be resolved. But the data presented in this chapter indicates that the violence in Croatia and Bosnia was not an expression of sentiments or relations within the communities that were torn apart by the war. Indeed, as we will see in subsequent chapters, the violence and wars were imposed onto these communities by political and military forces under the control of elites in Belgrade and Zagreb. Indeed, in both Croatia and Bosnia at the end of the 1980s the population was very much focused on their priority of reforming the political and economic system to be more responsive to the interests and needs of the wider population. Ethnic relations, while not perfect, were also not at the top of the agenda, nor were they so strained or overwhelmingly negative as to expect the outbreak of violent conflict along ethnic lines that would take place over the following several years. It was also clearly not the mere existence of "minority" populations in either place that caused the violence. Nor did the elections in 1990 in any of the republics result from an outpouring of popular sentiment for war, violence, or ethnic cleansing.

The following chapter looks at the political conflicts that were occurring within the League of Communists of Yugoslavia and the Leagues of Communists in Serbia and Croatia, with particular attention to how issues of ethnicity and nationalism entered the political dynamics of the period from 1960 to 1990.

CHAPTER 3

POLITICAL CONFLICT IN THE LEAGUE OF COMMUNISTS OF YUGOSLAVIA, 1960s–1989

Beginning in the 1960s and continuing up through the wars of the 1990s, the main axis of conflict in Yugoslavia was the future of the country's socialist-self-management political and economic system. This chapter examines two periods—the first beginning in the 1960s and lasting until the early 1970s; the second, starting with Tito's death in 1980 and continuing up through 1989–1990. In both periods, conservatives wanted to hew to an authoritarian, orthodox Marxist-Leninist line, keep a strong party hand on the economy, minimize reliance on market forces and material incentives, and maintain a centralized political system. Reformers, however, wanted to democratize the party at the micro level, to rely more on market forces in order to rationalize the economy, and to loosen party control and decentralize the country; in short, they sought to move away from Marxist-Leninist orthodoxy and to construct a democratic socialism and a more efficient economic system.[1]

In both periods, a deepening economic crisis brought the ascendance within the ruling party of advocates of fundamental change. In response, conservative forces in the League of Communists of Serbia tried to shift the focus of party debates toward alleged threats directed at Serbia and Serbs throughout Yugoslavia. Conservatives provoked, created, and fueled

---

[1] I will use the terms conservative and reformist in speaking about these two groupings within the League of Communists of Yugoslavia; Latinka Perović, head of the League of Communists of Serbia in the early 1970s, refers to them perhaps more accurately as the "authoritarian" and "democratic" tendencies or currents. Latinka Perović, *Zatvaranje kruga: Ishod Rascepa u SKJ 1971–1972* (Sarajevo: Svjetlost, 1991), 465.

conflict along ethnic lines in order to demobilize and marginalize those push-ing for change, thereby silencing and marginalizing them, as well as their supporters, both in the party and in the wider society. The strategic goal of conservatives was to recentralize the country by revoking the autonomy of the Leagues of Communists not only of the autonomous provinces but also of the other republics, hence recentralizing the League of Communists. Through such a move, the conservatives sought to prevent the changes that were being championed by reformists in Serbia and throughout the coun-try, changes that were proving very popular among the wider population.

At the end of the first period, Tito reversed his initial support for reform and intervened in order to end the process, which satisfied conservative forces. But at the same time, he further decentralized the SKJ and the fed-eration itself. In the second period, the conservatives faced a much graver economic crisis and in the absence of Tito, who could take their side against the ascendant reformists, the conservatives undertook an aggressive and sometimes violent strategy in an attempt to end the existence of sepa-rate republic-level communist party organizations.

Until 1990–1991, the immediate politically relevant population was the party elite. Thus conservative goals up until this point were focused on intra-party conflict. Legitimacy of position and of issues was not depend-ent on obtaining the direct support of the wider population, but rather on a majority of members of various party bodies and of Tito while he was still on the scene. The political strategies of this period were thus not focused mainly on mobilizing the wider population; nor was it necessary to demobilize them in the way that became crucial in the post-1989 period. It is in this period that conservatives who were opposed to and threatened by the officially accepted position of the party—under the doctrine of dem-ocratic centralism open opposition to this position was forbidden—used a strategy that shifted the focus of party debate to threats directed toward socialism, justice, and order within the country in order to end the incip-ient mobilization within the party (as well as outside of it). In the later period, conservatives stage-managed rallies not to mobilize the popula-tion but rather to put pressure through an implicit threat of violence on party leaderships that they wanted removed and replaced.

Round One: The Reforms of the 1960s

In the early 1960s, as an increasingly dysfunctional economic system began to exhibit its shortcomings, the conflict between reformists and conservatives came out into the open. Yugoslavia's socialist self-management system had been very successful in the 1950s and early 1960s. Centralized planning was very effective during the initial period of extensive economic growth; indeed, in that decade Yugoslavia had one of the highest growth rates in the world.[2] But by the early 1960s the need to shift to a more intensive use of resources was becoming clear.[3] In addition, the socio-economic structure of the population had changed, resulting in growing demands of urban, more educated and technically oriented social groups whose views and interests were quite different from the dominant partisan generation that tended to have little formal education and to come from rural backgrounds. This growing middle class had higher expectations not only of living standards but also of the meaningfulness of their work and participation in decisions affecting their lives.

At this time, reformists and technically trained managers within the SKJ proposed a far-reaching reform that pushed the party in the direction of radical change; they tended to be people who had the knowledge and skills that would enable them to succeed in a restructured environment with less party control, and thus whose control over and access to resources would be enhanced in a reformed system. Conservatives, whose access and control over resources was dependent on existing ways in which power was structured, responded to these trends by calling for moves that, in the words of one of the leading Serbian reformists of the time, would "lead to a strengthening of the power of the party over the state and society, and of the party bureaucracy (*aparat*) over the party."[4]

With Tito's backing, in 1965 the reformists' plans were adopted by the SKJ as the party's official policy. When it was revealed in 1966 that party conservatives, in particular those in the intelligence services, were undermining the reform efforts, Tito removed them (including most notably his close colleague Aleksandar Ranković) and reaffirmed his support for the reforms. Thus, beginning in 1966, the reformists in the SKJ dominated the policy process and began a radical restructuring of the Yugoslav political and economic system in earnest.

[2] For example, between 1958 and 1964 Yugoslavia's economy grew 80 percent; industrial production more than doubled; per capita income grew at an annual rate of 7.6 percent. Perović, *Zatvaranje Kruga*, 31.

[3] See for example Miko Tripalo, "Možda smo nešto pogriješili," in *Ljudi iz 1971.–Prekinuta Šutnja*, ed. Milovan Baletić (Zagreb: Vjesnik, 1990), 58–59, reprinted from *Iskra*, May 24 and June 16, 1989, 73, 74.

[4] Latinka Perović, *Zatvaranje kruga*, 7. Indeed, Perović refers to this stance as "the local variant of Stalinism."

At the local level, the reforms were a direct attack on party bureaucrats in enterprises and local administrative positions.[5] The reforms also involved a loosening of party control of society, including tolerance of more open expression of national sentiment.[6] The empowerment of reformist forces at the local level, in turn, served to reinforce the reformist strategy at the macro level, where the reform radically decentralized the federation by giving almost all decision making to the republic-level state organizations. This allowed the top party leadership to bypass the conservatives who dominated the central party and state bureaucracy and to rely instead on the republic-level leaders and central committees, which were dominated by young technocratically oriented reformists. Indeed, this decentralization was enthusiastically supported by all the party leaderships, including the leadership of Serbia.

The conservatives were extremely threatened by these proposals, a threat that was magnified by the popularity within the various central committees and among the wider population of the young republic-level reformist leaders who were championing change.[7] Indeed, the goal of the reforms had been in part to broaden the legitimacy of the communist party by building a base in that wider population; this meant, however, that conservatives were faced with leaders who could mobilize the broader

[5] Economic decisions were no longer to be made according to political criteria by party bureaucrats, but according to market criteria, and Tito himself openly dismissed "propaganda work," the mainstay of many party workers, and stressed instead the need for technical knowledge and "detailed understanding" of economics and management. See speech at fifth plenum of the SKJ CC, *Borba*, October 6, 1966, 2. Economic reform in turn was accompanied by political reform, including a radical restructuring of party relations at the local level. Such a move was meant to undermine the position of conservative party bureaucrats by bringing rank-and-file party members into the decision-making process, which dismantled the institutional bases of bureaucratic power at the local level (including the local party cells and regional party organizations). See Gagnon, *Ideology and Soviet-Yugoslav Relations*, 579–583; April Carter, *Democratic Reform in Yugoslavia: The Changing Role of the Party* (London: Frances Pinter Publishers, 1982).

[6] See Savka Dabčević-Kučar, from a series of interviews in *Nedeljna Dalmacija*, January 14, 21, 28, 1990; and Miko Tripalo, "Možda smo nešto pogriješili," 67–68.

[7] As Stephen Burg notes, "popular views on the central political issues of the mid-1960s in Yugoslavia corresponded quite closely to the general orientation of the liberal, reformist leadership then consolidating its control of the party. Inter-nationality relations ranked very low among the concerns of the population, especially in comparison with economic issues, and popular preferences on the issue of economic relations between the republics and provinces generally coincided with the current political platform of the central party. Moreover, the internationality tensions that did exist were perceived primarily as consequences of economic problems, and the population appeared to be generally satisfied with its economic prospects for the future." *Conflict and Cohesion in Socialist Yugoslavia* (Princeton: Princeton University Press, 1983), 50.

party membership as well as the wider population in support of irreversible radical changes to the structures of power. In response to these
threats, SKJ conservatives again tried to sabotage implementation of the
reform. Tito responded, at the urging of reformists, by purging conservatives from the party leadership for obstructionism. Following the purges,
the reforms became even more radically threatening to conservatives.

By the summer of 1971, the party leadership was discussing a further
decentralization of the party itself. At a meeting of the SKJ Presidency in
October of that year, many within the leadership were advocating for the
various republic and province party organizations to have the same measure of independence as the republican and provincial governments.[8] This
topic was put onto the agenda for the party meeting in November 1971.[9] If
implemented, the effect would have been to institutionalize reformism in
each republic, to remove all power from the conservatives who dominated
the center, and to eliminate even the possibility of a conservative comeback.[10]

It was at this point, when they had lost their ability to argue against the
reforms, when their efforts to block change were met with the threat of
expulsion, and when they were facing the most serious threat yet to their
interests, that conservatives in the Serbian party began to argue publicly
that the reforms were harmful to the Serbian nation and linked the reforms
to the "historical enemies" of Serbia.

Although some conservatives had been expelled from the party in 1968
for publicly opposing reform, by 1971, as the party faced the possibility
of radical decentralization, the remaining conservatives in the Serbian
party and army pointed, in particular, to the open expression of nationalist sentiment in Croatia that included some extremist views.[11] In this they
were aided by some in the Belgrade press who played up the alleged dangers of events in Croatia, portraying them as official policies of the SKH,
and thus as a revival of the Ustaša regime.[12] Conservatives blamed the

---

[8] Dušan Bilandžić, *Historija SFRJ* (Zagreb: Školska knjiga, 1979), 427.

[9] Ibid.

[10] For a fascinating look at the reform process and forces in this period at the local level
in Serbia, see Slobodan Krstić, *Niški liberali u jugoslovenskoj političkoj zbilji* (Niš: Gradina,
1993).

[11] One official history of the events written in the 1970s described the main sin of the
Croatian leadership not as specifically "nationalist excesses," but rather as the fact that
leaders were seeking to base their legitimacy on support from the wider population rather
than in party ideology. Bilandžić, 422.

[12] Miko Tripalo notes that the "excesses" of the nationalist forces in Croatia "were exaggerated, especially by the Belgrade press, and by the 'emissaries' who came from Belgrade
to Zagreb and heated up events such as attacks on Serbs, the creation of a republic army,
the entry of Croatia into the UN." "Možda smo nešto pogriješili," 67.

reformist and popular Croatian leadership for revival of Croatian nationalism.[13] These conservatives were allied with some conservatives in the
Croatian and Bosnian parties, party workers and war veterans who had
been forced into retirement, members of the central bureaucracy, elements
in the Yugoslav army, and Serbian nationalist intellectuals. They invoked
the massacres of hundreds of thousands of Serbs by the Croatian Ustaša
leadership during World War II and blamed the reforms for undermining
socialism and endangering Croatia's Serbs.

Given the political institutions of the time, the move to focus on threats
to Serbs was not meant to mobilize the population; indeed, the conservatives were accusing the reformists of exactly that heresy against the official party norms. Rather, the main target of this nationalist shift was within
the party itself—the goal was to shift political discourse by arguing that
the reforms, especially the loosening of party control over the state and
society, were extremely dangerous, since they would lead to nationalist
conflicts. Having lost the substantive, technical debate on the reforms—
that is, the debate about the most effective way to improve the economy—
conservatives shifted to a strategy that focused on the supposed unintended
negative consequences of the reforms. By linking the reforms to nationalism, and explicitly to the massacres of Serbs that occurred during World
War II, the conservatives were attempting to refocus the political discourse
of the party, and to convince Tito, the ultimate authority in the party, of the
alleged dangers that the reforms posed for stability and ethnic harmony
in the country, dangers that far outweighed any economic gain.

And indeed the conservatives in the security forces and in the army, in
particular, supplied (dis)information that convinced Tito to act against the
Croatian reformists for exactly those reasons.[14] The Croatian reformists were

[13] Although this period did see some extreme demands, including calls for a Croatian
army, a seat for Croatia in the UN, a division of Bosnia-Herzegovina, as well as some expression of chauvinistic Croatian nationalism, such demands were never made by the Croatian
party leadership, which rather appealed in a positive sense to material well-being, freedom
of expression, and cultural creativity. Pedro Ramet, *Nationalism and Federalism in Yugoslavia:
1963–1983* (Bloomington: Indiana University Press, 1984), 104–143; Ante Ćuvalo, *The Croatian National Movement, 1966–1972* (New York: East European Monographs, 1990).

[14] On the army's role in mobilizing war veterans against reformists in Croatia and in
other republics, see A. Ross Johnson, *The Role of the Military in Communist Yugoslavia: An
Historical Sketch*. Rand Paper Series, no. P-6070 (Santa Monica: Rand Corporation, January
1978), 31–33; on the army convincing Tito of the dangers of Croatian nationalism, see Robin
Remington, "Armed Forces and Society in Yugoslavia," in *Political-Military Systems: Compar-
ative Perspectives*, ed. Catherine McArdle Kelleher (Beverly Hills: Sage, 1974), 188, and James
Gow, *Legitimacy and the Military: The Yugoslav Crisis* (New York: St. Martin's Press, 1992), 58.
On the role of the security forces in supplying Tito with detailed information, see Zdravko
Vuković, *Od deformacije SDP do Maspoka i Liberalizma* (Belgrade: Narodna Knjiga, 1989), 586.

purged and tanks were sent onto the streets of Zagreb.[15] The following year
the Serbian reformists were also purged, despite very strong resistance from
the republic's central committee; and the reformists in the other republics
and provinces soon met the same fate. As a result, the local-level reforms
were effectively reversed, and a renewed ideologization took place.[16]

Casting the threat posed by reform in terms of a threat to Serbs was a
way for the conservatives to shift the focus of political debate away from
the cross-republic reformist project, and toward the alleged threats from
Croatian nationalism that was equated with counterrevolution, fascism,
and genocide against Serbs. This allowed conservatives to argue that radical reform had in fact brought the emergence of nationalism and thus
of counterrevolution.[17] Consequently, by equating liberalization and reform
with the unleashing of nationalism, they also tied the reforms to counterrevolution. By using a discourse of threat of external and internal enemies
of socialism defined in ethnic national terms, and by using their monopoly over intelligence information to exaggerate and even manufacture
examples of threats, the conservatives managed to divide the country's
strong reformists, to prevent the decentralization of the party, and to reverse
the essence of the reforms.[18] The fact that the decentralization of the federation itself remained and was enshrined in the 1974 constitution indicates that the main threat perceived by the conservatives was exactly
the radical reforms that would reduce the party's powers.

[15] Although there were demonstrations of extremist nationalism from outside the party
and even within it at lower levels, the leadership never took such a stand; indeed, despite
the official explanation, the Croatian party leaders never felt either party rule or socialism
to be in danger. The leader of the Serbian party at the time also subsequently admitted that
the purges of the Croatian leadership had been a mistake. See Dabčević-Kučar, interviews
in *Nedeljna Dalmacija*, January 1990; Miko Tripalo, *Hrvatsko proljeće* (Zagreb: Globus, 1990);
Perović, *Zatvaranje kruga*.

[16] Burg, *Conflict and Cohesion in Socialist Yugoslavia*, 181–183, 229. Since confederaliza-
tion remained in place, this meant that those economic mechanisms that were meant to
integrate the country were removed, resulting in eight statist and autarkic units. As a consequence, this marked the foundations of eight entrenched bureaucratic apparatuses
that would resort to extreme measures, in some cases, in order to retain control over
resources and privileges.

[17] The fact that they argued against the reforms, which were reversed, while the con-
federalization of the country remained even after the purge of liberals, indicates that the
main threat was exactly the reforms.

[18] Conservatives in Serbia also set the groundwork for a longer-term strategy, for example, by allowing Dobrica Ćosić, who had been purged for denouncing reform as anti-
Serbian in 1968, to continue to publish his nationalistically oriented works. Thus throughout
the 1970s he constructed a very specific version of Serbian nationalism whose theme was
that Serbs were the greatest victims of Yugoslavia; he portrayed them as a "tragic nation."
See, for example, his popular four-part series of historical fiction, *Vreme Smrti*,

An additional consequence of this conservative victory was that the Yugoslav Army now became a key political player; it had the official role of ensuring the domestic order against external and internal enemies. By 1974, 12 percent of the federal central committee were army officers, up from 2 percent in 1969.[19] The army thus cemented its position as natural ally of conservatives in the party.

Conclusion

The events of the late 1960s and early 1970s in Yugoslavia were the result of pressures for radical changes in the structures of power—within the League of Communists especially—that were being pushed by reformists, with Tito's backing. Having lost the political fight within the SKJ, and in the face of the strong popularity of the young reformist leaders and Tito's support for them, conservatives sought to prevent these changes by using images of threats to Serbs and Serbia, not in order to mobilize the population—which after all was not the main politically relevant audience in the existing political system—but in order to portray the reforms as an extremely dangerous loosening of party control. The conservative *portrayal* of Yugoslav society as on the brink of nationalist violence and separatism was an attempt to convince Tito—the most important politically relevant audience—to end the reforms and to purge the reformists. In this, they were successful.

But the perverse effect of their efforts was to make more concrete the institutionalization of autonomy of the Yugoslav republics and within each republic the structures of political and economic power on which conservative forces were based. While Tito ended the reforms, he retained the decentralization of power to the republics (and two autonomous provinces of Serbia). The result was eight unreformed republic-level economic and political systems with institutional interests in the maintenance

---

published in Belgrade between 1972 and 1979; it chronicles the tragedies of Serbia during World War I (during which it lost 25 percent of its population and 40 percent of its army) and portrays Serbia as the innocent victim of its neighbors: its supposed allies and other Yugoslav ethnic nations. In English, published as: *Into the Battle*, pt. 1 (San Diego: Harcourt Brace, 1983); *Time of Death*, pt. 2 (New York: Harcourt Brace Jovanovich, 1977); *Reach to Eternity*, pt. 3 and *South to Destiny* pt. 4 (San Diego: Harcourt Brace, 1983). See also the series of interviews in Slavoljub Đukić, *Čovek u svom vremenu: Razgovori sa Dobricom Ćosićem* (Belgrade: Filip Višnjić, 1989).

[19] Robert Dean, "Civil-Military Relations in Yugoslavia, 1971–1975," *Armed Forces and Society* 3, no. 1 (November 1976): 46.

of their institutional bases of power. But another result was the increasing dysfunctionality of the Yugoslav economy, which was kept afloat largely through international borrowing.

Round Two: The Post-Tito Debate

When Tito died in May 1980, the debate over reform broke out once again. The ending of reform in the late 1960s had made the economic situation even more dire than it had been previously, and, along with the decentralization of the federation, had resulted in an increased bureaucratization of the system. This system had greatly increased horizontally—there were now eight étatist systems rather than one—but also vertically. Moreover, each republic and province increasingly tended toward internal centralization. As a result, each republic's bureaucracy multiplied over the course of the 1970s. Relatively fewer workers were employed in the economic sector, while more were employed in non-economic units. The proportion of people who were chosen by political officials, based often on political criteria, was very high.[20] In the 1970s the situation had been temporarily ameliorated through foreign borrowing, including from the International Monetary Fund. In fact, by 1980 Yugoslavia had accumulated one of the highest per capita foreign debts in the world, amounting to US$20 billion (US$45 billion if adjusted to the year 2003). Much of that money had been spent on consumer goods or "political factories" (projects that did not necessarily make sense from an economic perspective but undertaken for political reasons), rather than on capital investment in export-oriented industries. At the same time, the economic situation continued to deteriorate: unemployment was skyrocketing (by 1984 it had reached one million, most of them young educated people); inflation was increasing; the standard of living was plummeting; and workers were increasingly mobilizing against the situation by going on strike.

As mentioned above, the selection of economic leaders and managers was fully controlled by local, regional, and republic-level party officials, and "managers' influence was dependent not on their ability but on their position in the political hierarchy."[21] The economic crisis that was triggered by the global recession of the late 1970s, the oil shock, as well as the

---

[20] Vladimir Goati, *Politička anatomija jugoslovenskog društva* (Zagreb: Naprijed, 1989), 43. See also Najdan Pašić, *Razgovori i rasprave o političkom sistemu* (Belgrade: "Partizanska knjiga"—Ljubljana, OOUR Izdavacko-publicisticka delatnost, 1986), 13–15.
[21] Goati, *Politička Anatomija Jugoslovenskog Društva*, 20–25.

negative results brought by ending reform in the early 1970s, all worked together with these domestic structural factors to compel radical systemic change. The major contribution to the pressure for change was the huge and growing foreign debt burden; given the importance of foreign trade to Yugoslavia's economy, and Yugoslavia's dependence on the outside, the debt burden made the need for change very urgent.[22] This need was reinforced by Yugoslavia's inability to keep up with its foreign debt payments, and the decision to seek further credits from the IMF, which in exchange imposed conditionality restrictions. These conditions in turn exacerbated the situation of the wider population.[23]

In response to these crises, the reformists' proposals were much more radical than in the 1960s, and their audience—managerial elites, democratically oriented intellectuals, and much of the party rank-and-file—was much more receptive. The proposals were therefore much more threatening to the conservatives than they had been in the 1960s, especially without Tito and the authority that enabled him to step in and moderate conflicts. This time the political conflict had become winner-take-all.

Serbia: The Decisive Arena

Serbian reformists were in the forefront of this struggle over the future of the social, political, and economic system of Yugoslavia. Indeed, by the early 1980s the Serbian party was among the most reformist in the country. Members of the Serbian party leadership called not only for the total removal of party influence at the local levels of the economy, but also for greater reliance on private enterprise and individual initiative; multiple candidates in state and party elections; free, secret elections in the party; recognition and adoption of "all the positive achievements of bourgeois civilization," i.e. liberal democracy.[24] From within the party leadership,

[22] For a discussion of this issue, see memoirs of Raif Dizdarević, who served as President of the Federal Yugoslav Parliament (1982–1983), as Yugoslav foreign minister (1984–1988), and as President of Yugoslavia (1988–1989): *Od smrti Tita do smrti Jugoslavije: Svedočenja* (Sarajevo: Svjetlost, 2000), 97ff.

[23] Although not as drastic as what came to be known as the "Washington Consensus" conditions imposed on countries in the 1990s, nevertheless the basic outline was very similar: a neoliberal emphasis on closing unprofitable enterprises, cutting government social spending, devaluing the domestic currency, reorienting the economy to produce goods for export for hard currency, and allowing greater foreign investment in the economy.

[24] These liberal positions especially linked the need for radical economic reform and a market system with an equally radical reform of the political system. See, for example, members of Serbian leadership Najdan Pašić, in *Danas*, October 12, 1982; and Mijalko

calls were also heard for private enterprise to become the "pillar of the economy," and even for a multi-party system. Reformists were also very critical of the Army's privileged political and budgetary position, and very early called for cutting that influence.[25]

Once again reformists were seeking to mobilize broader popular sentiment among party rank-and-file as well as the wider population at a time when the economic crisis had discredited the conservatives' ideological stance. The degree of threat posed by the reforms varied, in part by geographical region. In the early 1980s, those party officials and managers from more economically developed regions—Slovenia and Vojvodina—tended to be reformist, while those from less developed Montenegro, Macedonia, Kosovo, and Bosnia tended to oppose them. In Serbia, whose economy was very much split between underdeveloped regions in the south and more developed regions in the north, around Belgrade, and around other major cities in central Serbia, the party leadership was dominated by reformists, although there was a strong constituency of conservatives who were threatened by reform. Croatia, although more developed, was dominated by conservatives, mainly because of the 1971 purges, but the SKH also had a strong technocratically oriented group that attempted to be nonpolitical.[26]

Due to the consensus nature of federal decision making, the conservatives were at first able to hinder an outright reformist victory, but the terms of the debate nevertheless shifted in the favor of the reformists. Indeed by the mid-1980s, secret multi-candidate elections were being held for party

---

Todorović, who argued at one party meeting that the only solution to the economic crisis is "democratization of all political institutions." A report on this meeting noted that similar views were expressed also by Pašić and Draža Marković, head of the Serbian party, which indicated the position of the party. Cited in RFE #256, November 7, 1983; see also Pašić's letter to central committee on the political situation, November 1982, cited in RFE report. no. 125, June 1, 1983 and calls to purge the party of conservatives who blocked reform, *Politika*, September 10, 1984. See also Pašić's book, *Razgovori i rasprave o političkom sistemu* (Belgrade, 1986).

[25] For example, in December 1982 the army budget was openly criticized in the Federal Assembly for having been increased by over 24 percent without the Assembly's approval. *Politika*, December 15, 1982. The Young Slovene Communist Party organization even called in early 1984 for the abolition of the Yugoslav army. A. Tijanić, *Intervju*, March 30, 1984. Army officers enjoyed pay levels much higher than average Yugoslavs as well as housing privileges in a country where housing was in acute shortage. The budget was also quite high (around 4 percent of domestic product in the early 1980s at a time of sharp economic decline).

[26] For characterizations of the republic leaderships, see Pedro Ramet, "The Limits to Political Change in a Communist Country: The Yugoslav Debate, 1980–1986," *Crossroads* 23: 67–79.

officers, and even some state posts were chosen by way of multi-candidate popular votes.[27]

Conservatives in Serbia responded to this growing reformist influence with a three-pronged strategy. The first prong was to reemphasize orthodox Marxist themes, in an attempt to delegitimize liberal trends at the lower levels of the party. The second prong was to repeat their strategy of the early 1970s, that is, to attempt to defeat the reformists in the leadership by shifting the focus of attention away from reforms, toward images of the threat of nationalism and, in particular, Albanian nationalism as well as the alleged "genocide" against Serbs in the province of Kosovo. The third prong portrayed Serbia as the victim of Tito's Yugoslavia, setting the stage for an attack on the autonomy of other republics.

Although the conservatives were not very successful in the political debates over reform at the leadership level, at the local level in Serbia they imposed an orthodox ideological line, while at the same time raising the issue of threats to Serbs. Most notable was the Belgrade party organization, headed beginning in 1984 by Slobodan Milošević. Soon after coming to power, Milošević began a campaign stressing ideological orthodoxy,[28] and sent out warnings to all Belgrade party units urging vigilance against "the dangerous increase in anti-Yugoslav propaganda" from internal and external enemies, a warning that also dominated Yugoslav army leadership pronouncements.[29]

At the same time, a nationalist campaign began among Belgrade party members and "leftist" intellectuals, including Milošević's sociologist wife Mirjana Marković, who sought to defend "the national dignity of Serbia" and to "protect its interests" in Yugoslavia.[30] Belgrade also saw growing numbers of protests by Serbs from the province of Kosovo, claiming to be the victims of ethnic Albanian "genocide."[31] The fact that

[27] For example, Croatia and Slovenia had multicandidate party elections by 1986; Bosnia-Herzegovina held multicandidate popular elections for state presidency representative in 1989; and head of the Serbian presidency Ivan Stambolić proposed direct elections for top state positions in May 1987. *Put u bespuće*, 112.

[28] Slavoljub Đukić, "Trka za recenzentom," *Borba*, August 12, 1991, 11.

[29] Đukić, "Strogo pov. optužnica," *Borba*, August 13, 1991, 11. See also speech of Gen. Jovičić, head of the army's communist party organization, in *Politika*, December 15, 1984.

[30] Mira Marković, *Odgovor* (Belgrade, 1994); *Duga*, December 1993, cited in *Vreme*, February 7, 1994.

[31] Kosovo had been the heart of the medieval Serbian kingdom. But by 1981 it was 75 percent ethnic Albanian and had received a high degree of autonomy in 1974. In the late 1970s Serbian conservatives had used the issue of Kosovo's autonomy as a way of attacking reformist positions. In this they were supported by conservative Serbs from Kosovo who were being replaced by ethnic Albanians in party and government posts. In 1981 massive demonstrations by ethnic Albanians erupted throughout the province, which

the demonstrations took place without police interference was a sign that they were at least tolerated by the Belgrade party; in fact, these demonstrations were organized as part of an overall strategy by conservatives in the Serbian leadership, as part of their attempt to discredit the dominant reformist tendency in the party. As in the early 1970s, such moves were meant to create the image of threats to Serbs and to Serbia, thereby establishing a discourse meant to shift the focus away from the popular reformist position and to discredit the reformist leadership of Serbia.

Indeed, the problem of Kosovo was institutionally a difficult one; as a province of Serbia, Kosovo delegates sat in the Serbian parliament and voted on issues related to policies in Serbia. But as an autonomous republic with the de facto prerogatives of a full republic, policies in Kosovo itself were determined by the Kosovo parliament, without input from Serbia. These and other issues, however, were the subject of political discussions between the reformist minded head of the Serbian republic, Ivan Stambolić, and what he describes as "young, more educated, politically unburdened people of Yugoslav orientation" who came into the Kosovo leadership in the elections of 1986.[32]

The year 1986 represented a major turning point, as the reformist agenda became increasingly accepted at the federation level. Stambolić, a key player in these events, notes that the SKJ's 13th Congress in 1986 was a major victory for reformists.[33] Stambolić also noted that "we were moving in a good direction" on the Kosovo question; by 1986, the republic parliaments had decided to allow changes to the SFRY constitution and the constitution of Serbia on the relationship between Serbia and its provinces.[34]

The strategy of the reformist forces in this period was very much influenced by the conservatives' successes in stopping the reforms in the early 1970s. Stambolić notes that he had learned from the fate of the Serbian liberals in the early 1970s "that we cannot allow a rapid, sharp reform line in the direction of liberalization to call forth a strong defensive response

---

the Serbian conservatives cited as evidence of pervasive "Albanian nationalism." For background on Kosovo, see Magaš, *Destruction of Yugoslavia;* Banac, *National Question in Yugoslavia;* Elez Biberaj, "The Conflict in Kosovo," *Survey* 28, no. 3 (Autumn 1984); Ramet, *Nationalism and Federalism,* 156–171; essays in *Studies on Kosovo,* ed. Arshi Pipa and Sami Repishti (Boulder: East European Monographs, 1984); for the Kosovan Albanian view, see *The Truth of Kosovo* (Tirana: Encyclopedia Publishing House, 1993); for a Serbian view, see Miloš Mišović, *Ko je tražio republiku, Kosovo 1945–1985* (Belgrade: Narodna Knjiga, 1987).

[32] Ivan Stambolić, *Put u bespuće* (Belgrade: Radio B92, 1995), 89–90, 168–169. Interview with Stambolić, Belgrade, July 17, 1995.

[33] Author's interview with Ivan Stambolić, July 17, 1995, Novi Beograd.

[34] Stambolić, *Put u bespuće,* 89–93.

from dogmatic-nationalist and conservative line in the party and part of its leadership."[35] Yet, especially after the republic and federal league of communist conferences in 1986, he was convinced that

> a decisive breakthrough to reforms of the economic and political system was accomplished, and that the forces of change had won in all republics, that the preconditions were created for decisive steps. Individual talks which we had that autumn with all republican leaders only strengthened my belief.[36]

But despite Stambolić's awareness of the dangers of a conservative reaction, these reformist successes were provoking a backlash, as in the earlier period.

Indeed, faced with the progress being made on Kosovo and other fronts, conservatives, who opposed these outcomes and the reformists responsible for them, moved to undermine the reformist leaders. In this, they allied with hard-line nationalists in the Academy. As Stambolić points out, it was not a coincidence that the famous Memorandum of the Serbian Academy was released in draft form in October 1986, shortly after proposals were accepted to deal with the situation of Serbia and its provinces, proposals that represented a significant victory for the reformists.[37]

The Memorandum, an ideological manifesto written by some members of the Serbian Academy of Sciences and Arts in 1985, claimed to call for democracy. In fact, it actually advocated the restoration of the repressive, centralized socialist system that existed before the 1965 reforms. It sharply attacked the 1965 reforms as the root of all contemporary problems in Yugoslavia and as being aimed against Serbs. The Memorandum declared Serbs in Kosovo and Croatia to be endangered and denounced the "anti-Serbian coalition" within Yugoslavia.[38] As Stambolić points out, the only reason the Memorandum is now seen as influential is that it was accepted by the heads of the Serbian party:

> This Memorandum could, in the end, have remained just a piece of paper. . . . Thanks exactly to that warm acceptance in the top of the SK, the memorandum did not remain just an academic game of so-called immortals. . . . It was immediately clear to me that someone, through the Memorandum,

[35] Ibid., 104.
[36] Ibid., 109.
[37] Ibid., 175.
[38] For text, see "Memorandum SANU," *Naše Teme* 33, nos. 1–2 (1989): 128–163. On Milošević's quiet support for the Memorandum, see Slavoljub Đukić, "Čudno Miloše-vićevo ponašanje," *Borba*, August 21, 1991, 13.

wanted to politically destabilize Serbia so that it would turn its back on
its future and the future of Yugoslavia. . . . The Memorandum represents
a great watershed in the League of Communists between dogmatic (potentially nationalistic) currents and reformist currents.[39]

Indeed, for the conservatives, "it was necessary by all means to prevent a democratic solution that [. . .] had already legally and legitimately
[been] reached, but which had not yet taken full effect."[40]

The following year saw further successes of the reformist forces, as
an agreement was reached on federal constitutional changes on Provinces
and changes in Republic constitution. Stambolić notes that the serious and
substantive negotiations with the new Kosovo leadership had brought
positive results in a number of important areas and that compromise solutions to the most controversial conflicts were effectively reached by 1987.[41]
On September 10, 1987, Stambolić announced in a speech to the Serbian
assembly the agreements with the leaderships of Serbia's provinces on
constitutional change. The agreements were accepted, and the Assembly adopted his proposed changes to Serbia's constitution.

A mere ten days later, these successes were overturned when conservatives under the leadership of Slobodan Milošević managed to overcome
reformist dominance and began consolidating power in Serbia. The 8th
plenum, a twenty-three hour session of the Central Committee of the SKS
held on September 18–19, 1987, was a victory for the conservatives in Serbia. In January 1986, despite very strong opposition from within the party
leadership, Milošević had been elected head of the Serbian party's Central
Committee.[42] This period saw a Belgrade-centered coalition of conservative party members, orthodox Marxist intellectuals, and nationalist-oriented
intellectuals who drew increased attention to the issue of Kosovo by repeating the charges of "genocide" against Serbs in Kosovo.[43] Journalists who

---

[39] Stambolić, *Put u bespuće*, 131, 136.

[40] Ibid., 127, 131.

[41] Ibid., 89–90, 168–169; and author's interview with Stambolić, July 1995.

[42] For details of how Milošević and his allies overcame strong opposition, see Slavoljub
Đukić, "Kroz iglene uši," *Borba*, August 15, 1991, 11; "Pod okriljem Stambolića," *Borba*,
August 16, 1991, 11.

[43] Their main charge was that they were the victims of genocide by the majority Albanian population, which they accused of attempting to create an ethnically pure state through
rapes of women, children, and nuns, destruction of Serbian cultural monuments, and other
types of harassment which had resulted, they claimed, in a massive exodus of Serbs and
Montenegrins from the province. For details of the charges as well as a rebuttal of them by
an independent commission, see Srdja Popović, Dejan Janča, Tanja Petovar, *Kosovski čvor:
dresiti se ili seći?* (Belgrade: Chronos, 1990). See also Magaš, *Destruction of Yugoslavia*, 61–73.

were allied with Milošević, especially at the daily newspaper *Politika*, undertook a media campaign to demonize ethnic Albanians and to "confirm" the allegations of genocide.[44] Indeed, the issue of Kosovo now became the conservatives' main weapon against reformist forces within Serbia and in the wider federation, as Serbian conservatives insisted that Kosovo be the priority concern, and a political litmus test, not only of the Serbian party but at the federal level as well.[45]

The strategy of focusing on the situation in Kosovo—a situation that while clearly troubled, was being exacerbated and exaggerated by these same conservative forces—was meant to shift political discourse away from the reforms, to silence and marginalize opponents of the conservatives who would question their policies of putting the Kosovo issue at the top of the agenda, and who would instead continue to push the line of reform. The "movement" in Kosovo was stage-managed and organized from Belgrade by the conservative-nationalist allies; as Stambolić notes, "these unhappy people [Kosovo Serbs] were being terribly manipulated."[46]

One example of how the conservatives manipulated public opinion on Kosovo concerns the issue of rapes by Albanians of Serbs. This was one of the major themes of the conservative media in the late 1980s. Indeed, as one study of this issue put it, "the impression is created 'that Albanians rape anyone . . . in short that they rape everyone and everywhere,'" an impression that was supported in public opinion polling. Yet in actual fact, what researchers found was that in Kosovo there were two-and-a-half times fewer rapes than in "inner" Serbia, and two times fewer than in Yugoslavia; of the 323 reported rapes between 1982 and 1989, 31 (9.6 percent) were Albanians whose victims were Serbs or Montenegrins. There were no such rapes at all between 1987 and 1989.[47] The rate of criminality in Kosovo was actually markedly lower than in Yugoslavia as a whole.

Indeed, the report of the independent commission on Kosovo noted that the exaggeration of anti-Serb actions in Kosovo by the official Serbian media, which was controlled by conservatives, had as one of its major goals,

[44] For example, see Magaš, *Destruction of Yugoslavia*, 109.

[45] For example, in January 1986, two hundred Serbian intellectuals, including some who had previously been identified as socialist humanists, signed a petition accusing the (reformist) Serbian and federal party leaderships of complicity in what they described as "the destructive genocide" against Serbs in Kosovo. See Magaš, *Destruction of Yugoslavia*, 48–52.

[46] Stambolić interview with author July 1995; also in *Put u Bespuće*, 166.

[47] Srđa Popović et al., *Kosovski čvor: Dresiti se ili seći. Izveštaj nezavisne komisije* (Belgrade: Biblioteka Khronos, 1990), 39–42.

strengthening an authoritarian regime in Serbia, and doing that a) by stimulating repressive tendencies as such, by creation of a repressive mentality, b) by obtaining the widest and even special powers for the party in power and its leader; c) by marginalizing the opposition and by accusing the opposition of destroying national unity personified by the ruling party.[48]

Thus the issue in Kosovo was *how* to deal with its problems. The reformists were seeking compromises that would actually address the concerns of all sides. The conservatives, however, sought to exaggerate and exacerbate the situation and actively undermined the compromise solutions that had been reached. Clearly for the conservatives this issue was merely a means to a greater end.

At this time, within the central committee, Milošević worked to marginalize the reformist majority. As Stambolić explains:

> The central committee was no longer the one which elected him [Milošević] as its head. He destroyed it with some kind of his own central committee in the shadows, some parallel leadership. He did this in an unstatutory manner by bringing in large numbers of various people to Central Committee plenums who would then give speeches to the CC members. The CC was left only with voting on the decision.[49]

The day before 8th Plenum, the central committee of the army's party organization met and was clearly supportive of what was about to take place the next day.

The outcome of the 8th Plenum was partly the result of "behind the scenes chicanery," and partly of the playing up of "atrocities" such that anyone who called for moderation and rational approach to resolving Kosovo's issues was attacked for "betraying Serbdom."[50]

Within Serbia, the result of the conservatives' strategy was that questions of radical reform were shunted aside in order to deal with the pressing issue of "genocide" in Kosovo. Through a combination of press manipulation, stage-managed mass rallies, political manipulation, and a stress on Stalinist notions of democratic centralism, by 1988 Milošević managed to consolidate conservative control over the Serbian republic's party organization.[51]

---

[48] Ibid., 26.
[49] Stambolić, *Put u bespuće*, 162.
[50] Ibid., 188, 224–226.
[51] Reformists were purged for being "soft" on Albanians (because they wanted to negotiate a solution with the Albanians rather than impose one); for being openly critical of the media's enflaming of the Kosovo issue; for warning against the demonization of all ethnic Albanians; and for criticizing the chauvinistic version of Serbian nationalism being

Those parts of the Serbian media that had been relatively independent were taken over by conservative editors allied with Milošević.

However, it soon became clear that the conservative coalition's goals were not limited to Kosovo and Serbia. Indeed, given the nature of decision-making in Yugoslavia, to prevent the imposition of radical reform in Serbia, the conservatives would have to ensure that it did not take hold in the other republics and at the federal level. Their strategy was to attempt to recentralize the federation, in order to deprive the other republics of their autonomy.

The strategy of attempting to recentralize Yugoslavia in order to suppress reformist tendencies was one that had been on the agenda since at least the early 1980s; indeed, according to Martin Špegelj, a former member of the General Staff of the Yugoslav Army, plans to use military force to recentralize the country had been discussed as early as 1982; and the westward reorientation of the Army's military strategy in 1986 was aimed at the western republics.[52] Once conservatives had consolidated power in Serbia, they worked with conservatives in the Army to implement a recentralization.

At first, over the course of 1988 and 1989, the attempts to recentralize the country focused on taking over the leaderships of the communist parties of the other republics and provinces, replacing them with Milošević loyalists. The main strategy used to this end was the staging of mass rallies of tens of thousands in every major city in Serbia as well as in other republics and in front of party headquarters during party meetings. These rallies, which decried the "atrocities" in Kosovo and what was portrayed as bureaucratic corruption and betrayal of the population (thus the name "anti-bureaucratic revolution"), called for the party leaderships to step down. The rallies drew on social dissatisfaction caused by the increasingly poor economic situation, but refocused that dissatisfaction by shifting attention to the injustices and persecution of Serbs in Kosovo, and by blaming

---

used by conservatives. Dragiša Pavlović, "Potcenjuje se srpski nacionalizam," *Borba*, September 25, 1987, 3; *Borba*, September 11, 1987. See also the series of articles by Slavoljub Đukić in *Borba*, August 26, 1991, 11; August 27, 11; August 28, 13; August 29, 11.

[52] Martin Špegelj, interview in *Globus*, July 7, 1995, (54–63) notes that as early as 1982 the JNA leadership had discussed and agreed to use military force to recentralize the country; he also describes a meeting in 1986 at which the general staff was told that the country's strategic plans were shifting away from defense from an attack from the East, to a defense from an attack from the West, that is, from NATO. Špegelj describes other shifts in JNA strategy that he says meant that the reorientation was not aimed at NATO, but rather at the western republics (Slovenia, Croatia, Bosnia-Herzegovina) (p.56).

the targeted party leaderships for the deteriorating economic and social situation. Party leaders at the federal level and in other republics were denounced for tolerating these injustices and doing nothing to stop them. Some observers, including within Serbia itself, have characterized these rallies as being democratic mobilizations similar to the ones seen in other East European socialist states. But there were very significant differences.

For one, the rallies never criticized the ruling Serbian bureaucracy, and one of the most notable features of these rallies was the presence of many posters and slogans praising Milošević personally. This was not a coincidence, because the rallies were in fact organized and directed by the regime.[53] These "mobilizations" in fact had more in common with communist-era "mobilizations" than with the massive outpourings in other east European countries: workers were given the day off with pay, a bus ride to town, and free food (including beer and yogurt), in exchange for participating. Although, to be sure, many participants took part of their own free will, out of a true sense of liberation from perceived past oppression, it cannot be overlooked that this "mobilization" was organized by the existing power structures, and in that sense differed fundamentally from mobilizations in the rest of eastern Europe, as well as the mobilizations that were to be seen in Serbia once liberal political institutions were adopted in 1990.

In addition, the goals of these "mobilizations" were to support the existing regime only in an indirect way, rather than to get the active support of the population. The main goal was to overthrow the party leaderships at local, regional, republic, and even federal levels who disagreed with Serbia's conservatives, that is, opponents of the regime. The rallies most often took place at the same time as a party leadership meeting, in front of the building in which the meeting was taking place, and was used to instill fear into Milošević's opponents in these leaderships so they would step aside and allow new people loyal to him to be put in place. The cost to participants was relatively minor—since the rally was organized by the regime, there was no risk of confrontation or conflict with the police, for

[53] Magaš, *Destruction of Yugoslavia*, 206–207; Stambolić, *Put u Bespuće* (Belgrade: Radio B92, 1995), 168–181; interview with Dragoslav Marković, "Naš mir je, ipak, bio bolje," *Borba*, August 17–18, 1991. On the direct link between the regime's stage managed rallies and groups that were later used by the Serbian leadership to provoke conflict in Croatia and Bosnia, Mirko Jović, one of the organizers of the rallies, was also the founder of the guerrilla group "Beli orlovi," accused of numerous atrocities against civilians in Croatia and Bosnia from 1991 onward. See also "Zašto nismo pokorili Bosnu," *Naši dani*, June 21, 1991, 20; Raif Dizdarević, *Od smrti Tita do smrti Jugoslavije–Svedočenja* (Sarajevo: Svjetlost, 2000), 189–194, 201–205, 295.

example—and the psychic benefits were high. Notably, this mobilization also did not lead to violence along ethnic lines.

They were successful in their goals. The party leaderships in Vojvodina and Montenegro were ousted in October 1988 and January 1989. The Kosovo party leadership, which had been handpicked by the conservatives in Belgrade, was also pressured to acquiesce in the abolition of Kosovo's autonomy and the recentralization of Serbia. Although these moves provoked massive demonstrations and mobilizations among the province's Albanian population to protest the threat to its autonomy, in March 1989 the Kosovo assembly, subjected to fraud and manipulation by Belgrade, voted to end the province's autonomy.[54] This strategy was also used against the leaderships in Bosnia and in Croatia, moves that will be addressed later in this chapter.

The conservatives' strategy of consolidating control over the other republics through the use of aggressive rallies was accompanied by increasingly vehement media demonizations not only of Albanians, but also of Croats,[55] as well as an active campaign to portray Tito's Yugoslavia as specifically anti-Serbian.[56] It claimed that an authoritarian, Serb-dominated, and centralized Yugoslavia was the only way to ensure the security and interests of all Serbs. Not coincidentally, such a Yugoslavia would also ensure the power interests of the conservative Serbian elites.

Meanwhile the army, under Defense Minister Branko Mamula, openly sided with orthodox conservative positions and harshly attacked the political opposition. In the military itself, orthodox indoctrination was stepped up.[57] The army also endorsed Milošević's conservative economic

[54] *Yugoslavia: Crisis in Kosovo* (New York: Helsinki Watch, 1990); Michael W. Galligan, et al., "The Kosovo Crisis and Human Rights in Yugoslavia," *Record of the Association of the Bar of the City of New York* 46, no. 3 (April 1991): 227–231; Magaš, *Destruction of Yugoslavia*, 179–190.

[55] Stressed were images that evoked the specter of wartime Croatian fascists, including prime-time television broadcasts of previously unshown graphic films from the Ustaša concentration camps. The implication—and at times explicit conclusion—of these and other such images was that Croats as a people were "genocidal." On the television images, see Biljana Bakić, "Constructed 1990s Yugoslav Reality." MA thesis, University of Pittsburgh, 1992; see also Ivo Banac, "The Fearful Asymmetry of War: The Causes and Consequences of Yugoslavia's Demise," *Daedalus* (Spring 1992): 141–174.

[56] For example, see Robert M. Hayden, "Recounting the Dead: The Discovery and Redefinition of Wartime Massacres in Late- and Post-Yugoslavia," in *Memory and Opposition under State Socialism*, ed. Rubie S. Watson (Santa Fe: School of American Research Press, 1993); this cites Ljubomir Tadić, "Kominterna i Nacionalno Pitanje Jugoslavije," *Književne novine*, September 15, 1988.

[57] Anton Bebler, "Political Pluralism and the Yugoslav Professional Military," in *The Tragedy of Yugoslavia: The Failure of Democratic Transformation*, ed. Jim Seroka and Vukasin Pavlovic (Armonk, N.Y.: M. E. Sharpe, 1992), 126–127, 129.

and political program, stressing in particular continued monopoly of the communist party and recentralization of the state.[58] In cooperation with Serbian conservatives, the military openly attacked reformist calls to democratize the country, reduce the military's political role and to reform the military-industrial complex. Moreover, statements by top army officers "made clear that they viewed the Army's internal mission in orthodox ideological terms."[59]

The new pro-Milošević Vojvodina leadership proceeded to call for an extraordinary SKJ congress. As one party leader noted, "It seemed clear that they were preparing a coup against the leadership of the League of Communists of Yugoslavia."[60] Nevertheless, in the face of this pressure, reformist Ante Marković was chosen as federal prime minister by the Federal Parliament, which had not yet been taken over by conservatives, over Milošević ally Borisav Jović. Marković would prove to be one of the greatest threats to the conservatives.

In the conservative attempt to recentralize the League of Communists as a means to recentralizing the federation, perhaps the most destructive moves came in Bosnia; given the importance of Bosnia in the future course of events, I'll focus a bit on the Serbian conservatives' strategy in that republic.

The conflict between reformists and conservatives had a major impact on Bosnia-Herzegovina. The League of Communists of Bosnia-Herzegovina (SKBH) was one of the more conservative parties and had strong ties to the JNA; indeed, 60 percent of Yugoslavia's military industry was located in Bosnia, which had been the heartland of the Partisan resistance during World War II, and which contemporary Yugoslav military doctrine continued to see as the place to which self-defense forces would pull back in the event of invasion from outside. Many of the SKBH officials, from the local level, where military industries were located, to the very top, had close ties to the JNA. Thus, as the conservatives in the SKJ and JNA moved after Tito's death to recentralize the country in an authoritarian direction, it would have seemed that the SKBH would be a natural ally.

---

[58] Indeed, this platform, laid out in July 1989 by Defense Secretary Kadijević at the Conference of the JNA's party organization, was "the most conservative of all the explicitly articulated platforms in Yugoslavia and the most dogmatic as far as political pluralism was concerned." Bebler, "Political Pluralism," 129–131.

[59] Ibid., 130–131.

[60] Raif Dizdarević, *Od smrti Tita do smrti Jugoslavije–Svedočenja* (Sarajevo: Svjetlost, 2000), 303.

The Conservative Attack on Bosnia-Herzegovina

There are two reasons why this was not to be. First, although dominated by conservatives, the SKBH also was very much a defender of the autonomy of republics as defined in the 1974 constitution. This autonomy ensured not only that Bosnia-Herzegovina would not become a mere peripheral appendage whose fate was determined outside of its own borders, as tended to happen in the past, but it also ensured the balance of political forces in the republic, which in part took the form of an institutionalized "ethnic key," whereby all positions from the top down were carefully allocated across ethnicities. In effect, this ethnic key created an incentive structure whereby elites and prospective elites were ensured positions in the bureaucracy. This was based on their self-identification in terms of four categories: Muslim, Serb, Croat, or "Other" (which included Yugoslavs as well as other minorities: Gypsies, Slovaks, etc.).[61] Any change in the status of republics would threaten to disrupt this balance within the elite, though there would be minimal impact on the wider population.

This institutionalization of the ethnic key is one element that explains why, in social science polling, SKBH members were much more likely to have nationalistic feelings than the wider population: 29 percent vs. 8 percent.[62] It also helps explain why, despite the fact that ethnic ties were not a major fault line among the wider population itself, they remained important for elites and aspiring elites; it also helps explain the denunciations coming from the SKJ leadership in the 1970s and 1980s of the trend especially among young people, and especially in Bosnia-Herzegovina,

[61] Thus the BiH presidency included two members each from the three main national groups, plus one from the category of "other." Likewise, the BiH member of the Yugoslav presidency was chosen on a rotating basis from the three main groups; in 1989 the seat was to be held by a Bosnian Serb, so all of the prospective candidates came from among the ranks of the Serbian people in Bosnia. In ministries too there was a division and balancing such that each "group" was represented in all parts of the party and state bureaucracy and at all levels, from top to bottom. The result was ethnic heterogeneity in all party and state institutions. After the victory of the nationalist parties in the November 1990 elections, a kind of national key was maintained but implemented in a very different manner, whereby each party was "given" various institutions which it could then fill with its own followers. The result was a sharp shift away from heterogeneity to a kind of "ghettoization," whereby certain institutions became mono-ethnic. This very different implementation of the institution of ethnic key also caused very different outcomes.

[62] Report on survey undertaken by Ibrahim Bakić and Ratko Dunđerović, Institute for the Study of National Relations in Bosnia, "Građani Bosne i Hercegovine o međunacionalnim odnosima," in *Oslobođenje*, March 22, 1990, 2.

of declaring themselves Yugoslavs.[63] Any change in the status of Bosnia-Herzegovina as a republic, as was being proposed by the Serbian conservatives, was thus potentially very disruptive and against the interests of most of Bosnia's elite.

The other reason for the lack of an open alliance between the SKBH and the Serbian conservatives was the nature of the strategy the latter were using. From the early 1980s onward, but especially after the victory of Milošević at the 8th Plenum in September 1987, the conservatives used the issue of threats to Serbdom and, in particular, Kosovo as a way to discredit party leaders who did not agree with Milošević. Just as in Vojvodina and Montenegro, the so-called "anti-bureaucratic revolution" was an attempt to recentralize the SKJ by destabilizing and then replacing current SK leaderships in the republics and provinces. The mass meetings were stage-managed and meant explicitly to discredit party leaderships by accusing them of being self-serving bureaucrats out for themselves and not dealing with—or in fact abetting—the "genocide" against Serbs in Kosovo. Indeed, the scenario played out in Bosnia was very reminiscent of the scenario in Kosovo, in that Serb conservatives began airing accusations that Serbs were being victimized in the republic, including being subjected to "genocide." The Serbian secret police became involved in this by the summer of 1989 when it acted on its own within the borders of Bosnia in a way that served to create conflict along ethnic lines.

While this strategy was successful in Montenegro and Vojvodina, the anti-bureaucratic revolution clearly was also a threat to party leaders in Bosnia in a number of ways. First was the very real possibility that they would suffer the same fate as their colleagues in Vojvodina and Montenegro. But another threat, one that was even more dangerous, was that by following a strategy that constructed the political landscape—and not just positions within the bureaucracy—in ethnic terms, by focusing on threats to Serbs, they would destabilize the republic(which of course was exactly the goal of the Serbian conservatives). Indeed, this was the same reasoning that led conservative Croatian Serbs in the SKH to denounce Milošević and his strategy of creating conflict along national lines. In the case of Bosnia, the reformists in the party opposed Milošević regardless of nationality. On the other hand, some Serb conservatives, with close ties to the conservative JNA and with Milošević's conservatives in Serbia, cooperated with

---

[63] On the increasing hostility of the Party toward growing expressions of Yugoslavism, see Ana Dević, "Nationalism and Powerlessness of Everyday Life: A Sociology of Discontents in the SFR Yugoslavia Before the Breakup." Presented at "Living with the Beast: Everyday Life in Authoritarian Serbia," Clark University, Worcester, Mass., April 2000.

the Serbian conservatives in their attempts to undermine an autonomous Bosnian party leadership.

Thus, despite its conservative stance, the SKBH became a target of the conservative forces that would eventually be led by Milošević. The strategy of the conservatives was multifold. One of the earliest was to discredit and remove those SKBH leaders who were older and authoritative, who carried weight at the federal level. Thus a number of "affairs" were uncovered or cooked up in order to discredit various SKBH leaders. For example, Hamdija Pozderac, the head of the constitutional commission that was to rewrite the Yugoslav constitution, was a strong advocate of republic and province autonomy, and he had refused to give in to conservative calls for recentralization. As a way to discredit him, the Agrokomerc scandal broke. Likewise, Mikulić and others were targeted with various other scandals. The result was that by 1988 much of the old SKBH elite had been targeted.[64]

Nevertheless, since the anti-bureaucratic revolution was about maintaining structures of power in Serbia and in Yugoslavia as a whole through authoritarian means, such concerns did not stop the Serb conservatives from threatening to export it to Bosnia and from pursuing other policies meant to destabilize the republic. Indeed, by the end of 1988 it had become clear that there were two diametrically opposed views of how the SKJ should proceed: one, championed by the Slovenian SK as well as some within the SKH, was for a pluralistic, democratic liberalization in politics and the economy. This is the line that was supported by Ante Marković following his election as federal prime minister in March 1989. The other line was that of the Serbian conservatives, who were seeking a recentralized authoritarian system in which a monolithic SKJ held all the reigns of power. In this conflict, the SKBH was in the middle; its membership was split between these two positions, and the leadership consistently called for a negotiated solution, a compromise between the two positions. And since Milošević had attempted to "ethnicize" these political positions, that is, to identify them as pro-Serb and anti-Serb, the result within Bosnia-Herzegovina was to impose this ethnification onto the SKBH.

The instrumental nature of the anti-bureaucratic revolution's meetings is made clear in an interview with Miroslav Šolević, former party secretary, the "commander of the antibureaucratic revolution," organizer of mass demonstrations in Serbia, Kosovo, Montenegro, and Vojvodina that led to the fall of reformists and other opponents of Milošević. He described how the

---

[64] Author's interview with Ivan Stambolić, July 1995. Interview with Raif Dizdarević, "I Bosna i Bošnjaci su dužni Titu," in *Dani* (Sarajevo) 126 (October 29, 1999); "Kako je otišao Hamdija Pozderac: U pozadini afere Agrokomerc," *Valter* 22 (January 12, 1990), 8–9.

plan was to export the demonstrations to Bosnia as well, beginning in September 1988 with a planned meeting in Jajce. But the demonstration did not happen, because the leadership of the SK Serbia struck a deal with the SKBH leadership: in exchange for its three votes in the CKSKJ presidency—three votes that would give Serbia a majority position—the "mitinzi" (demonstrations) in Jajce and Bosnia would be called off.[65] Thus the mere threat of exporting the "mitinzi" to Bosnia seemed enough to ensure the votes of the SKBH.

But the efforts by the Serb conservatives did not stop there, as they continued their attempts to destabilize Bosnia. One notorious example had to do with claims that Bosnia was a repetition of what had happened to Serbs in Kosovo, namely, that the SKBH leadership was tolerating and even encouraging the emigration of Serbs out of the republic, proof that it was leading an "anti-Serbian policy." As part of this campaign, the Serbian secret police that was secretly operating in eastern Bosnia collected information that was alleged to support the claim that Serbs in Bosnia were "threatened" (*ugroženi*). These efforts were seen within Bosnia as an attempt by the SPS leadership in Serbia to create conflict and to destabilize Bosnia.[66]

Further evidence of pressure coming from Serbia's conservatives onto Bosnia was seen in early to mid 1989. The SKBH more and more vocally denounced attempts to homogenize people, especially in the SKBH, by nationality;[67] attempts were made to set up "paternalistic" relationships of peoples from their "mother" republics;[68] and other actions were taken

[65] "... the Serbian party leadership reached an agreement with the Bosnian leadership on voting. . . . that they would support the Serbian positions and in return we would refrain from holding the 'miting' in Jajce. . . . We immediately withdrew." "Zašto nismo pokorili Bosnu," *Naši dani,* June 21, 1991, 20.

[66] For the reaction of the SKBH, see statement of the SKBH Presidency in *Oslobođenje,* October 26, 1989, 4.

[67] For example, Milan Uzelac, member of SKBH presidency and SKJ central committee, denounced "strong pressure on this Central Committee to divide up along national basis, and on the public as a whole, on citizens, youth, on workers of Bosnia-Herzegovina, to divide along national lines." "Pritisak na medunacionalne odnose," *Oslobođenje,* April 6, 1989, 44.

[68] See the communiqué following a meeting of leadership delegations from Serbia and Bosnia. It was clear that the Bosnia leadership's concerns included attempts to export the "anti-bureaucratic revolution" to Bosnia; reports in the Serbian press that distorted the situation in Bosnia, reports described as "tendentious, incorrect or imprecise information" and the "constant tendency" to focus on "the alleged threats to Serbs in Bosnia, measures to defend Serbs," the "alienation of the Bosnian leadership from the people and the constant heating up (*podgrijavanje*) of that mistrust; the inadequate and tendentious insistence on national problems alongside the pronounced forcing of the supposed threatened Serbs in Bosnia; claims by the Serbian leadership that any criticism of its policies was "Serbophobia" and anti-Serbian; attempts to destabilize Bosnia through a "propaganda war" that focused in part on "affairs" such as Agrokomerc and Moševac. "Nemamo paternalistički odnos prema BiH," *Oslobođenje,* July 20, 1989, 3.

"whose essence and whose means of existence, execution and continuation are exactly the production of conflicts [and] confrontations."[69] Conservatives were also putting forth claims that Bosnia was seeing the appearance of Islamic fundamentalism.[70]

An additional move by conservatives was their attempt to prevent a young, reformist, and democratically oriented Serb from filling the Bosnia seat in the Yugoslav presidency. The seat was scheduled to be filled with a Serb from Bosnia, on the principle of rotation and ethnic key, and was to be determined in an open and contested election in which all citizens of Bosnia-Herzegovina were to vote. The two candidates were Milan Škoru, an older party official a few years from retirement "who has had a significant part in creating Bosnia's policies in the last two decades," and Nenad Kecmanović, a political scientist and the youngest dean ever at the University of Sarajevo. Unexpectedly, Kecmanović was ahead in the polls in over half the municipalities of the republic and in the largest cities, receiving a majority in eighty municipalities against Škoru, who achieved a majority in only fifteen. At this point, less than a week before the election, Kecmanović became the target of attacks in the press concerning his private life and political positions; he was urged to withdraw from the race to prevent further compromises, and his opponent, although urged to speak out on this, remained silent.[71] Kecmanović ended up withdrawing from the race. The election, finally held in June 1989, was however won by Bogić Bogićević, who would prove to be one of the strongest opponents of Serbia's conservatives.

Thus Bosnia too became the site of Serbia's conservative strategy to recentralize the federation. The conflicts in Bosnia were the result not of ethnic hatreds, but rather of purposeful attempts by the Serbian regime to foment conflict as a way of imposing a conservative leadership that would allow recentralization of the federation. These moves were adumbrations of the more violent strategy that Serbia would pursue just a few years later and set the stage for that strategy.

Croatia: The Last Years of the SKH in Power: 1980–1989

The events in the Serbian party had an enormous impact on the League of Communists of Croatia (SKH). In Croatia, as in the rest of Yugoslavia,

[69] Nijaz Duraković, President of the Presidency of the Central Committee of the SKBH, quoted in "'Politika' proizvode sukobe," *Oslobođenje*, August 28, 1989, 3
[70] "Nemamo paternalistički odnos prema BiH," *Oslobođenje*, July 20, 1989, 3.
[71] Goran Todorović, "Bosansko hercegovački watergate," *Valter* 10 (April 7, 1989), 2.

the focus of political conflict throughout the 1980s was the clash between different visions of the future of the country and of its socialist self-management system. As in Serbia, the conflict in Croatia too was one between conservative forces who sought to reconsolidate a more authoritarian and orthodox form of state socialism, thereby preserving the structures of party and state power that ensured their control over and access to resources, and those who sought not a wholesale shift to capitalism and liberal democracy, but rather a reform of the existing system in a direction that would nevertheless fundamentally alter these structures of power and thus threaten the bases of power of the conservatives.[72]

In the 1970s and 1980s, the SKH had been one of the more conservative of the Yugoslav communist parties. After the events of 1971, in which the reformist SKH leadership was charged with allowing Croatian nationalism to threaten the socialist order, the Croatian party adopted a style of decision making that was marked by the lack of open conflict. Conflicts that did exist were worked out behind closed doors in a more consensual manner, which gave the advantage to the conservatives. But as explained above, with the death of Tito in 1980, and the concomitant escalation of the economic crisis, including a growing number of workers' strikes and the need to repay $20 billion in hard currency loans to the IMF and Western banks, pressure for significant reform mounted, both from the international community as well as from within Yugoslavia.

In the face of such pressure, the initial reaction of the SKH conservatives was, as would be expected, very strong resistance to such changes not only within Croatia but also at the all-Yugoslav federal level. But perhaps even more than elsewhere in the country, in Croatia there was much

[72] At this time there is very little evidence that the wider population supported a wholesale adoption of the kind of neo-liberal capitalism that would come to dominate Western policy in the region, with its focus on rapid and wide-spread privatization of state enterprises, and the reduction or elimination of state intervention in the economy; rather, they wanted a more democratic form of the existing socialist system. For example, in a poll of Zagreb residents in 1988, when asked what the best way would be to overcome the economic crisis (asked to pick three), only 18.1 percent of respondents said "allow free working of the market without state direction and control"; the top answer, at 39.3 percent, was "stimulate personal initiative and develop the so-called 'small economy,'" while 35.1 percent responded, "consistent application of the principal of reward for work and results of work" Bahtijarević et al., 1989. While these results may have been the result of perceptions about what was possible at that time, subsequent polling (cited later in this chapter) indicated that, among the Croatian population, there was and remains very strong support for, at the very least, a social market system, as opposed to the neoliberal model that was initially adopted in much of the rest of the region. Even ten years later, polling showed that the large majority of Croatia's citizens, while accepting capitalism, also strongly valued other goals such as social justice that require a significant role for the state in the economy.

support among the wider population, as well as among the SKH's rank-and-file membership, for major reform of the economic system.[73] Pointing to the economic crisis and the widespread sentiment in favor of change, in the mid-1980s the reformists made significant headway; indeed, in 1986, for the first time since the late 1960s, the SKH held party elections that were contested.[74]

As one Croatian political analyst noted, this period between 1985 and 1989 saw the previously hidden split in the ruling elite, between the conservative "orthodox communist faction" and the reformist "pragmatic faction," erupt into public view. At first, the orthodox retained their dominance and imposed a strongly anti-liberal and anti-pluralist position, as well as "an ideological dictatorship which was stronger in Croatia than in any other part of Yugoslavia."[75] But the reformist faction of the SKH, "helped by the liberal political and cultural currents outside of Croatia, especially in Slovenia and Serbia," nevertheless continued to grow in strength.[76]

At the same time, as described above, conservatives within the Serbian party were battling in a much more open and confrontational way with the much stronger Serbian party reformists. Indeed, the Serbian reformists at this time were openly arguing for political and economic liberalization, which would in effect radically change the structures of power within the party, the state, and the economy. Their economic plan included a kind of liberalizing economic centralization—a common Yugoslav economic space rather than the existing six or eight largely separate spaces that had come into existence since 1974.

---

[73] For example, in a survey of public opinion in Zagreb undertaken in December 1988, asked to rank the importance of various reforms, 49 percent put economic reform first and 16 percent ranked political reform first. Forty-four percent put political reform in second place. Štefica Bahtijarević, Ivan Šiber, Mladen Zvonarević, "Javno mnijenje Zagreba '88." *Naše teme* 33, nos. 7–8 (1989): 1967.

[74] The idea for such multi-candidate elections within the party was raised between 1980 and 1982 in the Zagreb party committee; and when the idea was pushed in 1985 it was first accepted by the local party organizations of the cities of Croatia. Eventually, it "achieved such popularity among SKH members and among citizens that 'we couldn't have turned back even if we'd wanted to.'" Arguments in favor of such a policy were: democratization of SKH and society; bringing new and younger people into positions; and increasing the quality of chosen functionaries. Eugen Pusić, Josip Kregar, Ivan Šimonović, "SK u razvoj komunalnog sistema grada Zagreba," *Naše teme* 32 no. 12 (1988): 3009–3041.

[75] The main support for this orthodox position came from the ideological apparat, especially in the schools, science and academia, and cultural areas. Its main spokesperson was Stipe Šuvar. Mirjana Kasapović, "Strukturna i dinamička obilježja političkog prostora i izbora," in *Hrvatska u izborima '90*, ed. Ivan Grdešić, Mirjana Kasapović, Ivan Šiber, and Nenad Zakošek (Zagreb: Naprijed, 1991), 28–29.

[76] Ibid, 30.

The Croatian conservatives seized on this aspect of the Serbian reformists' plans and portrayed it as an attack on the status quo of republic auton- omy. By painting Serbian party reformists as equivalent to Serbian author- itarianism and expansionism, the SKH conservatives attempted to hinder an alliance between reformists in the two largest republics. Despite this, however, the economic problems and the specific situation of Croatia, with its relatively more developed economy, pushed the SKH as a whole toward a gradual change. More crucial to this shift, however, were the attempts by Serbian conservatives to deprive the republic parties of autonomy and to recentralize Yugoslavia under their own control.

As described above, from the early 1980s onward, Serbia's conserva- tives used the discourse of threats to Serbs in Kosovo to justify the aboli- tion of that province's autonomy, as part of their battle to fight off the danger of reformism in Serbia. Along with other republic leaderships, the SKH leaders seemed at first to have believed that Milošević's concerns about Kosovo's autonomy were mainly an internal Serbian matter and that his takeover of Kosovo would resolve the problem. Most of them apparently did not perceive it as a move by conservative forces in Serbia to end auton- omy elsewhere, although SKH head Šuvar was supportive of this strategy, perhaps seeing it as a way to crush reformism throughout the country.

But this sentiment shifted sharply when, after consolidating power in Serbia at the end of 1987 and 1988, Milošević and his allies sought to impose their conservative line on the country as a whole by attempting to under- mine the autonomy of the other federal units. By 1989 they had succeeded in overthrowing the reformist leaderships in Montenegro and Vojvodina. Croatia too was targeted in this period, as Milošević's allies in the veter- ans' association and among conservative army generals and former par- tisans from the rural regions of Croatia channeled weapons to local allies via the JNA, seeking to undermine the SKH's autonomy in an almost direct replay of the strategies in Montenegro and Vojvodina.

As elsewhere, Serbian conservatives used the issue of Kosovo in their attempts to undermine party autonomy and reformist trends at the local level throughout Yugoslavia, including in the SKH.[77] In February 1989, Belgrade orchestrated a series of demonstrations in Serb-populated regions

---

[77] For example, in reports on meetings of regional and local SKH organizations, what becomes clear is a split between reformists, who focus on the need for change in the polit- ical and economic system and in the role of the party, and those who oppose reform, and who try to push the focus toward the situation in Kosovo, following the line of Belgrade on this issue. For example, see the report on the Sisak municipality committee of the SKH, Lj. Ahmetović, "Za jasan i odlučan stav," *Jedinstvo* (Sisak), March 9, 1989, 3.

of Croatia, busing people in from Serbia. These demonstrations were organized by the same people who had stage-managed the "meetings of truth" that had toppled the leaderships in Vojvodina and Montenegro. A large rally held in June 1989 in the small town of Kosovo in Croatia was likewise attended by groups from Serbia who held aloft posters of Milošević. At the same time, the media in Serbia, which was also seen and read in Croatia, was filled with images that demonized Croats, evoking the specter of World War II, and explicitly accusing the SKH leadership and the Croatian people of being genocidal.[78] Clearly if even the SKH was being accused of being Ustaša and anti-Serb, then no matter who won the upcoming elections, the policy of demonization of Croats and Croatia would continue as long as there was resistance to the Serbian conservatives' line.

Indeed, this targeting of Croatia led even the conservative head of the SKH Stipe Šuvar to realize the need for change. Likewise, Dušan Dragosavac, a Serb who fought with the Partisans during World War II, a leading conservative in the Croatian party leadership and member of the SKJ Central Committee, denounced Milošević for creating national hatreds.[79] In response, he was attacked by Milošević's allies as an Ustaša.[80] Similarly, other Serb officials in the SKH at this time sharply criticized Belgrade's attempts to "help" Croatian Serbs, arguing that such "aid" was actually creating new problems and worsening any already existing ones.[81]

---

[78] These included prime-time television broadcasts of previously unshown graphic films from the Ustaša concentration camps. On the television images, see Biljana Bakić, "Constructed 1990s Yugoslav Reality," master's thesis, University of Pittsburgh, 1994; also see Ivo Banac, "The Fearful Asymmetry of War: The Causes and Consequences of Yugoslavia's Demise," *Daedalus* (Spring 1992): 141–174.

[79] *Danas*, December 13, 1988.

[80] See "Saopštenje," *Lički Vjesnik*, March 1, 1989, 12, and Dragosavac's response, "Saopštenje," *Lički Vjesnik*, May 1, 1989, 12. See also his denunciation of Milošević's strategy in *Danas*, December 13, 1988, cited in Branka Magaš, *The Destruction of Yugoslavia*, 216. The fact that Serbs like Dragosavac, who had fought in the Partisans against the Ustaša, were now being labeled as such, is an indication of the overwhelmingly political nature of this policy, as opposed to the discourse of ethnicity that was being deployed by Belgrade.

[81] Borisav Mikelić, SKH party official, Serb from Petrinje, near Sisak: "I have been in Croatia's political structures for a long time. Exactly for that reason I am offended by the appraisals that Serbs in Croatia are threatened and assimilated Serbs are the ones who are in power.... We can resolve our own problems..., we don't need any help from outside, especially if it is insulting." "Uvredljive ocjene o ugroženosti Srba," *Jedinstvo*, September 28, 1989, 2; and report on speech by Mira Krajnović, an official in the Gospić party organization, denouncing "writings, pamphlets and speeches by certain groups ... who claim to be defending Serbs, alleging that they in Croatia are threatened, that they are losing their identity," responding, "We do not need such support and help, because Serbs themselves know their own situation in this Republic best." "Stabilni međunacionalni odnosi," *Lički vjesnik*, March 1, 1989, 1.

The Serbian conservatives' strategy of creating conflict along ethnic lines as a way of recentralizing the Yugoslav party thus pushed even SKH conservatives, both Croats and Serbs, closer to the reformists' line, since such a policy, by provoking conflict between Serbs and others in Yugoslavia along ethnic lines, posed a grave threat to the existing positive state of inter-ethnic relations in Croatia.[82] Indeed, by the late 1980s liberalization

> was largely an expression of the panic and stress to which Croatian communists were exposed because of the ever stronger Serbian nationalist movement . . . The liberalization of political life [in Croatia] thus had the special purpose of providing scope for a more vocal and explicit resistance to Serbian politics in Yugoslavia through the institutions of civil society.[83]

In other words, the SKH conservatives agreed to open up and liberalize in large part to gain support and legitimacy among the wider population in the face of attempts by Serbian conservatives to undermine the SKH's autonomy.

In addition to this threat to SKH autonomy coming from Belgrade, trends within Croatia were adding to the pressure to accept radical change, such that by 1988 the SKH was actively considering the introduction of multiparty elections. The economic situation continued to deteriorate despite the conservatives' attempts to stem the slide. There was also a sharp decrease in legitimacy of the SKH, as indicated by a drop in participation in elections. Support for reformist positions among Croatian communists as well as among the wider population was growing; in a striking example of this, in March 1989 Croatian reformists in the federal parliament allied with reformists from other republics, including from Serbia (Milošević had not yet been able to replace them) to elect Ante

[82] A particularly interesting case of a conservative Serb who refused to jump over to Milošević's instrumentalization of nationalism is Borisav Mikelić, from Petrinje. A conservative who headed the Petrinje općina and was a member of the top leadership of the SKH, Mikelić was very openly critical of Milošević's provocation of conflict in Croatia. When the SKH as a result moved toward a reformist line, Mikelić was stuck. He at first attempted to form his own conservative communist party, but as Belgrade and its allies put increasing pressure on Serbs in the region to leave the SKH and join the SDS, and especially after the violent establishment of "Krajina," Mikelić became caught up in the politics directed from Belgrade, sometimes as a target, sometimes as a participant (he served as the prime minister of Krajina for a period). The HDZ also targeted him, returning the enterprise that he had managed and built up, Gavrilović, to its prewar owners.

[83] Mirjana Kasapović and Nenad Zakošek, "Democratic Transition in Croatia: Between Democracy, Sovereignty, and War," in *The 1990 and 1992/93 Sabor Elections in Croatia: Analyses, Documents and Data*, ed. Ivan Šiber (Berlin: Sigma, 1997), 16.

Marković, a strong reformer, as federal prime minister over Milošević's candidate and close ally, Borisav Jović.

By late 1989, Belgrade's attempts to undermine the SKH by using the issue of Kosovo and the image of threatened Serbs, along with the growing economic problems facing Croatia, led to reformists taking control of the SKH. The final reformist victory came at the 11th SKH Congress in December, which, in a close vote, nevertheless officially called for holding multiparty elections in the spring of 1990.

Meanwhile, the economic situation continued to deteriorate, especially in the least developed parts of the republic. In the summer of 1989, the Lika region was hit with a series of strikes; in Gračac half of all employed workers went on strike for several days demanding higher pay.[84] Indeed, the economic situation in the entire region was serious, with output tumbling, unemployment mounting, and more and more enterprises operating in the red.[85] Given the perception that the elections would improve the economic situation, whoever came out victorious would be faced with growing expectations on this front.

The End of the League of Communists

By early 1990, when the Extraordinary 14th Congress of the League of Communists of Yugoslavia was held, the lines within the ruling party had been clearly drawn. On the one side were the conservatives in Serbia, under the leadership of Slobodan Milošević, who were insisting on a more centralized party, a more centralized political and economic system, and a more authoritarian role for the party in society. This faction used tactics of intimidation and fear in order to silence its opponents. On this side also were the newly installed leaderships of Vojvodina, Montenegro, and the

---

[84] "Ni Lika nije imune," *Lički tjednik*, September 15, 1989, 1.

[85] For examples of local reports on the serious problems in the local economies, see, M. Čuljat, "Pola gubitaša," *Lički vjesnik*, May 15, 1990, 3, which pointed out that output of the Gospić economy had fallen in 1989, with the decrease picking up at the end of the year, for a total fall of 18 percent, while at the same time employment fell; it also noted that the decline had continued to accelerate in the first months of 1990; and Veljko Kekić, "Visok nivo gubitaka," *Lički vjesnik*, May 15, 1990, 1, which pointed out that 92.2 percent of the total losses in the entire Lika region came from five of the twenty enterprises which worked at a loss, in Lički Osik, Perušić, and Gospić., all of which were in the Gospić općina (which had a majority Croat population of 64.7 percent, Serbs 30.9 percent, and in Otočac, 65.4 percent Croat and 31.1 percent Serb). Sixty-nine percent of losses were in Gospić, 29 percent in Otočac, and 1 percent each in T. Korenica, Donji Lapac; Gračac had no enterprises working at a loss.

JNA. The Bosnian party was split, not so much along ethnic lines—
some of the strongest opponents of Serbia's conservatives were themselves
Serbs—but along the reformist/conservative axis. Croatia's party by
this time was dominated by reformists and indeed had already scheduled
multiparty elections for the spring.

Slovenia too, which had been in the forefront of calls for radical restructuring of relations within the party and the federation, was also determined to ensure a reformist line. But unlike Croatia and Bosnia, there
seemed to be little commitment on the part of the Slovene leadership to
maintain Yugoslavia as a state. In fact, Slovenia and Serbia of all the
republics seemed most determined to have their way: Slovenia, through
separation from Yugoslavia if necessary, Serbia, through the use of force
to impose its will on the rest of the country. The two republics themselves
seem to have struck a deal: Dizdarević notes that one of the basic lines
of Milošević's policies in 1989–1990 was that "Serbia had nothing against
Slovenia leaving Yugoslavia if it wished. . . . Yugoslavia can survive without Slovenia."[86]

The 14th Congress ended in stalemate. Slovenia's delegation walked
out when it became clear that Milošević's allies were refusing to even consider anything that did not result in a recentralization of the party and a
tightening of the party's control over society. Indeed, the conservatives'
position seemed as if it were meant to purposely ensure Slovenia's walk-
out. But what they had perhaps not counted on was that the Croatian,
Bosnian, and Macedonian party delegations would refuse to continue the
Congress without the Slovene delegation. While for the conservatives
Yugoslavia existed regardless of Slovenia's presence, for these other
republics, decisions could only be made if all members of the federation, including Slovenia, were present.

Following the breakup of the 14th SKJ Congress, Belgrade once again
attempted to take control of local party organizations in Croatia and elsewhere. The conservative argument now was that the SKJ no longer existed
as a party of republican parties, but rather as a party of individual SK
members, who as individuals should decide the fate of the SKJ and its
policies. The plan was to gain the support of a majority of SKJ members
in Yugoslavia as a whole and then declare a "legitimate" victory. This
attempt to recentralize the SKJ was, however, soon overtaken by the
course of events and was superseded by more direct action on the part
of Belgrade.

[86] Dizdarević, *Od smrti Tita*, 291.

By the time of the April and May 1990 Croatian elections, Serbia's conservatives were still attempting to undermine local party organizations
in Croatia (and Bosnia) by using the issue of Kosovo. In areas with significant Serb populations, the Kosovo question and the attitude toward
the rallies organized by Belgrade in the region were litmus tests and cor-
related directly with support for or opposition to the reformist line in
Zagreb. These splits indicated the degree to which local SKH organizations were allied with Belgrade on issues of reform vs. orthodoxy, but
also demonstrated how Belgrade's policies were succeeding in creating
rifts within the SKH.[87]

In this sense, the 14th Congress marked the end of an era. While Serbia unsuccessfully attempted to hold subsequent sessions, and as noted
above, tried to argue that the SKJ was made up not of republic party organizations but rather of individual members, it was clear even before the
Congress that the era of unchallenged one-party rule was over. The Croatian and Slovene parties had already scheduled multiparty elections, and
pressure was also growing in Serbia itself for such a move. The dynamics
of Yugoslav politics, and thus the strategies pursued by the conservative
forces in the ruling party, changed to reflect those shifts.

Conclusion

From the early 1980s onward, the main axis of conflict in Yugoslavia was
the fate of the existing political and economic system. As the balance
of forces shifted in the favor of reformist forces who sought to fundamentally reform the existing structures of power, conservative forces in
the Serbian party resorted to a strategy of conflict by which they sought
to demobilize that movement within the party by shifting the focus of
political discourse away from issues of reform toward the threat of nationalism, in particular, the threat to innocent Serbs in Kosovo, Bosnia, and
Croatia. In this campaign, they accused reformists and even conservative Serbs in other republics, who opposed their strategy, of being in

[87] In Sisak, for example, while the local veterans committee denounced the HDZ and
supported federal efforts to stabilize Kosovo, it also denounced the "meetings of truth" in
Karlovac, Knin, and at Petrovo Gore as worsening relations and threatening a "Kosovo-
ization" of Croatia. "Protiv raspirivanja nacionalne mržnje," *Jedinstvo*, March 8, 1990, 2. In
Dvor, however, the local SKH committee opposed reformist moves to change the SKH's
name to include "Party of Democratic Changes," and fully supported the meetings. Milan
Đurić, "Naziv bez dodataka," *Jedinstvo*, March 15, 1990, 3; "Demokratska zajednica," *Jedinstvo*, March 29, 1990, 2.

league with the antirevolutionary extremist nationalist forces that were victimizing Serbs throughout Yugoslavia. They organized mobs and demonstrations that openly supported the Serbian conservatives, while calling for the resignation of leaderships that did not agree to the conservative recentralization as a means to pressure those leaders to resign. This threat of mob violence against communist party leaderships succeeded in Vojvodina and Montenegro, but created backlashes in Bosnia and especially in Croatia. The result was the final breakup of the League of Communists of Yugoslavia and the scheduling of multiparty elections in the northern republics.

The following chapter documents the strategies used by Serbia's conservatives, given the threat to their control over the structures of power in Serbia by massive anti-regime mobilizations. Chapter 5 will focus on the reaction of the Croatian leadership to these changes and to the strategies followed by the Croatian Democratic Union (HDZ), once it came to power in the May 1990 elections.

CHAPTER 4

SERBIA AND THE STRATEGY OF DEMOBILIZATION, 1990–2000

Between 1991 and 1995, the wars in Croatia and Bosnia-Herzegovina were characterized in the Western media, and much of the scholarly work on the conflict, as the result of ethnic hatreds whose source was identified particularly with the Serbs. The focus has been on Serbian President Slobodan Milošević, seen as mobilizing Serbs into violent conflict against non-Serbs by appealing to their hatreds and resentments. Much of this coverage has also focused on historical symbols and events that tap into deep-rooted aspects of Serb identity. According to this story, the resulting mobilization allowed Milošević to stay in power at a time when communist parties in the rest of eastern Europe were being replaced.

This chapter shows that the violence that Serbia perpetrated in Croatia, Bosnia, and Kosovo was not the result of ethnic hatreds or solidarity, nor was it a means by which the ruling party in Serbia sought to mobilize its population. Rather, these wars were part of a strategic policy on the part of the conservatives who dominated the ruling party. These elites were indeed faced with the same kind of anti-regime popular mobilizations seen throughout eastern Europe, based on the same kinds of values and preferences. But faced with these mobilizations, the Serbian ruling party and its allies responded by attempting to *demobilize* their population, to silence and marginalize those who were calling for fundamental changes to the structures of power. The images of violence that were portrayed in Serbia's state-controlled media, and the actual violence itself in Croatia and Bosnia, were parts of this overall strategy. The immediate goal of this strategy was to demobilize the population: to prevent an immediate overthrow of the existing structures of power through the reconstruction of political space, that is, through the creation of a political space in which the only legitimate and authentic political and ideological position was the one held by the ruling party. In contrast, at times when the ruling conservatives needed to actively mobilize support in elections, they presented themselves as moderate, concentrating on economic issues and declaring their desire for peace and stability in relations with the other Yugoslav republics and peoples. But when faced with popular anti-regime mobilizations, they consistently pursued a strategy of conflict.

In addition to the goal of demobilizing the population, the strategy of conflict also served to redraw the contours of the political space that had been Yugoslavia, in an attempt to destroy the notion of Yugoslavia as a federation of equal provinces and nations and reconstruct in its place a smaller space: a strongly centralized polity ruled from Belgrade and controlled by the conservatives. This new state would in effect be an enlarged Serbian state with a large majority of Serbs. Because many of them would suffer in the resulting wars, the conservatives could continue to use appeals to the injustices suffered by Serbs as a means of demobilizing opposition, thereby preserving the existing power structure.[1] In pursuit of this goal they actively collaborated with the conservative HDZ-controlled government in Croatia.

In addition, the reconstruction of political space was a means to what was perhaps the ultimate goal, namely, to maintain power structures in Serbia itself. This included taking control over what had formerly been classified as "socially owned property," as well as using positions within the ruling party, its allies, and the state, to transfer wealth from the state and the wider population into the private hands of the ruling elite. While, from the perspective of the well-being of Serbia and of Serbs throughout Yugoslavia, this strategy was disastrous,[2] from the perspective of the

[1] Since Serbia itself was only 65 percent Serb, by bringing the 25 percent of Serbs who live outside Serbia into the republic, and by expelling from their territories all non-Serb populations, the SPS would have been able to increase that percentage to 73 percent, a large proportion of whom are from economically underdeveloped regions with little education—the SPS's largest constituency within Serbia itself. In the end, Milošević did succeed in uniting most Serbs in Yugoslavia in one state, but rather than through territorial expansion this was accomplished through Serbs leaving or being expelled from places outside of Serbia and moving into Serbia itself.

[2] For example, at the end of 2000, Serbia's GDP was one-half the level of 1989; the average wage had fallen below 90 DEM; unemployment was more than 30 percent; industrial production was at 30 percent of the 1989 level; foreign debt was larger than the GDP; the country was isolated and had no access to international financial organizations. Aaron Presnall, Milko Stimac, eds., *Economic Review* (Group 17 and East-West Institute) 1.1, no. 9 (September 2000): 1, 8. In addition, Serbs in the rest of what was Yugoslavia are much worse off than they had been prior to the wars.

conservative elites it was strikingly successful, enabling them to maintain control long beyond the time when conservative elites in the rest of eastern Europe had lost power.

The strategy of demobilization proved effective until the end of the war in Bosnia. In the last section of this chapter, I will show how the return of mass anti-regime mobilizations, combined with decreasing standards of living, led the regime to revert to overtly authoritarian strategies, including the use of violence against domestic opposition. In fact, the war in Kosovo was part of that strategy and represented once again an attempt to demobilize increasingly organized and popular opposition forces. Following that war, however, the regime had again come to rely on authoritarian rule, on open repression of the opposition, including assassination. The elections of September 2000 were lost by the ruling SPS and its allies for a number of reasons, including their inability to demobilize opposition voters, their overconfidence in the likelihood of victory, and the defection to the opposition of a crucial part of the power elite—those whose control over and access to resources was no longer dependent on their relationship with the SPS or on the SPS's control of the state.

New Challenges:
Electoral Competition and Popular Mobilization, 1990–1991

We have seen that Serbia's conservatives had, from the time they took power in 1987 until the 14th Congress of the LCY in January 1990, focused on recentralizing the country in order to prevent the dominant reformist faction of the party from imposing significant changes in the structures of political and economic power. In this period conservatives had arranged mass rallies to pressure recalcitrant or reformist party leaderships and had used images and a discourse of Serbs as innocent victims of grave injustices in order to shift the focus of political discourse and competition within the League of Communists away from issues of reform and toward the alleged threat to innocent Serbs and to the socialist system itself from nationalist, anti-revolutionary forces.

This strategy succeeded in overcoming the reformist challenge from within the League of Communists of Serbia (SKS) and allowed Serbia's conservatives to replace party leaderships in Montenegro and Vojvodina with officials subservient to Belgrade. But it also had the effect of creating a backlash in the other republics, most notably in Slovenia, Croatia, and Bosnia. The resulting failure of the 14th Congress to reimpose a

centralized party structure fundamentally changed the political landscape
that Serbia's conservatives were facing, since the strategy of recentralizing Yugoslavia by taking over the communist parties of the other republics
was no longer feasible.

   At the same time, in the rest of eastern Europe massive street rallies
and the mobilization of large parts of the population against the ruling
communist parties had resulted in non-communists taking power throughout the region. These events had an enormous impact within Yugoslavia,
especially in Serbia, and form the background for what was to be the
greatest threat yet to the conservative Serbian coalition: the emergence
of a political system in which the wider population would choose political representatives and leaders through competitive, multiparty elections. Now, rather than fighting their battle within the framework of the
League of Communists, Serbia's conservatives would have to contend
with a much larger political field that included the active participation
of the wider population.

   The specific threats that Serbia's conservatives were facing now came
from three directions. The first was the fact that in the spring 1990 elections in Slovenia and Croatia, openly anti-socialist parties, which were
committed to a loosening rather than a tightening of political ties, had
taken power, due in large part to a backlash against Milošević.[3] Federal
decision-making bodies thus now included representatives from these
two republics, marking the introduction of an irreconcilable ideological
difference in terms of economic and political viewpoints. Indeed, the
Slovene and Croat governments soon put forward formal proposals for
reorganizing the country into a confederation, rejecting out of hand Serbia's calls for recentralization. Given the pressure for multi-party elections
in the other Yugoslav republics, and the fall of communist parties throughout the rest of eastern Europe, as well as the extent to which Serbia's strategies were threatening their autonomy, it seemed likely that other republics
would join these calls.[4] If reformist forces came to power in the other

   [3] On the Slovenian election, see Cohen, *Broken Bonds*, 89–94; Milan Andrejevich, "On
the Eve of the Slovenian Election," *Report on Eastern Europe* 1, no. 16 (April 20, 1990): 32–38;
on Croatia, see Milan Andrejevich, "Croatia Goes to the Polls," *Report on Eastern Europe* 1,
no. 18 (May 4, 1990): 33–37; and Cohen, *Broken Bonds*, 94–102. On Milošević's role in the
victory of the HDZ in Croatia, see interview with former Croatian party head Stipe Šuvar,
in "Jugoslavija nije razbijena i neće biti," *Nedeljna Borba*, May 5–6, 1990, 12.
   [4] Even the Bosnian communist party, formerly quite conservative, denounced Serbian
presidency member Jović's statement that democratization was endangering the constitutional order of Yugoslavia. Enver Demirović, "I vanredni kongres obnove," *Borba*, May
18, 1990, 3.

Yugoslav republics that were not controlled by Belgrade, it would become virtually impossible to resist this reformist line within the existing institutional framework.

The second set of threats came from the policies of federal Prime Minister Marković. By early 1990 these policies had proved quite successful in lowering inflation and improving the country's economic situation, and he was very popular, especially within Serbia.[5] Taking advantage of these successes, and looking ahead to multi-party elections, Marković pushed bills through the Federal Assembly allowing the privatization of state-owned firms and legalizing a multi-party system in the entire country. In July 1990, Marković formed his own political party to support his reforms.[6] The reforms that Marković was championing were exactly the kinds of changes that were most threatening to the conservatives who had taken control of Serbia at the end of 1987, and Marković's popularity in Serbia itself showed the extent to which these changes were potential points of mobilization against the regime.

The third and most serious source of threat to Serbia's conservatives came from within Serbia itself. Encouraged by the fall of communist parties in the rest of eastern Europe, and by the victory of non-communists in Croatia and Slovenia, opposition forces in Serbia began demanding competitive elections. Political parties were founded in the first months of 1990,[7] and the opposition called for multi-party elections, holding massive protest rallies in June 1990 in order to force the conservatives to accept a multiparty system.

Thus suddenly the relevant political audience now included the wider population. Within Serbia this meant that the ruling party needed to counter those elites outside of the SKS who were mobilizing large parts of the wider population for change. Just as in the rest of eastern Europe, so too

---

[5] In May 1990, Marković's popularity in Serbia surpassed that of Milošević; while the Serbian leader received a 50 percent approval rating, the federal prime minister's positive rating in Serbia was 61 percent. *Borba*, May 21, 1990.

[6] Marković named his party the "Alliance of Reform Forces." Cohen, *Broken Bonds*, 103.

[7] In the first public opinion poll about opposition parties carried out in Belgrade, the Institute for Political Studies in April 1990 found 37 percent of respondents saying they would vote for the ruling party, 27 percent undecided, and the remaining divided among the then-existing opposition parties. It is important to note however that about 50 percent of respondents had never heard of the largest opposition parties. Milošević, however, was popular, with 90 percent having a positive view of him. Ante Marković in this same poll received a positive evaluation from 92 percent of respondents. Slobodan Antonić, "Promene Stranačkog raspoloženja građana Srbije 1990–1993," in *Srbija između populizma i demokratije: Politički procesi u Srbiji 1990–1993*, ed. Slobodan Antonić et al. (Belgrade: Institut za političke studije, 1993), 6.

in Serbia most of the population wanted fundamental changes in the structure of political and economic power. Unlike communist parties in the rest
of eastern Europe, however, in Serbia the ruling party was unwilling to
allow changes to take place; unlike in Hungary, the conservatives did not
see that they could maintain access to and control over resources in a new
liberalized system; and unlike in Czechoslovakia and East Germany, they
did have alternatives to giving up power. Their alternative was to use a
strategy of conflict in order to demobilize the challengers.

The period from 1990 onward thus saw a marked shift in the strategy
of Serbia's leadership. In order to meet these new challenges, the conservatives abandoned their attempt to recentralize the country, instead
shifting to an alternative strategy whose goal was to destroy Tito's federal Yugoslavia and on its ashes to build a smaller more centralized state
dominated by Belgrade. In the new circumstances, the destruction of
Yugoslavia seemed to be the only way to prevent reform from being
imposed on Serbia from the federal level, as Prime Minister Marković was
already attempting to do.

A major obstacle to such a move, however, was the fact that the idea of
Yugoslavia was popular among Serbs, especially Serbs outside of Serbia. Thus publicly the SPS and its allies loudly proclaimed that they were
attempting to preserve Yugoslavia, blaming other republics and the international community for destroying the federation. As will be seen below,
their actual policies, however, were very much aimed at ensuring the
destruction of the Yugoslav federation. Another major obstacle was the
challenge to the ruling party coming from within Serbian society itself, as
the policies of Prime Minister Marković proved to be very popular, and
as opposition leaders mobilized the wider population against the regime
and for fundamental change. Part of their goal was thus to discredit
Marković, to undermine the reforms that he was attempting to implement,
and to demobilize the opposition forces at home.

The conservatives' decision to destroy Yugoslavia was reached shortly
after the victory of the HDZ in Croatia. According to Borisav Jović, at the
time president of the Yugoslav presidency and close ally of Milošević, by
June 1990 Milošević, Jović and federal defense minister Veljko Kadijević had decided to "throw Slovenia and Croatia out" of Yugoslavia by
using military force, thereby ensuring the conservatives and their allies
a majority of the votes in the Yugoslav party and state presidencies.[8]

[8] Jović notes that on June 27 he proposed to Veljko Kadijević "that I would most happily through the use of force throw [Slovenia and Croatia] out of Yugoslavia, by simply
cutting the border and proclaiming that they created this situation through their own

Milošević's idea was "to undertake the 'cutting off' or 'severing' of Croatia such that the municipalities in the regions of Lika, Banija, and Kordun, which have created a separate community [*zajednicu*], will stay on our side. Then later the people there will decide in a referendum whether they want to stay or to leave."[9] The stage was thus set for the start of the Yugoslav wars.

Accompanying this shift in strategy came a campaign against the new Croatian ruling party, the Croatian Democratic Union (HDZ). Beginning shortly after Croatia's May 1990 election, the Serbian conservatives accused the HDZ of planning to massacre its Serbian residents.[10] Throughout the summer of 1990, the Serbian media also ran stories detailing the anti-Serb massacres of the World War II Ustaša regime, furthering the implicit link with the HDZ.[11]

Shortly afterward, Belgrade and its allies began to implement their strategy of destroying Yugoslavia. They began by provoking and imposing violent conflict in the Serbian populated areas of Croatia. In the May 1990 elections only a small minority of Croatia's Serbs had supported the Serbian nationalist party, the Serbian Democratic Party (SDS).[12] Between July 1990 and March 1991, Belgrade's allies took over the SDS, forcibly replacing moderate leaders with hard-liners. It portrayed the HDZ as genocidal Ustaša; rejected all compromises with Zagreb; held mass rallies and erected barricades in those regions of Croatia they claimed as "Serb lands"; threatened and intimidated moderate Serbs and non-SDS members who refused to go along with the confrontational strategy; provoked armed incidents

---

actions." He further proposed, and Kadijević agreed, that Serbs in Croatia would hold a referendum "on the basis of which it would be decided to undertake the redrawing of borders." On the next day, Jović proposed the same thing to Milošević, who "agreed to the idea of 'throwing out' Slovenia and Croatia from Yugoslavia" but worried about whether the army would follow such orders. Jović responded that he was not worried about that, but rather about how to ensure a majority in the SFRY Presidency for such a decision. Borisav Jović, *Poslednji dani SFRJ: Izvodi iz dnevnika* (Belgrade: Politika, 1995), 159–161.

  [9] Ibid., 161.

  [10] Magaš, *Destruction of Yugoslavia*, 262.

  [11] Hayden, "Recounting the Dead," 13.

  [12] In the 1990 elections, most of Croatia's Serbs, especially those who lived in ethnically mixed and more economically developed parts of the republic, had rejected the overt nationalism of the Serbian Democratic Party (SDS), and had voted instead for multi-ethnic parties. Although 23 percent of Croatia's Serbs preferred the SDS, 46 percent preferred the reform communists, and 16 percent preferred the Coalition of National Reconciliation. Both of the latter advocated harmonious interethnic relation and improved material-well being; they rejected Milošević's strategy of recentralizing the country. Ivan Siber, "The Impact of Nationalism, Values, and Ideological Orientations on Multi-Party Elections in Croatia," in *Tragedy of Yugoslavia*, ed. Seroka, 143.

with the Croatia police, and stormed villages adjacent to the regions already controlled by Serbian forces and annexed them to their territory.[13] Throughout this period, conciliatory moves by moderates in the Croatian ruling party were rejected, while moderate Serbs who disagreed with Belgrade's conflictual strategy were branded as traitors.[14] Although the campaign rhetoric and the actions of hard-liners in HDZ did give Serbs cause for concern, and while HDZ conservatives with similar goals as the SPS were in many ways just as responsible for the violence, Belgrade worked to exacerbate the Croatian Serbs' concerns rather than fostering negotiation and compromise with Zagreb.

By the time of the December 1990 Serbian election, the violent strategy in Croatia had resulted in armed clashes within territory that was forcibly blocked from Croatian authorities, and the organization of armed groupings in other ethnically mixed regions of Croatia. At the same time, Serbia's media portrayed the events in terms of injustices and dangers to innocent Serbs who were victims of a neo-ustaša regime.

Indeed, what was most striking about the public rhetoric that accompanied the new strategy of violent conflict was its defensive nature. The political rhetoric of the Serbian leadership was most inflammatory and nationalistic exactly in the period when it did not need to actively mobilize the wider population to support it, that is, in the period when the politically relevant audience was limited to within the communist party, before late 1990. During that period, Milošević and his allies actively appealed to resentment, organized mass rallies, and in the media resorted to these racist images of ethnic others to support their contentions. That

---

[13] Cohen, *Broken Bonds*, 131, 134; Miloš Vasić, "Labudova pesma dr Milana Babića," *Vreme*, February 10, 1992, 13–15.

[14] For example in June 1990 the HDZ offered SDS leader Jovan Rašković a position as vice president of the parliament; Belgrade's pressure on Rašković and other SDS members led him to reject the offer and walk out of the assembly, and to end negotiations with Zagreb on Serbs' status in Croatia (Cohen, *Broken Bonds*, 86.) During the referendum on sovereignty in August, though Zagreb condemned the voting, it made no move to stop it, or to remove the barricades that Serbian forces had thrown up around the territory (Cohen, *Broken Bonds*, 134). Indeed, outside observers note that despite Serbia's accusations of a genocidal regime, Zagreb continued to moderate its rhetoric and act with "restraint." Helsinki Watch, "Human Rights in a Dissolving Yugoslavia," January 9, 1991, 7. In October, moderate SDS representatives from areas outside of Krajina (Slavonia, Baranja, Kordun, Istria) in negotiations with Zagreb received official recognition of the SDS as the legitimate representative of Croatia's Serbian population and the promise (later confirmed) that the draft Croatian constitution would not include the description of the republic as the "national state of the Croatian people," one of the Serbs' main grievances. The HDZ delegation also promised to resolve all other disputed questions quickly. SDS hard-liners from Knin, however, denounced the moderate Serbs as traitors. Vasić, "Labudova pesma."

earlier period did not however see the outbreak of violent conflict along ethnic lines, much less full-scale war.[15]

But when the political arena dramatically shifted in 1990 to include the entire adult population, and when the conservatives needed to gain the active support of a majority of voters in a system of multiparty elections, both the rhetorical line and the actual policies shifted. The rhetoric in this period focused almost exclusively on injustices being perpetrated against innocent Serb women, children, and old people outside of Serbia. Those parts of the political rhetoric of the ruling SPS that made specific reference to ethnic or national sentiment were structured in a very specific way around this concept of justice. Rather than appealing to some preexisting or abstract sense of ethnic solidarity, these appeals instead constructed images of terrible injustices by relying on distortions of reality, drawing on specious historical parallels, and resorting to outright lies.

Of course, in the case of Serbia there certainly were real grievances and injustices from the period of Tito's Yugoslavia that political elites could draw on for popular mobilization. In particular, the repression of public expression of national sentiment, to the point where peasants who sang nationalist songs faced imprisonment, was perceived as a grave injustice by a significant part of the population. In order to reinforce the ethnic nature of the grievance—and thus to redefine the meaning of being a Serb in Yugoslavia in a way that portrayed that meaning in homogeneous terms, as "victim"—the SPS portrayed those injustices as being essentially based on ethnicity, as having been inflicted on Serbs by non-Serbs—since Tito was identified as a Croat, and all top Yugoslav leaders after 1966 were identified as either Croats or Slovenes.[16] From the mid-1980s onward, the Serbian conservatives had managed to portray the federal and other republics' party organizations as the agents of injustice. The Serbian party, in contrast, portrayed itself not in terms of expressing ancient ethnic hatreds, but rather as the instrument of righting those injustices.

Yet this redress of injustices against cultural expression was not in itself sufficient to mobilize the population and certainly not enough to bring about violent conflict. Once those grievances were resolved, the rhetoric

[15] The province of Kosovo was put under virtual military occupation by Yugoslav and Serbian military and police. But what is significant is the almost total lack of violent conflict in Kosovo between ethnic Albanians and Serbs on an individual level. For statistics on the extremely low-level of inter-ethnic violence in Kosovo, see report of the independent commission, Srdja Popović, et al., *Kosovski čvor: drešiti ili seći?* (Belgrade: Khronos, 1990). There was also a complete lack of organized, sustained violence along these lines.

[16] Similar arguments were made in other republics where the injustices of cultural suppression were blamed on central authorities, who were identified with Serbia.

of injustice shifted its focus to the alleged extreme injustices against the 30 percent of Yugoslavia's Serb population that lived outside of Serbia's borders, echoing a major theme of the 1986 Memorandum of the Academy of Arts and Sciences.

Serbs in those places, especially after the 1990 elections, did indeed have legitimate concerns. But just as they did with regard to the negotiations on Kosovo in 1986, rather than trying to address those concerns Milošević and his allies exacerbated them, instrumentalizing them to create images of injustice, and portrayed the SPS as the only force standing up for these defenseless victims. The federal government and other republics were at the same time portrayed as either indifferent or actually complicit in the injustices. This image was driven home in a very powerful way through the ruling party's control over the mass media, especially television. The discourse itself was structured around injustices that Serbs outside of Serbia were suffering only because they were Serbs, at the hands of crazed, bloodthirsty extremists defined in ethnic and/or religious terms. Innocent Serb women and children were not safe in their own homes, while the outside world was doing nothing or was actually complicit in these injustices. Moreover, the outside was unjustly criticizing and punishing Serbia for helping these innocent victims. An important part of the strategy was the denial of any guilt whatsoever.

Serbian television, and the ruling party's control of it, played a crucial role in constructing this image of an unjust world.[17] Once conflict was provoked in Croatia and then in Bosnia, the media then "spun" these events in this way not only for viewers in Serbia but also for the victims themselves, who, in turn, repeating the official version of events then reconfirmed the impressions of terrible injustices back to their friends and relatives in Serbia.

This discourse served not only to justify military intervention into Croatia, but it also served as part of a strategy to demobilize the population of Serbia. At the same time the conservatives were attempting to provoke the violent dissolution of Yugoslavia, they were also facing, as explained above, demands from within Serbia itself for multiparty elections. Although Milošević argued that elections could not be held until the Kosovo issue

---

[17] As one respected polling institution noted about the influence of television within Serbia, "Television . . . has very great influence on public opinion even though its credibility is widely challenged." Cited in *Vreme*, November 16, 1992, 26–28: "TV's influence on the ghostly voters," by Dr. Miladin Kovaćević and Srdjan Bogosavljević. On how Serbian television managed to gain credibility, see Biljana Bakić, "Constructed 1990s Yugoslav Reality," MA thesis, University of Pittsburgh, 1994.

was resolved, by June the Serbian regime recognized the unavoidability of elections.[18]

In the face of this serious challenge, the regime also resorted to the issue of Kosovo, in particular, working assiduously to provoke violent resistance from the Albanian population.[19] At the same time, as described above, they were also heating up the situation in Croatia, provoking violence while at the same time pointing to that violence as evidence of the injustices and threats facing Croatia's innocent Serb population. This turning up the heat on Kosovo and Croatia was part of the SPS's strategy to deal with the growth of opposition forces and the mobilization of Serbia's population in favor of multiparty elections by both nationalist parties on the right (most notably the Serbian Renewal Movement, SPO, headed by writer Vuk Drašković), as well as civically oriented democratic parties. Despite this attempt at demobilization, however, the demands for elections continued, and the ruling party finally recognized the inevitability of an electoral contest.

In the face of this prospect, and in order to win the necessary two-thirds of the Serbian vote (since the party had alienated the 33 percent non-Serb population of the republic), the Serbian conservatives first undertook a strategy of averting a split of the communist party into a large pro-reform social democratic party that would more credibly appeal to the population's economic interest, and a small hard-line party (as happened in the rest of eastern Europe). To this end, in July 1990 the League of Communists of Serbia (SKS) was renamed the Socialist Party of Serbia (SPS), and Slobodan Milošević was elected as its president. At the same time, however, alongside the strategy of conflict, and the images of injustices being suffered by Serbs in Croatia, the ruling SPS and in particular its leader, Slobodan Milošević, presented themselves as peacemakers and reformers, concerned primarily with the stability and well-being of the population.

Indeed, in the election campaign itself, when it needed to mobilize voters to support it, the SPS's main appeal was to their material well-being, arguing for the continuation of a socialist system that provided social

[18] Dušan Radulović and Nebojša Spaić, *U Potrazi za Demokratijom* (Belgrade: Dosije, 1991).
[19] In July, Serbia dissolved the Kosovo Assembly and took over all institutions of the province; all Albanian language media was closed down; all Albanians were fired from positions of responsibility and replaced with Serbs, many fanatically anti-Albanian; Albanian workers were fired without cause; and there was a general harassment of the Albanian population. Galligan, "The Kosovo Crisis," 231–234, 239–258; Magaš, *Destruction of Yugoslavia,* 262–263.

security and economic growth.[20] It positioned itself as "the party of moderate change," and with the slogan, "With us there is no uncertainty,"
appealed to the fear that economic reform would bring instability.[21] The
SPS focused on the dangers of unemployment and economic insecurity,
blaming existing economic problems on the "anti-Serbian" policies of federal prime minister Ante Marković. The SPS emphasized that it would
ensure social security and especially job security. Milošević also criticized
the reformist opposition parties for wanting to turn Serbia into a colony
of the West, declaring for example that

> We want to belong to the modern world . . . but we must not allow our-
> selves to become dependent on anybody in Europe or the world under the
> pretext of so-called integration within Europe. . . . Serbia can cooperate
> with anybody in the world in the sphere of politics, economics, and cul-
> ture on an equal footing.[22]

The conservatives thus portrayed the reformist policies of the opposition
parties as dangerous, as ensuring increased unemployment and insecurity,
and as a means by which Yugoslavia would be deprived of its independence
and be turned into a colony of the West. At the same time, since the economic
situation was quite dire (in large part because the SPS was blocking the
implementation of Marković's reforms), the government just before the
December elections also printed the equivalent of US$2 billion in dinars for
overdue worker salaries, funds taken illegally from the federal treasury.

On issues of nationalism, the SPS had already very much distanced itself
from the policies of Tito, especially those which forbade public expression
of national sentiment. This fact, plus the fact that Yugoslav agriculture had
remained in private hands, ensured the SPS of most of the vote of peasants
and those one generation off the land, a majority of the voters, and thus
dampened anticommunist sentiment against it.[23] The SPS also portrayed
itself as a modern, moderating, and progressive force opposed to nationalist excesses.[24] Milošević compared the main opposition nationalist party,
the Serbian Renewal Movement (SPO), to Serbian extremists during World

---

[20] Sixty-six percent of those who voted for SPS gave priority to developing a strong
economy, and 59 percent to improving the material conditions of life. "Glasali ste, gladu-
jte," *Vreme,* January 6, 1992, 12–13.

[21] Slavujević, "Election Campaigns," in Goati, *Challenges of Parliamentarism.*

[22] "Srbija napreduje," *Politika,* November 22, 1990, 1–2.

[23] "Sto dana višestranačke Srbije," *NIN,* March 29, 1991, 77–79.

[24] Forty-nine percent of SPS voters stressed the importance of good inter-ethnic relations. *Vreme,* January 6, 1992.

War II, and accused it of wanting to drag Serbia into war and of seeking to "provoke confrontation and incite hatred toward other peoples and nations." Milošević portrayed this election as a fundamental choice:

> Serbia finds itself before elections that will determine whether we will be for peace and economic and cultural prosperity, or for conflicts and hatreds which will block all the efforts that we've made to date to come out of the crisis and to have a better life.[25]

Milošević also declared that the SPO's focus on Serbian history was counterproductive, because "the past can't resolve the problems of the present" and "should be left to history."[26] His victory, Milošević argued, was what would ensure peace at home and good relations with the other Yugoslav republics. Using this strategy, the SPS managed to win an overwhelming majority of parliamentary seats with the support of 47 percent of the electorate (72 percent of Serbia's Serbs).[27]

Thus the SPS, in the first multiparty elections held in Serbia since 1945, appealed to the population in terms of their economic interests and desire for stability and security and openly rejected a strategy based on conflict and violence, and on appeals to the past. This is not to say that these themes were not of importance to parts of the population. It is evidence, however, that in the December 1990 elections the SPS calculated that the most effective way to mobilize voters to support it was not to "play the ethnic card" or try to ethnically outbid the opposition, but rather to appeal to their clear priorities, priorities that were reflected in the social science polling cited in chapter 2: material well being, economic security, and positive coexistence with the other republics and peoples of Yugoslavia. In contrast, the SPO, which attempted to portray itself as more nationalist (and aggressively so) than the SPS, received 16 percent of the vote, while the Serbian Radical Party (SRS), which openly called for expulsion of non-Serbs from Serbia and for a war to create an enlarged Serbia, received only 2 percent of the vote.

Of course the SPS's control of the television and radio networks and major newspapers, its ability to design a winner-take-all electoral system that did not require a majority of votes to ensure control of parliament, its

[25] Milošević campaign speech in Niš, cited in Dušan Radulović and Nebojša Spaić, *U pótrazi za demokratijom* (Belgrade: Dosije, 1991), 147.

[26] Speech in Niš, November 21, 1990, in *Politika*, November 22, 1990, 1, 2. For other examples, see his speeches at Bor, November 1, and in Kragujevac, November 27.

[27] For a detailed description of how the SPS managed to subvert the elections and cripple the opposition, see Radulović and Spaić, *U Potrazi za Demokratijom*.

control of economic policy, and its proliferation of other political parties, all served to fragment the opposition and to ensure that the SPS had an advantage going into the election. But what is more interesting in the broader context is that the SPS saw that its best chance to mobilize votes was to stress themes of peace and security, rather than appealing to themes of ethnic hatreds and conflict.

1991: The Threat of Popular Mobilization

Following Milošević's December 1990 victory in the Serbian elections, the situation in Croatia became even more confrontational as a hard-line group within the Serbian Democratic Party in Croatia (SDS), working closely with Belgrade and armed by the Yugoslav Army, began to provoke armed conflicts with Croatian police in areas where Serbs were not in the majority. Indeed, Jovan Rašković, one of the founders of the SDS, was quite upset by this takeover, declaring that "I warned that this radical group which wanted to take over the SDS is a danger for us and that war will definitely result if they exacerbate things."[28] Croatian Serbs were increasingly pressured to toe the SDS line, and Croats in Krajina were besieged by Serbian armed forces and pressured to leave.[29] These purposefully provoked conflicts were publicly characterized by Belgrade in its communications with the outside world as "ethnic conflicts," the result of ancient hatreds, and the Yugoslav army was portrayed as having been called in to separate the "feuding ethnic groups." In Serbia, these conflicts were portrayed as evidence of the Croatian regime's intentions to rid itself of its Serb population, and that the actions of the JNA and the paramilitary forces were heroic attempts to protect those innocent lives. At the end of February 1991, Krajina proclaimed its autonomy from Croatia.

These Serbian moves gave Croat hard-liners an excuse to step up their repressive actions against Serbs in areas where the ruling HDZ controlled

---

[28] Rašković notes that at a February 26 meeting of the SDP leadership, 38 out of 42 members supported his call for moderation, against extremist Milan Babić, who advocated a hard-line confrontational and military approach and who was in direct contact with Belgrade. Babić the next day proceeded to found his own party, the "SDS Krajina." See interview with Rašković, *Globus*, February 14, 1992, 14–15. Shortly after this armed clashes with Croatian police broke out in Pakrac, in western Slavonia, and at the Plitvice Lakes national park on the edge of Krajina.

[29] One example of this was the Croat majority village of Kijevo outside Knin, which was besieged for eight months. Srđan Španović, "Čudo u Kijevu," *Danas*, March 12, 1991, 18–20.

the local government. In turn, these actions were pointed to by Belgrade's allies as proof of the threat to Serbs.[30] Despite calls by Croatian hard-liners to use military force, Zagreb lacked significant stocks of weapons (although it was actively seeking sources), and Croatian president Franjo Tudjman reportedly feared providing the Yugoslav army with an excuse to crush the Croatian government.[31] He was thus forced to accept the army's gradually expanding occupation of the areas where the SDS's authoritarian rule prevailed. This period saw the groundwork for a similar strategy being laid in Bosnia by Belgrade's ally there, Radovan Karadžić, head of that republic's SDS.[32]

As conflict heated up in Croatia, in negotiations over the future of Yugoslavia, Milošević and his allies took a hard line in refusing to budge from the conservatives' call for a more tightly centralized federation. He declared that if his demand were rejected, then the borders of Serbia would be redrawn so that all Serbs would live in one state.[33] The result of this conflictual strategy was exactly as intended, to further the destruction of Yugoslavia. The provocations and repression of even moderate Serbs in Croatia increased the territory under JNA control and provoked reactions on the part of extremist Croats that were then pointed to as justifying military action.

This apparently successful strategy was suddenly interrupted when the opposition and students succeeded in mobilizing large numbers of people against Milošević and his government in the form of massive protest rallies in Belgrade from March 9 to 14.[34] Appealing to the wider popula-

---

[30] For example in western Slavonia, some hard-line HDZ members from Herzegovina, "former petty criminals," were put into the police force and began harassing Serbs, although even local Croats were frightened. The result was that the SDS, which had little support in the region before, began to attract many Serbs. Zoran Daskalović, "Skupljenje povjerenja," *Danas*, March 12, 1991, pp. 13–14; Milan Bečejić, "Forsiranje straha," *Danas*, March 12, 1991, 16–17.

[31] On Croatia's efforts to obtain weaponry, see Martin Špegelj, *Sjećanja vojnika* (Zagreb: Znanje, 2001), 131–132.

[32] Karadžić openly declared the goal of drawing ethnic borders, citing the Krajina experience, but ignoring the Muslims as a factor. Yet Bosnia's population was so ethnically intermixed that there really were no ethnic borders. See Stjepko Golubović, Susan Campbell, and Thomas Golubović, "How Not to Divide the Indivisible," in *Why Bosnia? Writings on the Balkan War*, ed. Rabia Ali and Lawrence Lifschultz (Stony Creek, Conn.: Pamphleteers' Press, 1993), 209–232. Karadžić also declared that "we have given Milošević a mandate to represent Serbs in Bosnia-Herzegovina if Yugoslavia disintegrates." *Borba*, February 26, 1991, 7.

[33] *Vreme*, March 4, 1991.

[34] See Helsinki Watch, "Yugoslavia: The March 1991 Demonstrations in Belgrade," May 1, 1991; Zoran Miljatović, "9. mart, zvanična verzija," *NIN*, March 29, 1991, 11–13.

tion, the opposition, led by Serbian Renewal Movement chief Vuk
Drašković, threatened to oust the conservatives by force of street rallies.
The bottom line demand of the protesters was that the SPS step down from
power as other east European communists had done. These events represented extremely serious threats to the ruling party and to the structure
of power that they relied on, and political commentators in Belgrade were
predicting the imminent fall of the regime.

Initially called to denounce the SPS's tight control and manipulation of
the media, the rallies also condemned Milošević's disastrous economic
policies and his policy of provoking conflict with other republics.[35] Indeed,
what is most striking about this mobilization is that it marked a shift in the
strategy of Drašković, who had previously pursued a strategy of ethnic
outbidding, that is, trying to attract support by claiming to be more mil-
itantly nationalistic than the ruling party. At the March demonstrations,
however, Drašković began pursuing a strategy of ethnic *underbidding*, that
is, trying to seem more moderate on national questions than the SPS. While
not renouncing his nationalist viewpoint, Drašković accused the SPS of
war-mongering and called for peaceful negotiations to realize the interests of Serbs and of Serbia in Yugoslavia. By the end of the summer,
Drašković went so far as to publicly question the need for the war that
Serbia had provoked in Croatia, and criticized the destruction of civilian
targets and whole cities by Serb forces in Croatia.[36] Some question
Drašković's sincerity in this shift; but his sincerity is less important than
his calculation that the way to mobilize support was to seem more moderate, not more aggressive, on ethnic issues

What is interesting about these events is that the wider population was
being mobilized not on ethnic issues, and not through the classic image
of leaders playing the nationalist card. Rather, a nationalist leader of an
opposition party was ethnically underbidding the ruling powers, and the
population was mobilized in massive numbers around political demands
for a free media, a more open political system, and economic demands for
basic reform. There was also anger that Milošević's policies were undermining relations between Serbia and the other Yugoslav republics. Rather
than ethnic solidarity or "playing the nationalist card," these rallies were
very much focused on the kinds of issues the polling cited in chapter 2
indicated were a priority.

[35] For list of initial demands, see Milan Bečejić, "Rafali u demokraciju," *Danas*, March
12, 1991, 29–31; see also "Objava mira umesto rata," *Politika*, May 8, 1991, 8.
[36] See interviews with Drašković in *Vreme*, November 4, 1991, 9–11, and *Danas*, February 18, 1992.

Although Milošević's immediate reaction to the protests was to call on the army to put down the demonstrations, the military refused to use massive force against the unarmed population.[37] This marked the start of the democratic opposition's rapid rise in popularity and the beginning of an open split within the ruling SPS by democratic, pro-reform forces.[38] Shortly thereafter, massive strikes (including one of 700,000 workers) aimed specifically against Milošević's rule, shook Serbia.[39] Given the refusal of the army to use force, Milošević was forced to negotiate with his opponents. He accepted limited economic reform, printed more money to pay workers, and discussed the formation of a multi-party Serbian national council.

At the same time, in response to one of the protesters' demands, he shifted to a much more conciliatory rhetorical line in the inter-republic talks on the future of Yugoslavia. In April, Milošević, after months of refusing to budge from his insistence on a more centralized federation, accepted the principle of a confederation, and in talks over the future of Yugoslavia in early June, he agreed to the principles on which such a confederation would be based.[40] Belgrade also pressured its Serbian allies in Croatia to negotiate with Zagreb, although they refused to reach an agreement.[41] Thus in terms of public rhetoric and actions, Serbia's conservatives seemed to be heeding the protesters and adopting their moderate demands.

Behind the scenes, however, Milošević was gearing up his strategy to demobilize the opposition, by marginalizing and silencing it, and to ensure that in the short term the structures of power remained intact, while at the same time ensuring his ability to realize the long-term strategy of creating an enlarged centralized state ruled from Belgrade. To this end, in late March, Milošević secretly met with Croatian President Tudjman to agree on a division of Bosnia-Herzegovina, thus removing the possibility

---

[37] On use of force, see Helsinki Watch, "Yugoslavia," May 1991.

[38] On the SPS split, see *Politika*, May 12, 1991, 12; Toma Đodić, "Istočno od partije," *NIN*, April 26, 1991, 28–29.

[39] Života Đorđević, "Optužen nije došao," *NIN*, April 19, 1991, 34–35.

[40] See "Kompromis i ustupci korak ka rešenu," *Borba*, June 7, 1991, 1, 3; and interview with Bosnian president Izetbegović, co-author (along with Macedonian president Gligorov) of the compromise plan, "Država na ljudskim pravima," *Vreme*, June 17, 1991, 12–14.

[41] Tanjug, April 15 and 16, 1991, in FBIS-EE, no. 73–91 and 74–91; this occasion was used, however, to further purge the SDS of moderates with the accusation of being "traitors" for having talked with Tudjman. This same period saw further marginalization of other moderates, including Rašković, who was sent to Belgrade. Vasić, "Labudova Pesma," 14.

of Tudjman taking advantage of Milošević's then weak position.[42] The
two leaders also reportedly agreed to try to remove Ante Marković as a
political factor, since Marković's policies were threatening to the interests
of both leaders.

Simultaneously, the strategy of provoking conflict along ethnic lines
was also stepped up. Milošević himself labeled the protesters "enemies
of Serbia" who were working for Albanians, Croats, and Slovenes to try
to destroy Serbia, and he ominously stressed the "great foreign pressures
and threats" being exerted on Serbia that gave "support to the forces of
disintegration of Yugoslavia."[43] The media stepped up its portrayals of
Croatia as a fascist Ustaše state, and, in April, graphically reported on the
opening of caves in Bosnia-Herzegovina filled with the bones of thousands
of Serb victims killed in the 1940s by the Ustaše; in August it broadcast the
mass interment of the remains, thus vividly illustrating its argument that
Serbs were and continued to be the innocent victims of evil forces that had
to be opposed.[44] By linking the opposition to these evil forces, Milošević
sought to portray the opposition as not caring about and even complicit
in the injustices.

This period was also one of close cooperation between elements in
the Yugoslav army, the Serbian conservatives, and the Bosnian SDS, as
the three sides implemented "Project RAM," the conservatives' plan
to use military force to expand Serbia's borders westward and create
a new Serbian Yugoslavia.[45] Thus in Bosnia in the spring of 1991, the
SDS set up "Serbian Autonomous Regions" that were declared no longer

[42] See reports of the testimony of Stipe Mesić at the International Criminal Tribunal at
the Hague on October 1, 2002, in "The Courtroom Summit," *Tribunal Update of the Institute
for War and Peace Reporting* 283 (October 9, 2002). <http://www.iwpr.net/index.
pl?archive/tri/tri_283_1_eng.txt> (accessed October 11, 2003). See also report on the testimony of former Prime Minister Ante Marković, "Plan to Divide Bosnia Revealed," *Tribunal Update* 330 (October 24, 2003). http://www.iwpr.net/index.pl?archive/tri/
tri_330_4_eng.txt (accessed October 25, 2003).

[43] Milošević speech to Serbian parliament, *Politika*, May 31, 1991, 1–2.

[44] The funeral, presided over by the Serbian Orthodox patriarch, included a proces-
sion of coffins that stretched for one-and-a-half kilometers. Hayden, "Recounting the Dead,"
p. 13.

[45] On SDS cooperation with the Yugoslav army, see "Skica pakla," *Vreme*, March 9,
1992, 25. On project RAM, see *Vreme*, September 30, 1991; and stenographic notes of federal cabinet at which this plan was discussed, in *Vreme*, September 23, 1991, 5–12.
Related to RAM, just after the March 1991 street protests, Defense Minister Kadijević held
secret talks in Moscow with Soviet Defense Minister Yazov (who would several months
later lead the coup attempt), and without the knowledge of civilian officials arranged for
a large quantity of weapons, including planes, rocket systems, and helicopters to be delivered to the Yugoslav army (ibid., 7).

under the authority of the republic government, a repetition of the Krajina strategy.[46]

The SPS at this time also began an open alliance with the neo-fascist Serbian Radical Party led by Vojislav Šešelj, ensuring Šešelj's election to the Serbian parliament in a by-election.[47] Šešelj's guerrilla groups were active in the ensuing escalation of conflict in Croatia. In this period, Belgrade also exerted growing pressure on moderate Serb leaders in Croatia's ethnically mixed Slavonia region (where Serbs were not in the majority) to accept its confrontational strategy; in May, Krajina held a referendum to join with Serbia, and Belgrade supported guerrillas, including Šešelj's "Chetniks," flowed into Croatia, terrorizing both Serb and non-Serb populations in the more developed regions of eastern and western Slavonia (neither of which had Serb majorities).[48] These forces attacked Croatian police, in at least one case massacring and mutilating them, and began a policy of forcible ethnic expulsions in areas coming under their control. Moderate SDS leaders denounced Belgrade for provoking and orchestrating this confrontational strategy.[49]

In the face of this pressure, and in preparation for the new confederal agreement, in late June the Croatian government declared the start of a process of disassociation from Yugoslavia, specifically stating that it was not an act of unilateral secession and that Zagreb continued to recognize the authority of federal organs, including the army.[50] When the army attacked Slovenia following its own declaration of sovereignty,

[46] Momčilo Petrović, "Odlučivaće sila?" *NIN*, April 19, 1991, 11.

[47] Miloš Vasić, "Falsifikat originala," *Vreme*, June 17, 1991, 8–9. Šešelj appealed to a virulent Serbian nationalism that demonized other nationalities, especially Albanians and Croats, called for building a Greater Serbia including all of Croatia "except what can be seen from the top of Zagreb's cathedral," and advocated expulsion of non-Serbs from Serbia. See program of his "Chetnik movement" in *Velika Srbija*, July 1990, 2–3.

[48] Other Belgrade-supported paramilitary groups include those of Arkan ("Tigers"), and of Mirko Jović ("White Eagles"). On Belgrade's support of these groups and the local Serbian forces, see, "Helsinki Watch Letter to Slobodan Milošević and General Blagoje Adžić," January 21, 1992, in *War Crimes in Bosnia-Herzegovina* (New York: Human Rights Watch, August 1992), 275. On the referendum, see *Politika*, May 13, 1991, 1, 5. For an excellent study of the military units that used "volunteers" that were organized by political parties, the Serbian State Security forces, and the Yugoslav army, see Aleksandra Sasha Milićević, "Joining Serbia's Wars: Volunteers and Draft-dodgers, 1991–1995," Ph.D. diss., University of California at Los Angeles, 2004.

[49] Vojislav Vukčević, head of the SDS organization in the Baranja region of Croatia, bordering on Serbia, in *NIN*, April 19, 1991, 14. Former SDS leader Rašković also denounced the hard-liners who had taken over the party as well as Belgrade's strategy of conflict. *NIN*, May 3, 1991, 15.

[50] See report Chuck Sudetic, "2 Yugoslav States Vote Independence to Press Demands," *New York Times*, June 26, 1991, A1, A6.

Croatia did not help the Slovenes in order to avoid giving the army an excuse to attack Croatia.[51]

Nevertheless, the Yugoslav army, despite its promises not to attack Croatia,[52] escalated and intensified the conflict in Croatia, and Serbian forces continued their strategy of provoking conflicts in Slavonia and on the borders of Krajina, terrorizing civilian populations, destroying Croatian villages and Croat parts of towns, bombing cities to drive out the population, and forcing Serbs on threat of death to join them and point out Croat-owned houses.[53] These forces included units of the "Special Operations Forces" or "Red Berets," which were under the direct command of the Serbian State Security and were funded and directed from Belgrade; volunteer units of the Yugoslav National Army; and volunteer units that were attached to political parties and that were partially controlled by State Security.[54] Serbs who openly disagreed with these policies were terrorized and silenced.[55] Helsinki Watch noted that in the period through August 1991, when the Croats finally went on the offensive and Croat extremists themselves undertook atrocities against civilians, by far the most egregious human rights abuses were committed by the Serbian guerrillas and the Yugoslav army, including indiscriminate use of violence to achieve their goals of terrorizing the Serb population into submission and driving out the non-Serb population.[56] This policy, by provoking

[51] These Yugoslav army attacks seemed in part to be the result of U.S. Secretary of State Baker's declaration in Belgrade that the most important U.S. priority continued to be a united Yugoslavia. This declaration was apparently crucial in assuring the army that the international costs of military action would not be unbearable. For his statement, see Thomas Friedman, "Baker Urges End to Yugoslav Rift," New York Times, June 22, 1991, 1, 4. Indeed, the reliable independent Belgrade weekly Vreme reported that just before Baker's visit the United States had sent special emissaries to offer the Yugoslavs the help of the 82nd airborne division in Munich if necessary; and a few days before the visit assistant secretary of state Eagleburger mentioned the possibility of NATO or CSCE aid to Yugoslavia. Roksanda Ninčić, "Kraj druge Jugoslavije," Vreme, July 1, 1991, 6.
[52] Cited in Danas, July 23, 1991, 7.
[53] See "Helsinki Watch Report on Human Rights Abuses in the Croatian Conflict," September 1991, in War Crimes, 230–273; and "Helsinki Watch Letter to Milošević and Adžić," 276–302.
[54] For information on the special forces that were under the direct control of the Second operative directorate of the Department of State Security of the Ministry of Internal Affairs of Serbia, see Igor Salinger and Aleksandar Radić, "Od Arkana do Gumara," Vreme, April 3, 2003, and "Tajna avijacija državne bezbednosti," Vreme, April 10, 2003. For information on volunteers to all three types of units, see Milićević, "Joining Serbia's Wars."
[55] See NIN, November 8, 1991, 15; Vreme, November 4, 1991, 12–15; and interview with moderate Zagreb-based Serbian Democratic Forum leader Milorad Pupovac in Vreme, October 21, 1991, 12–14.
[56] Helsinki Watch noted that "the majority" of human rights abuses by Croats "involved discrimination against Serbs," where individual managers demanded that Serb workers

extremist forces in Croatia into action—or more accurately, giving them an excuse to carry out their own strategy of conflict—thus in effect became a self-fulfilling prophecy as the Serbian regime pointed to those atrocities as proof of their original charges.[57]

The violence in Croatia was thus not the result of spontaneous outbursts of ethnic hatreds, nor was it the result of ethnic elites mobilizing the "ethnic masses" into violent conflict. Rather, the bloodshed and "ethnic cleansing" that took place over the summer of 1991 was a purposeful strategic use of military force on the part of elites in Belgrade and Zagreb that had the immediate goal of destroying heterogeneous communities in the most ethnically plural parts of Croatia. This war policy also destroyed the chances for Marković's reforms to succeed. Although Slovenia and Croatia, along with Serbia, had been trying to block implementation of many aspects of his reform, the JNA and Serbian guerrilla attacks ended support for a continued Yugoslavia even among those who had advocated it, while Milošević's moves to take over the Federal presidency and marginalize the federal government by September 1991 led Marković to the conclusion that he had no choice but to resign.[58] By the summer the army was also draining the federal hard currency reserves and taking up a vast proportion of the federal budget, which had been carefully managed by Marković.

One of the main effects of the war was that it greatly helped Milošević in his domestic crisis, effectively demobilizing the opposition. In April 1991, the democratic opposition had been at a high point, the ruling party was facing a split, and commentators were predicting the imminent fall of the SPS. But the SPS used charges of genocide and the subsequent war in Croatia, along with its control over the media, to suppress internal party

---

sign loyalty oaths to Croatia or be fired, as well as some police beatings; while abuses by the Serbian forces involved "physical maltreatment" and "egregious abuses against civilians and medical personnel," including the use of civilians as "human shields" in battle. It also accused the Yugoslav army of "serious human rights violations by attacking civilian targets with Serbian forces," including the mortar bombing of such cities as Vukovar and Osijek. "Yugoslavia: Human Rights Abuses in the Croatian Conflict," September 1991. See also Blaine Harden, "Observers Accuse Yugoslav Army," on EC observers' similar charges, *Washington Post,* January 17, 1992, A23.

The head of the main democratic nationalist party in Serbia, Vuk Drašković, has publicly stated that "there was no particular need for war in Slavonia." *Danas,* February 18, 1992. See also his denunciation of the war in *Vreme,* November 4, 1991, 9–11.

[57] For details of atrocities and abuses by Croatian forces, see Helsinki Watch report on abuses in Croatia, above; and "Helsinki Watch Letter to Franjo Tudjman," February 13, 1992, in *War Crimes,* 310–359. See also chapter 5.

[58] For example, by September 1991 all Croats in the federal diplomatic service had been fired. Mihailo Nicota, "Lončar bez baze," *Danas,* 502 (October 1, 1991), 46.

dissent and to marginalize the democratic opposition by drowning out concerns about economic and political reform and by charging those who questioned the war with treason. Indeed, part of the opposition played right into the SPS's strategy, shifting away from demands for reform toward trying to appear more patriotic than the SPS.

The regime also used the war to try to physically destroy the opposition: it first sent reservists to the front from municipalities that had voted for opposition parties. Opposition leaders and outspoken anti-war activists were sent to the front, and any criticism was met with physical threats and violence from neo-fascist gangs.[59] The regime also targeted the Hungarian minority in Vojvodina (an absolute majority in seven counties), which, although only 3 percent of Serbia's population, represented 7 to 8 percent of reservists at the front and 20 percent of casualties.[60]

By September the army was attacking Dubrovnik, and thousands of reservists were wandering Bosnia-Herzegovina, terrorizing the Bosnian Muslim population.[61] But at this same time there was growing discontent in Serbia about the war, discontent that was increasingly being expressed in public.[62]

Indeed, what is striking about this war was the response of Serb men to the army's efforts to draft them to fight against Croatia. At a time when the Serbian media was filled with images of genocidal ustaše massacring innocent Serb women and children, the attempts to mobilize young men and reserve forces in Serbia to fight in Croatia were stunningly unsuccessful.

According to figures from the Belgrade Center for Anti-War Action, turnout rates in Belgrade were 5 percent, while rates in smaller cities and the countryside were somewhat higher, around 20 percent. Other reports give an overall figure of about 50 percent. As Stephen Burg and Paul Shoup point out,

> the inability of the JNA to mobilize, train, and motivate Serb recruits from
> Serbia proper to fight in Croatia was critical. . . . General Kadijević in his
> memoirs identified the failure of the Serbs to fight in Croatia as a major

---

[59] Milan Milošević, "Srbi protiv Srba," *Vreme*, October 21, 1991, 8–11; Helsinki Watch, Letter to Milošević and Adžić, *War Crimes*, 302, 304; Milan Milošević, "Panonska pobuna," *Vreme*, November 18, 1991, 12–15.

[60] In addition, 25,000 Hungarians fled Serbia. The leader of Serbia's Hungarian community described this policy as "violent changing of the ethnic structure" of Vojvodina. "Bekstvo od rata," *Vreme*, January 20, 1992, 31.

[61] On reservists, see Mladen Klemenčić, "Srpska kama u trbuhu Bosne," *Globus*, September 27, 1991, 9.

[62] For polling data, see Milan Milošević, *Vreme*, September 23, 1991, 29–33.

factor contributing to the poor performance of the JNA. . . . The Belgrade opposition weekly *Vreme* reported in late September that the Serbian parliament had been informed in a closed meeting that only 50 percent of the reservists in Serbia and only 15 percent in Belgrade had obeyed orders to report for duty.[63]

Thus between 50 and 85 percent of Serb men called up to fight in Croatia either went into hiding or left the country (200,000 men reportedly went abroad to avoid the draft) rather than fight. In addition, about 50,000 reservists who did go into the army deserted from the front.[64] This hardly fits with the typical model of ethnic mobilization.

The result of the various parts of the SPS strategy was that the summer of 1991 saw a sharp decline in the opposition. Whereas they seemed poised to overthrow the SPS in April, by July they had been effectively silenced and marginalized. Their supporters were demobilized not only by the atmosphere of war and fear but also by the military mobilization for the war. Consequently, the structures of power in Serbia remained intact.

As long as the conflict was going on in Croatia, this demobilization remained effective. But Belgrade began to run into a number of obstacles to a continuation of this strategy. In August, the SPS's hard-line allies in Moscow had failed in their attempts to seize power.[65] By November 1991, the European Community was threatening economic sanctions against Serbia, and Croat forces began taking back territory. When the conflict in Croatia came to an end with the arrival of UN peacekeepers, the demands of the Serbian population surfaced once again.

[63] Steven Burg and Paul Shoup, *The War in Bosnia-Herzegovina: Ethnic Conflict and International Intervention* (Armonk, N.Y.: M. E. Sharpe, 1999), 84, citing Veljko Kadijević, *Moje viđenje raspada* (Belgrade: Politika, 1993), 138–139, 143, and *Vreme*, September 30, 1991, 6–10 and October 21, 1991, 8–11.

[64] See Dragan Todorović, "To nije njihova kolubarska bitka," *Vreme*, October 7, 1991, 24–26; Milan Milošević, "Marš preko Drine," *Vreme*, October 7, 1991, 20–22; Torov, *Danas*, October 1, 1991, 32. For an excellent study of those who refused to respond to the call-up of reservists as well as those who deserted after being called up, see Milićević, "Joining Serbia's Wars."

[65] In fact, the SPS was also the only ruling party in Europe to have openly supported the attempted coup, declaring the beneficial effects of its success for the Serbian regime. See Stojan Cerović, "Staljinizam bez Kremlja," *Vreme*, August 26, 1991, 16–17; for specific comments by SPS officials supporting the coup, see Hari Štajner, "Jeltsin preuzeo Gorbačova," *Vreme*, August 26, 1991, 4–6; in *Vreme*, September 2, 1991; and in "Točak istorije ne može nazad," *Borba*, August 21, 1991, 4. As mentioned earlier in this chapter, in March 1991 Yugoslav Defense Minister Kadijević held secret talks in Moscow with Soviet Defense Minister Yazov (who was one of the leaders of the coup attempt against Gorbachev). Without the knowledge of Soviet civilian officials, Yazov arranged for a large quantity of weapons, including planes, rocket systems, and helicopters to be delivered to the Yugoslav army. *Vreme*, September 23, 1991, 7.

1992: The Renewed Threat of Popular Mobilization

By January 1992, as the war in Croatia was ending, the opposition in Serbia was again gaining momentum, drawing on the anti-war sentiment,
economic decline, and continued authoritarian attitudes of the SPS to
mobilize large numbers of people against the ruling elite. Condemning
the SPS's economic policy, its war in Croatia, and even the conflictual policy in Kosovo, the opposition by February was gathering hundreds of
thousands of signatures calling for Milošević's resignation and the con-
vening of a constitutional assembly. The opposition also called for new
elections, and once again mobilized thousands of supporters into the streets
of Serbia's major cities.[66] While those who were calling for Milošević's
ouster included nationalists critical of him for betraying the interests of
Serbs, the majority of those who mobilized against the SPS regime did so
for reasons similar to the March 1991 protests. Indeed, as mentioned
earlier, at this time SPO leader Drašković apologized for the actions of
Serb forces against civilian targets in Croatia.

In the face of this massive mobilization, the SPS repeated its strategy
from the previous year. Once again, the regime publicly moderated its
line: it allowed UN troops to move into Krajina; put pressure on hard-
liners in Knin and allowed moderate Serbs to negotiate with Zagreb;[67]
called for talks with Croatia; and set up meetings with the remaining
four Yugoslav republics to negotiate a future Yugoslavia.[68] Because of
the international recognition of the independence of Croatia, Slovenia,
and Bosnia, Serbia and Montenegro in April decided to form the Federal Republic of Yugoslavia.

But at the same time, Serbia's conservatives stepped up the pressure on Bosnia. Indeed, the same scenario was beginning in Bosnia that
had been carried out in Croatia the previous year, with the difference
that this time the enemy was the allegedly fundamentalist Muslim population of Bosnia, who were said to be seeking to impose an Islamic state
on the Serbs of the republic.[69] The SPS instituted an economic blockade

---

[66] Milan Milošević, "Događanje potpisa," *Vreme*, February 17, 1992, 9–14; Mirjana Prošić-
Dvornić, "Enough! Student Protest '92: The Youth of Belgrade in Quest of 'Another Serbia,'" *Anthropology of East Europe Review* 11, nos. 1–2 (Spring–Fall 1993): 127–137.

[67] See interview with chairman of HDZ executive council Stipe Mesić, in *Globus*,
February 7, 1992, 6–7.

[68] "Četiri republike za zajedničku državu," *Politika*, January 22, 1992, 1.

[69] One example of this propaganda came in March 1992, at the end of the Muslim holiday of Ramadan, when the SDS's press agency cited a made-up Koran verse in which
Muslims are called on to kill Christians at the end of Ramadan. Ejub Štitkovac, "Kur'an po

of the areas not controlled by its Bosnian SDS allies.[70] In December, the SDS stated its intention to form a Serb republic,[71] and in January 1992 an independent "Serbian Republic" was declared in the 66 percent of Bosnian territory that the Bosnian SDS controlled there, the "Serbian Autonomous Regions" that had been formed the year before. SDS leader Radovan Karadžić at this time declared that Bosnia would never again be undivided.[72] Objecting to a referendum on independence to be held in those parts of the republic not under SDS control, Serbian guerrilla forces began armed attacks on Croat and Muslim civilians in early March.[73] In early April, a massive, multi-ethnic peace march in downtown Sarajevo was fired upon by SDS snipers, killing eight and wounding fifty. The following day the streets of many other Bosnian cities were filled with similar peace marches. But those marches were not enough to stop the conservatives' strategy of destroying Bosnia.

Over the next two months, guerrilla groups and paramilitary forces backed by the SDS and the SPS were sent into multiethnic communities where they carried out massive atrocities, expelling and murdering non-Serbs, mostly in areas already controlled by the SDS.[74] Once again, special operations forces directly under the control of the Serbian Ministry of Internal Affairs were responsible for much of the violence.[75] By September 1992, Belgrade's Bosnian Serb allies had increased their holdings by less than 10 percent, to about 70 percent of the territory of Bosnia-Herzegovina. As in Krajina, almost the entire non-Serbian population was expelled

'SRNI,'" Vreme, April 27, 1992, 33. For information on the relationship of Bosnian Muslims to Islam, see Ivo Banac, "Bosnian Muslims: From Religious Community to Socialist Nationhood and Postcommunist Statehood, 1918–1992," in The Muslims of Bosnia-Herzegovina, ed. Mark Pinson (Cambridge: Harvard University Press, 1994), 129–153.

[70] Helsinki Watch, War Crimes, 26.

[71] "Priprema formiranja srpske BiH," Oslobodjenje, December 22, 1991, 3.

[72] The "Republic of the Serbian People of Bosnia-Herzegovina" was declared to include areas where Serbs were in a majority as well as "those areas where the Serbian people is in a minority because of the genocide against it during the Second World War." Zehrudin Isaković, "Spor oko 'ako,'" Vreme, January 13, 1992, 17–18.

[73] See Helsinki Watch, War Crimes, 27–29.; "Drugi Sarajevski atentat," Globus, March 6, 1992, 3–6.

[74] For details of the atrocities and war, see War Crimes in Bosnia-Herzegovina, vol. 2 (New York: Helsinki Watch, April 1993); Zahrudin Isaković, "Pocrveneli ljiljani," Vreme, April 6, 1992, pp. 6–7; testimony at the International Criminal Tribunal, available at Tribunal Report, archived online at the website of the International War and Peace Report, at <http://www.iwpr.net/>.

[75] Igor Salinger and Aleksandar Radić, "Od Arkana do Gumara," Vreme, April 3, 2003, and "Tajna avijacija državne bezbednosti," Vreme, April 10, 2003.

or killed, while Serbian dissenters were silenced and repressed.[76] Just as in Croatia, the violence seen between the spring of 1992 and the end of 1995 was neither the result of ancient hatreds bursting to the surface nor of elites mobilizing the population to violence. Rather, it was a purposeful policy imposed on communities from outside of those communities. Under orders from Belgrade, paramilitary forces and special operations forces controlled by Belgrade were sent into Bosnia to carry out what came to be called "ethnic cleansing" against non-Serb populations. These attacks spawned a spiral of violence, as many of those on the "receiving" end of the violence sought to organize and retaliate.

The effect of these events was once more to demobilize the opposition, as the focus of attention once again shifted away from demands for fundamental change toward the war in Bosnia and the economic sanctions that the United Nations Security Council placed on Yugoslavia as punishment for its involvement in the war in Bosnia. In the May 1992 federal elections, held at the moment that the UN sanctions were announced, 44 percent of the eligible voters did not take part, boycotting the election. Of those who did participate, 43 percent voted for the SPS (24 percent of eligible voters), while 30 percent voted for the SRS (about 17 percent of eligible voters), with which the SPS had allied and which was portrayed in the SPS-controlled state media as a moderate nationalist party.[77] The result was that Milošević and the SPS remained in power, and the new constitution of the Federal Republic of Yugoslavia in many ways increased his formal authority. Attempts by the opposition to organize further resistance to the SPS over the summer of 1992 failed in the face of a population politically demobilized by war in Bosnia.

Elections for the parliament of Serbia held in December 1992 renewed the sense of threat to the SPS, which received only 28 percent of the vote, a lower total than it had received in the 1990 elections. Indeed, as political sociologist Zoran Slavujević notes,

---

[76] See, for example, Blaine Harden, "In Bosnia 'Disloyal Serbs' Share Plight of Opposition," *Washington Post*, August 24, 1992, 1, 14.

Because this work is focusing on the strategy of the SPS and its goals in Serbia, it does not fully explore this part of the Bosnian conflict. While the war also involved political dynamics within Bosnia itself, it is clear that the violence was imported into Bosnia and into the communities worst hit by violence as part of a purposeful strategy on the part of conservatives in Croatia and Serbia to destroy Bosnia and to destroy the existing social realities in those communities.

[77] Srecko Mihailovic, "The Parliamentary Elections of 1990, 1992 and 1993," in Goati, *Challenges of Parliamentarism*, 52–53; Slobodan Antonić, "Promene stranačkog raspoloženja," 27–36.

The SPS did worst in the 1992 elections, when it radicalized its policies on the national question and war and promoted the extremist SRS. However, after softening its national policy the SRS was able in 1993 election to win over as many uncommitted voters as all the opposition parties put together.[78]

Thus in terms of domestic political strategy, the SPS's strategy of moderation and portraying itself as not rabidly nationalist proved to be the key to its success, while shifts to the right on the nationalist issue made a serious dent in its vote totals.

This point was most clearly seen in the December 1992 presidential elections, in which Milošević was challenged by Serbian-born U.S. businessman Milan Panić. Panić had been named federal prime minister of the new Yugoslav state in July 1992, in part because of his appeal to the international community. While in that office, he consistently took an almost anti-nationalist line.[79] In the December presidential election, Panić ran on a platform that explicitly stressed economic issues, called for immediate economic liberalization and privatization and, in particular, stressed the absolute necessity of ending the UN economic sanctions that had been placed on Yugoslavia to punish it for involvement in the Bosnian war. Panić harshly criticized the SPS's policies as being disastrous for Serbia and for Serbs outside of Serbia. Milošević's response was to emphasize that the sanctions had positive effects (for example, allowing "infant industries" to develop) and that Serbia had its own resources and the ability to withstand sanctions.[80] He stressed the importance of economic development as a key goal, and again printed billions of dinars to pay workers who had not received a paycheck in months. The SPS accused Panić of being a foreign agent and stressed that Serbia would never bow to foreigners who try to tell her voters how to behave.[81]

[78] Zoran Dj. Slavujević, "Election campaigns," in Vladimir Goati, *Challenges of Parliamentarism*, 162.

[79] For example, in his first speech as prime minister in July 1992, Panić called for demilitarizing Bosnia-Herzegovina, declared that "there simply is no idea in this world which would be worth killing for at the end of the 20th century," stated as a priority the restoration of cooperation and trust between the new, Serbian Yugoslavia and the other former Yugoslav republics, and put most emphasis on the need for radical economic reform and true democratization. *Review of International Affairs*, 1005–6: 4–6.

[80] See the following speeches by Milošević: December 8, 1992, at campaign rally in Srem, Belgrade radio (Foreign Broadcast Information Service daily report: East Europe-92–238, December 10, 1992, 44–45); talk to businessmen, December 14, 1992, Belgrade TV (FBIS-EE-92–241, December 15, 1992, 50–52).

[81] For example, see interview with Serbian prime minister (and SPS member) Božović, in Novi Sad daily *Dnevnik*, reported by Tanjug, December 12, 1992 (FBIS-EE-92–240, December 14, 1991, 73–74).

On "ethnic issues" Panić called for an immediate end to the war in Bosnia and recognition of existing republic borders, improving relations with the West, and (in an uncanny repetition of Milošević's own rhetoric from the December 1990 campaign) called on Serbs to look toward the future rather than the past. He noted that Serbia had to be concerned with the fate of Serbs outside Serbia, but pointed out that their negative situation was due precisely to the past policies of the SPS. In response to SPS claims that Kosovo was being subverted from abroad, Panić pointed out that no country recognized Kosovo as independent of Serbia.

Rather than trying to ethnically outbid Panić, Milošević instead stressed ethnic tolerance, the equality of all citizens of Serbia, and even stated, while in Kosovo, that most Albanians were blameless, and only a small minority of separatists, aided by Tirana, were the cause of problems. Indeed, he even implied that the Kosovo problem was basically resolved since the Serb population there was increasing and thus the ethnic balance was more "natural."[82] Milošević also stressed that Serbia had no territorial claims against any other state, vehemently denied charges of ethnic cleansing by Serbs as impossible, and pointed out that Serbia was extending hospitality to refugees of all nationalities.

Thus in his political rhetoric Milošević consistently recognized the continuing primacy of non-ethnic issues. His stress on social justice, economic development, and ethnic peace all belie hypotheses that would expect a political rhetoric of ethnic outbidding. In fact, the rhetoric of ethnic injustice came to the fore especially in periods *after* elections, or when the opposition was mobilizing people against the regime. It was precisely in these periods that Serbian forces would begin to provoke conflict along ethnic lines, which was then pointed to as evidence of injustices. The very fact that the provocation of such incidents was necessary to divert attention from economic and peace issues in itself is evidence that ethnic issues, though not unimportant, are not so central as to exclude people's other non-ethnic interests.

Although the wave of opposition seen in the spring 1992 was submerged under the rising tide of "injustices against innocent Serbs" in Bosnia, the appearance on the scene of Milan Panić shows clearly the explanatory weakness of the concept of ethnic outbidding. Indeed, during the election campaign for the Serbian presidency between Panić and Milošević in November and December 1992—it was a time when the most vocal anti-

---

[82] See series of Milošević speeches in Kosovo, December 17, 1992 in Tanjug (FBIS-EE-92-244, December 18, 1992, 38–39).

war and liberal elements of the country had fled abroad and images of innocent Serbs under attack from Mujehedeen and Ustaše flooded the air-waves—the SPS strictly limited Panić's access to the broadcast media.

The ethnic conflict literature, with its hypotheses about the dynamics of ethnic outbidding and the priority of ethnic solidarity, would have predicted that the Serbian leadership should have given Panić all the air time he wanted, since his rhetoric alone would have discredited him. Yet the regime was clearly quite afraid of Panić's challenge. Not only did it severely limit his access to the media, it demonized him as a foreign agent sent by the West to subvert Serbia's independence.

Nevertheless, at the start of the campaign, in October, Panić had a favorable rating of 76 percent, while Milošević's was 49 percent.[83] In the election itself, 5–10 percent of voters, mostly younger ones who were most likely to support Panić, were turned away from the polls, and many people's names had disappeared from the voting lists in Belgrade, the center of Panić's support. Yet despite massive fraud, exit polls taken during the voting itself showed an even split of 47 percent each for Panić and Milošević.[84] This result is even more striking if we keep in mind that this 47 percent for Panić does not include the massive numbers of young men who had fled the country to avoid being drafted to the war in Croatia, and who would have been natural supporters of Panić. A further indication of the inaccuracy of the official statistics is that in Belgrade, exit polls showed that between 80 to 90 percent had voted for Panić, while the official figures for Belgrade showed 55 percent for Milošević and 33 percent for Panić, with Milošević winning at almost every polling place in the city. The regime's official results gave Milošević 56 percent of the votes compared to Panić's 34 percent.

Over the course of the next year, the SPS shifted back toward a position of peacemaker, signing a peace plan for Bosnia put forward by the international community. In the campaign for the December 1993 parliamentary elections, the SPS stressed peace in Serbia, political stability, the fight against criminals and growing differentials in wealth, denounced the "looting of state property" and called for a review of all privatizations to date; it managed to obtain 38 percent of the vote, or 27 percent of the

[83] Poll by Institute of Social Sciences, cited in *NIN*, November 27, 1992, Bogdan Ivanišević, "Our Topic: Opposition against Itself: Running for the Arrow," 10–12 (FBIS-EE-92–243, December 17, 1992, 45–48).

[84] Douglas E. Schoen, "How Milošević Stole the Election," *New York Times Magazine*, February 14, 1993. Schoen is an American campaign consultant who worked for Panić during this election. His figures are based on exit polls conducted throughout the country by the respected Institute for Social Sciences in Belgrade.

electorate.[85] This resulted in an increase of its parliamentary seats from
the 101 it won in 1992 to 123. Whereas after the 1992 elections it had formed
an alliance with the Radical Party, after the 1993 elections in order to gain
a majority the SPS formed an alliance with the small moderate New Democracy party, which had been part of the DEPOS opposition coalition. The
Radicals, who were no longer in coalition with SPS and had been presented by Belgrade television in their true colors (as war criminals, etc.),
received 10 percent of the vote, and their number of seats in parliament
was almost halved. The SPS media had promoted a new chauvinistically
nationalist party, the Party of Serbian Unity (SSJ), headed by war criminal
Arkan, giving it much positive coverage on television, but it received less
than 2 percent of votes cast. The one real opposition party that attempted
to exploit the national question in a strategy of ethnic outbidding, the
Democratic Party of Serbia (DSS), received only 5 percent of votes cast.
Thus, in the 1993 elections, only 15 percent of the electorate voted for blatantly chauvinistic parties; 27 supported the SPS based on its moderate
focus on peace, stability, and economic well being; while at least 47 percent of the republic's Serbs supported either democratic opposition parties or abstained from voting, hardly a massive mobilization based on
ethnic outbidding.[86]

While the ethnic or national question was clearly one part of political
discourse at times of elections, and the "Serbian question" was one that
all candidates had to address, there was no automatic mobilization of "Serbian ethnic solidarity" leading inexorably toward greater conflict, no
rising up *en masse* of "the Serbian nation" against other ethnic groups.
Indeed, while the SPS and its allies managed in rigged elections and quite
favorable circumstances (virtual control of mass media) to receive the votes
of less than 50 percent of the population, their emphasis on non-ethnic
issues, their shift in 1993 back to a focus on moderation, the way in which
ethnic issues were framed, and the quite obvious fear of the anti-nationalist candidacy of Milan Panić does put into doubt an image of ethnic politics spiraling inexorably toward ever more extreme and conflictual policies
due to the need to gain electoral support or to mobilize the wider population. The dominant image of Serbs under threat of genocide in Bosnia
and Croatia, and the outside world's complicity in this injustice, makes
these findings even more intriguing.

[85] For election result figures, see Milan Milošević, "Maratonci trče počasni krug," *Vreme*,
December 27, 1993, 10–14.
[86] See campaign ad in *Vreme*, December 13, 1993. DEPOS and the other democratically
oriented opposition parties received about 35 percent of the total vote.

The strategy of demobilization of the population worked quite well while the war in Bosnia raged on. This strategy, as explained above, was meant to prevent mobilization against the existing power structures, thus giving status quo elites the chance to preserve their power by transforming power and capital from the old system into forms of power relevant for the coming system. In addition to the political demobilization, there was also what sociologist Eric Gordy has termed the elimination of alternatives, that is, the active attempt by the ruling SPS to destroy any alternatives to its own rule and the hegemony of its views of society.[87] Indeed, Gordy shows how during the period of the Bosnian war and in its aftermath, the support for the SPS continued to decline, as the SPS pursued policies that were extremely detrimental to the vast majority of the population, including disastrous economic policies that, while serving to enrich the elites, impoverished the vast majority of the population while at the same time reinforcing their demobilization. The policy of war in Bosnia and the economic disasters served, however, to ensure that there would not be anti-regime mobilization. Gordy also documents quite clearly how the internationally imposed sanctions, meant to punish Serbia for its involvement in the war in Bosnia, in fact served to strengthen the existing structures of power by making anti-regime mobilization even less possible as they worsened an already dismal economic situation. As he points out, "parents who spent all day trying to purchase food for their children . . . were not thinking about whether they approved of wars carried out in their names or about the monopoly of administrative and corporate positions by a single political party."[88]

The demobilization of the opposition also achieved one of the conservatives' major goals: it gave Serbia's prewar elites the time to further cement their grip on power. In part, this was achieved by giving personal control over large state-owned enterprises to SPS members and allies:

> The highest ranks of power, using their political power and various forms of state and quasi-state ownership (the remaining "socially owned" property, joint stock companies with state firms as majority shareholders, etc.), managed to preserve their monopoly over the overwhelming majority of the country's economic resources. . . . The escalation of the war in Bosnia-Herzegovina, and particularly the imposition of international sanctions, gave a specific group of people the opportunity to plunder the economy

---

[87] Eric Gordy, *The Culture of Power in Serbia: Nationalism and the Destruction of Alternatives* (University Park: Pennsylvania State University Press, 1999).

[88] Ibid., 197.

directly (the spoils of war, for example), or indirectly (state-generated hyperinflation . . .) to gain control of enormous wealth. This stratum largely originated from the circles of the ruling hierarchy . . . (as many as two-thirds of elite entrepreneurs belonged to the previous nomenklatura or were members of their families—or had close connections with it).[89]

Thus the SPS elite and its allies used this period to consolidate control over state-owned assets. As political scientist Vladimir Goati noted in 1995,

> in Serbia the SPS survived the old regime and remained in power [which explains why] in Serbia there was relatively little change in the ruling political elite. In the most important positions in the managerial-administrative apparatus of the state, the army, the large public enterprises and media under state control remained mainly the same people who were there before the first elections. To the extent that there were between 1990 and 1994 personnel changes, openings were filled by individuals from the SPS . . . [As] in the time of the old regime, one can speak about the 'personal union' between the SPS and the state.[90]

The conservatives also used their control of monetary policy and inflation to enrich themselves, in part, by draining US$4 billion of citizens' hard currency savings into their own coffers.[91]

Another way by which the ruling elite realized its goal of preserving control over the bases of power was by using their positions in the old system to accumulate the kinds of resources that would be the bases of power in a new liberalized economic system, or, in the words of sociologist Mladen Lazić, "the transfer of social wealth into private ownership":

> [T]he old political elite is adapting to new times. It is, as one researcher notes, "as a group attempting to preserve some levers of the command system, but at the same time many of its members (especially from the management level) are 'transferring over' to sectors in which status is based on new principles (on the ownership of capital)." (Lazić, 1994: 254)[92]

[89] Mladen Lazić, "Introduction: The Emergence of a Democratic Order in Serbia," in *Protest in Belgrade: Winter of Discontent*, ed. Mladen Lazić (Budapest: Central European University Press, 1999), 7–8.

[90] Vladimir Goati, "Socijalna osnova političkih partija u Srbiji," in *Potisnuto civilno društvo*, ed. Vukašin Pavlović (Belgrade: Eko Centar, 1995), 201.

[91] Mladan Dinkić, *Ekonomija destrukcije: Velika pljačka naroda* (Belgrade: VIN, 1995).

[92] Vladimir Goati, "Socijalna osnova političkih partija u Srbiji," in Vukašin Pavlović, *Potisnuto civilno društvo* (Belgrade: Eko Centar, 1995), 201.

Thus alongside the consolidation of control over state owned assets by members of the ruling elite, there was also the formation of a new sector of elite whose power was based on actual ownership of private assets. Their control over private assets was made possible by what could be called "insider privatization," where certain assets of the state were basically handed over to businessmen supportive of or close to the ruling party. As sociologist Mladen Lazić notes, this new private elite, who are popularly called the "tycoons," was very much dependent on the state, and was thus also dependent on the maintenance of the SPS in power:

> The founders of the new, private enterprise elite, also (because of the war and sanctions) to a significant degree are oriented toward the state. Their interest is primarily directed to those forms of regulation that will ensure them further unobstructed accumulation (for which, it has been shown that, in some circumstances, they can more quickly proceed in conjunction with the apparatus of the government, and with at least partly unstable legal-political order on which they are parasites).[93]

In other words, even those parts of the elite that had shifted over to formal ownership and private non-state activities were dependent for their success on the existing structures of state power.

Another part of the elite which was able to use this time to consolidate control was made up of underground organized crime networks. The international sanctions, in particular, enabled them to accumulate enormous wealth, since the ruling party relied on them to ensure that basic consumer goods and other commodities were available, despite the sanctions. These smuggling networks, which had very close ties with the special operations units of the police, represented a new part of the elite that was dependent for its power on control over networks of distribution rather than over actual assets.

The strategy of demobilization gave all of these elites the time and opportunity to either consolidate their control over the structures of economic power, either by taking control of state-owned firms, or by transferring their power resources from those that were most important in the old system—positions within the party and state (nomenklatura)—to those that mattered in the new system—ownership of property, capital and wealth, and control over distribution networks. The quote from Lazić

---

[93] Mladen Lazić, *Razaranje društva: Jugoslovensko društvo u Krizi 90-ih* (Belgrade: Filip Višnjić, 1994), 254–255.

above shows that this transfer was well advanced by the time the regime faced the massive protests in the winter of 1996–1997.[94]

Indeed, by 1996 ruling elites had a much firmer grasp on the structures of power than they had had prior to 1990. In this sense, the strategy of demobilization had proven a great success. Especially given the demands and pressures from the population for change, this continuity of power resources is striking, and was made possible exactly by the conservatives' strategy of demobilization.

From Dayton to Kosovo: The Limits of the Demobilization Strategy

At the end of 1995, the dynamics of the situation in Serbia changed radically as the military conflict in Bosnia came to an end. Beginning in 1994, Washington pursued a strategy meant to put pressure on the SDS leadership in Bosnia to end the conflict and come to the bargaining table. In the summer of 1995, the Croatian army took back Krajina, and subsequent offensives by the Bosnian Croat Army and the Army of the Bosnian Republic, with NATO air support, later that summer took land held by SDS forces. As these forces approached Banja Luka, the largest city in the SDS-held territory, the SDS leadership agreed to a ceasefire and peace talks.

What was striking about the military offensives of the Croatian army was Serbia's role in them. In the case of Krajina, information from people in Krajina indicates that the military forces received orders from Belgrade to pull back into Bosnia, effectively surrendering all of the territory to the Croatian army.[95] In Serbia itself, there were no massive rallies or popular mobilizations over this loss of what had come to be called "Serbian lands," and official Serbian media played down the loss of those territories, as well as the subsequent mass exodus of the Serb populations of those territories. Nor was there any massive volunteer movement to go fight on the fronts. Rather, in the summer of 1995, as HDZ and then Bosnian army forces advanced on SDS-held territories in Croatia and Bosnia, police in Serbia searched the cities and towns for men with any kind of

[94] See also Milan Milošević, "Moćni i nečasni," *Vreme*, July 27, 1996, 12–15, which surveys a number of studies that look at the ways in which elites managed to convert their positions in the old system into the kinds of capital that are the bases of power in the new.

[95] See interview with Milan Martić, then-President of the "Serbian Republic of Krajina," in "Milošević nas je izdao," *Vreme*, August 3, 1996, 20–21. This was confirmed to me in personal conversations I had with a number of people who were in Krajina at the time of the Croatian army's offensive in the summer of 1995.

Bosnian connection, forcibly inducting young men who had even the most tenuous link to Bosnia into the SDS army, gathering them onto buses and sending them across the Drina.[96]

The Dayton peace talks held in November 1995 brought together Miloše-vić, Croatian President Franjo Tudjman, Bosnian President Alija Izetbe-gović and the heads of the Bosnian HDZ and SDS. The result was a treaty that brought an end to the military conflict in Bosnia and brought the international recognition of Bosnia within its pre-war boundaries.[97]

Once the Bosnian conflict ended, a popular mass mobilization movement once again surfaced in Serbia. As before, the focus of this mobilization was not the issue of nationalism, the loss of what had been portrayed as "Serbian lands" in Croatia and Bosnia, or the expulsion of Serb populations from those lands, but rather the attempt by the government to subvert electoral results, where opposition parties had won elections in almost every municipality in the country but the SPS had, through fraud, declared the opposite. In response, the grievances that had existed since at least 1990 but which had been demobilized by the wars and the images of threat now burst into the open. In addition, the extent of transformation in the rest of eastern Europe, and the degree to which Serbia, which as part of Yugoslavia had enjoyed standards of living higher than much of the rest of the socialist bloc, had now fallen so far below those standards, further reinforced the preferences of the wider population that had been so clearly expressed in the polling at the end of the 1980s.

The trigger came at the time of the November 1996 local elections. The results of the second round of voting were striking, as the opposition swept to power in virtually every major city in the country, winning a majority of seats in at least 34 local councils in Serbia, including cities and municipalities which together accounted for over 60 percent of the population. The SPS-dominated Electoral Commission, however, refused to accept this result; for example in Belgrade, it annulled the results of 33 of the 60 seats (out of 110) that the opposition Zajedno coalition had won. The SPS then scheduled new elections to be held later in the month. In response, the opposition coalition called for a boycott of the new elections, as well as for massive popular mobilization against the SPS. At the same time, student organizations separately began massive protests against the SPS and its attempts to impose its rule on the universities as well.

[96] See Filip Švarm and Miloš Vasić, "Danajski poklon," *Vreme,* July 3, 1995, 16–18.
[97] For the text, see "The General Framework Agreement for Peace in Bosnia and Herzegovina," <http://www.ohr.int/dpa/default.asp?content_id=380> (accessed October 14, 2003).

These moves marked the beginning of what turned out to be three months of massive anti-SPS protests throughout the country. Beginning in late November 1996, hundreds of thousands of people took to the streets of every major city in Serbia in the largest public demonstrations ever seen. The protests were marked by mass participation, that is, participants came from across the social spectrum.[98] Social science polling conducted in the first month of the protests showed that the main goal of most of the marchers was for the regime to recognize the results of the local elections, while their main motivations were to ensure their rights to participate in the political process, and to express their desire for nonviolence and tolerance.[99] In general terms, "this protest displayed an aspiration to change both the political and economic systems; a wish for rapid change; the focus on political change as a precondition for economic transformation."[100]

The ruling party responded to the protests by trying to portray them as undermining stability in society, as carried out by just a small group of "provocateurs and hoodlums."[101] Citing pressure being put on the SPS by the United States, the ruling party also used the slogan, "Serbia will not be ruled by a foreign hand," attempting to identify the protesters as agents of enemy foreign powers who were working to destabilize the country.[102] The SPS expelled elected SPS officials who expressed sympathy or support for the protesters. It also called in the police, including units of the special forces unit, resorting to violence against the protesters. Notably, representatives of the Army promised the opposition that the military would remain neutral in the dispute. After it became clear the protests would continue despite the use of force, Milošević eventually recognized the opposition's control of 14 of the republic's 19 largest cities, including Belgrade.

The result of this mass mobilization was crucial to the further course of events and the strategy of the regime.

[T]he regime was partially delegitimized; in the course of the protests . . . the means by which the ruling group had come to power and held onto it

---

[98] For a breakdown, see Marija Babović, "Potential for an Active Society," in Lazić, 33–59. See also Ivana Spasić and Đorđe Pavićević, "Građanski protest–malo posle," *Republika* 162 (April 15–30, 1997): II.

[99] Spasić and Pavićević, II, cites polling undertaken by the Institute for Sociological Research of the Faculty of Philosophy, University of Belgrade.

[100] Vladimir Vuletić, "Citizens in Protest," in Lazić, 94–95.

[101] Lazić, *Protest in Belgrade*, 215.

[102] Ibid., 219.

was revealed. Its populist basis and its pretensions—proclaimed over the previous ten years—that it enjoyed "plebiscitary support" was debunked. This demystification [was] for the first time made known publicly and massively.[103]

At this same time, the protests greatly improved the position of the opposition parties that set about to solidify their coalition and to work together toward their common goal.

Another crucial change came at this time when Milo Djukanović, the prime minister of Montenegro and previously a Milošević ally, broke with the SPS and came out in support of the opposition. Djukanović criticized Milošević for isolating Yugoslavia and called for fundamental political and economic reforms. Djukanović subsequently ran for president of Montenegro, defeating the pro-Milošević candidate in the elections of fall 1997. This defection marked a major challenge to the conservatives because Montenegro, despite its small size (population of 800,000 compared to Serbia's population of 10 million) had equal representation with Serbia in the federal parliament and in the federal defense council.

This period thus marked not only a major threat to the existing structures of power but also a major turning point. The combination of mass popular mobilizations, the coming together of opposition parties, and Djukanović's joining the opposition seemed to show that the conservatives' ability to hold onto power in a nominally democratic environment had reached its limits. The conservatives' response to this challenge was to revert to more openly authoritarian forms of rule, using repression and violence against opposition parties and organizations as well as against the independent media.[104] Official media devoted intense coverage to the SPS and its ruling partners, virtually ignoring the opposition. In the face of these challenges, the opposition parties and Montenegrin prime minister Djukanović continued to work to unite and strengthen the opposition.

It is in this context of an increasingly threatened ruling elite in Serbia, and an increasingly organized opposition, that the conflict in Kosovo in 1998 and 1999 must be seen. Kosovo had been relatively quiescent, under virtual military occupation since its autonomy had been revoked in 1990. The Albanian political leadership had decided to pursue a policy of peaceful and passive resistance, and to that end had set up an underground

---

[103] Spasić and Pavićević, II–III.
[104] Goati, "The Nature of the Order and the October Overthrow in Serbia," in Spasić and Subotić, *Revolution and Order*, 48–51.

unofficial society, complete with hospitals, schools, businesses, and a
university, and an underground Kosovo government. The Kosovar leadership, under Ibrahim Rugova, had been supported in this peaceful strategy by the United States, and was under the impression that the United
States would look out for the interests of Kosovo.

But when the Dayton accords were signed in November 1995 without any mention of Kosovo, a dispute that had long been simmering in
Kosovo's Albanian community broke out into the open. The Kosovars had
believed they had an implicit promise from the United States that it would
support their claims to independence if they followed a peaceful path.
When it became clear that Kosovo was not included in the overall peace
agreement, Kosovo Albanians who had become increasingly skeptical and
critical of the peaceful path became more vociferous in their demands for
a new confrontational strategy. They argued that by refusing to resist
the occupation, the Albanian leadership was in effect allowing Serbia to
pick the timing of what they saw was an inevitable armed conflict. This
group argued that the Kosovars themselves should choose the timing of
the conflict, and they called for armed resistance to the Serbian forces in
the province. By 1997 the Kosovo Liberation Army (KLA) began making
armed attacks on Serbian police, Serbian civilians, and Albanians who
cooperated with the Serbian state.

At the time, there were rumors that the KLA had been set up by Belgrade as a means of provoking conflict in the province. Such a move
would certainly fit the pattern set by Belgrade in the other conflicts.
Nevertheless, many Albanians were ready for a more confrontational
approach with Belgrade, and so despite its origins, the KLA had no
problem attracting recruits, stepping up its attacks on Serbian targets
in the province. In late February 1998, Serbian police attacked Albanian villages, killing at least 16 people in retaliation for a KLA ambush
that killed four Serbian police officers.[105] It was at this point that the
conflict began to escalate.

Meanwhile, faced with growing dissatisfaction and anti-regime mobilization at home, Milošević pointed to the growing unrest in Kosovo as
evidence of a continued threat. Milošević sent more Serbian police and
military forces into the province to crack down on what he characterized
as terrorists; these forces in turn attacked Albanian villages, provoking violent responses from the Albanian population. The result was an escalation

---

[105] "Yugoslavia: Again the Visible Hand," *International Crisis Group Report*, May 6, 1998.
<http://www.crisisweb.org/home/index.cfm?id=1747&1 =1> (accessed October 25, 2003).

of the conflict, an escalation that was highlighted in the officially controlled mass media in Serbia. The pattern of stoking conflict as a means to demobilize the opposition was once again set in motion.

As the conflict escalated, however, the international community became involved in a way they had not in Croatia and Bosnia. By late 1998, the United States had given an ultimatum to Milošević to sign a peace agreement or face military action. Milošević refused to sign the treaty at Rambouillet, and the United States responded by bombing targets in Serbia. Apparently the United States believed that Milošević's stubbornness was merely for domestic consumption, and that after a couple of bombs were dropped on Serbia he would relent and sign the agreement. In fact, matters proceeded rather differently, and the bombing continued for eleven weeks before Milošević relented; but even then he did so only after the Rambouillet agreement had been modified.

What the United States failed to realize was how conflict was a central part of the Serbian conservatives' strategy of demobilization, and how NATO's threats, and the bombing itself, played into that strategy. Indeed, the NATO intervention came at just the right moment for Milošević. It confirmed his long-standing claim, which previously had seemed outrageously paranoid, that NATO was the enemy of Serbia and of Serbs. This in turn reinforced his claims that the opposition, which had received assistance and support from the United States, was, in fact, an agent of the enemies of Serbia. Serbs were not convinced by U.S. claims, including Madeleine Albright's, that Milošević was the target of the bombing, not the Serbian people.

As in the previous conflicts, the main result of this conflict too was to demobilize the opposition. The fact that NATO dropped bombs not only on clear military targets but also in downtown Belgrade, Novi Sad, and Niš, places that had consistently been the center of popular resistance to the conservative regime, showed Washington's fundamental lack of understanding of the political dynamics of Milošević's hold on power. The military attack was apparently aimed at motivating the Serbian people to overthrow Milošević and the ruling SPS. The result, though, was the opposite, as almost the entire political spectrum, even people whose whole careers had been spent opposing the conservatives, condemned the bombing and rallied around the president.

Indeed, the result of the bombing, in the words of human rights activist Vojin Dimitrijević, director of the Belgrade Center for Human Rights, was to destroy much of the progress that the opposition had made over the previous years in their efforts to build the bases for popular mobilization against the SPS.[106] During the bombing, the SPS cracked down on the opposition, arresting and harassing opposition figures, forcibly sending activists and opposition political figures to the front. Once again, Milošević's strategy of demobilization worked as planned, though this time with the help of NATO rather than extremists in Croatia or Bosnia.

Following the end of hostilities, however, the opposition continued its attempts to unite: in January 2000 they jointly demanded that the regime call special elections and cease "all acts of state terror and lawlessness in all forms," and in April they mobilized 200,000 people in Belgrade to demand elections.[107] The demobilization effect of the loss of Kosovo thus proved to be extremely limited, and indicated that the ability of the regime to use a strategy of demobilization had come to an end.

The conservatives responded by stepping up their repression and violence against the opposition. In February, at the Congress of the SPS, Milošević characterized the opposition as

> a group of corrupt weaklings and thieves, who, taking advantage of the difficult times in which many people are not leading easy lives, and using considerable financial resources brought from abroad, are manipulating the feelings and needs of a certain number of people, . . . lying to them that there can be no relief from the difficulties without bending before the force that has subjugated the entire world.[108]

This was followed by "an intensification of repressive measures against opposition parties, on the basis of which it can be concluded that Serbia had ceased to 'tolerate an opposition.'"[109] One example is that between January and June about 700 young people, mostly members of the Otpor student opposition group, were arrested or beaten on the streets.[110]

The extent of this repression was shown even more graphically in the two assassination attempts against opposition leader Vuk Drašković, and

---

[106] He noted that "In one night, the NATO air strikes have wiped out ten years of hard work of groups of courageous people in the non-governmental sector and democratic opposition": Vojin Dimitrijević, "The Collateral Damage Is Democracy," Institute for War and Peace Reporting, March 30, 1999, online at <http://www.iwpr.net/index.pl?archive/bcr/bcr_19990402_5_eng.txt> (accessed October 15, 2003).

[107] Goati, "The Nature of the Order," 53.

[108] *Politika*, February 18, 2000, quoted in Goati, 51.

[109] Goati, 51. See also "Serbia: The Milosevic Regime on the Eve of the September Elections," *Report of the International Crisis Group*, August 17, 2000.<http://icg-beta.web.easynet.be/home/index.cfm?id=1738&1 =1> (accessed October 12, 2003).

[110] Dragoš Ivanović, "Političke promene u Srbiji 2000. Godine," *Republika*, 274–275 (December 1–31, 2001): 24.

the successful assassination in August 2000 of former Serbian president Ivan Stambolić, who had been helping the opposition and who was at the time rumored to be thinking about challenging Milošević in the upcoming presidential election. According to information from Milošević's secret police, Milošević personally ordered Stambolić's assassination.[111]

As part of his strategy to disempower Montenegro now that it was under the control of reformist forces, Milošević had changed the process of selection for the post of president of Yugoslavia. Whereas previously the president had been selected by the Federal Assembly, where Montenegro had equal representation with Serbia, now the president was to be elected by popular vote; given that Montenegro's population was less than 10 percent the size of Serbia's, this effectively marginalized the smaller republic's influence in the outcome.

Although Milošević's term as president did not expire until July 2001, he decided to move up the date of the presidential election to coincide with previously scheduled elections for the Federal Assembly and local governments, apparently indicating strong confidence that he would easily win the vote. During the electoral campaign, conservatives continued to accuse the opposition of being agents of NATO and enemies of Serbia, and continued their strategy of harassment and threats.

As returns came in from the first round of voting in September, it became clear that the opposition had won a majority in the Federal parliament and had once again swept in local elections. At the crucial presidential level, the opposition candidate, Vojislav Koštunica, won a clear majority of the vote. But the SPS once again attempted to subvert the results, this time by having the electoral commission determine that he had fallen short of 50 percent of the vote necessary to win in the first round (they reported that Koštunica had received 48.96 percent, and gave Milošević 38.62 percent). Based on this result, the electoral commission declared that a second round of voting would be required between these two top candidates.

As the date of the second round of the presidential election approached, miners once again went on strike to protest the rigging of the process. As it became clear that the opposition would probably win the election,

---

[111] The Belgrade weekly *NIN* reported after investigation that former head of State Security Rade Marković has stated that Milošević personally ordered Stambolić's assassination, and that the same people who killed Stambolić had also been responsible for the attempts on Drašković's life, and that the assassins were members of the Special Operations Unit of State Security, the so-called red berets. Slobodan Ikonić, "Milošević lično naređivao Legiji," *NIN*, September 11, 2003, 26–28. These are the same forces and people who would three years later assassinate reformist prime minister Zoran Đinđić. Miloš Vasić, "Jedinica za specijalna ubistva," *Vreme*, March 27, 2003.

the SPS annulled the results of the first round and canceled the second round of voting, declaring that there would be new elections some time in the future.

Washington claimed that the 2000 electoral defeat of Milošević was the direct result of the NATO bombing. In fact, it is extremely difficult to substantiate that claim. First, as pointed out above, the bombing was actually an enormous setback for the opposition. Second, a close study of the election itself reveals a number of factors that are of more importance. One is miscalculation by the regime. Just as in Croatia in 2000, so too in Serbia the ruling party was extremely overconfident. Clearly it badly misjudged the outcome of the election.[112] Because of this miscalculation, the conservatives did not make the kinds of efforts they had made in the past to ensure a victory.

The government also miscalculated its economic policy; whereas in the past just prior to elections it had followed policies that increased real wages, this time real wages fell right before the election, marking the first time the SPS was not able to raise real wages before an election.[113] In addition, "Milošević had entered pre-election silence with a hint of chaos on the foreign currency market and inflation that was escaping control," and Russia had cut off gas exports to Yugoslavia, which caused "a shortage of oil derivatives that it was not able to solve."[114] In short, the economic situation had deteriorated to the point where the SPS was not able to manipulate the economy to its advantage prior to the election.

As pointed out above, the first reaction of the SPS to the electoral results was to reject them, and to resort to annulling the election and calling for new elections. The DOS coalition responded by once again calling for massive protests and civil disobedience in order to force the SPS to acknowledge the results. Hundreds of thousands of citizens took to the streets of Belgrade and other major cities, and 13,000 miners also went on strike in support of the protests.[115] When the government threatened to bring the military in to force the miners back to work, the miners were joined by thousands of citizens, and the military refused to follow Milošević's orders to use force against them. Meanwhile the opposition leaders had already

[112] Goati, "The Nature of the Order," 54, notes that "The ruling elite . . . was wrong in its judgment of the balance of strength among the electorate and convened presidential elections despite the fact that the presidential mandate was not due to expire until July 2001. It did so in the belief that it would win an overwhelming electoral victory."

[113] "Macroeconomic Review," *Economic Review* (G-17 and East-West Institute, Belgrade) 1.1, no. 9 (September 2000): 6.

[114] Ibid.

[115] Goati, "The Nature of the Order," 55.

spoken with the special police units, who informed them that they would not obey orders from above to use force against the protesters.[116]

Indeed, a crucial factor in the final outcome—a transfer of political power from the SPS and its allies to the opposition—was the defection from the SPS of critical parts of the post-war power structure in Serbia: the mafias, the so-called "tycoons," and the special services unit of the State Security police.[117]

The defection of powerful economic actors to the side of the opposition showed that the conservative elite had become fragmented and that parts of it no longer felt threatened by the prospect of the political opposition taking power. This was so in part because the structures of economic power had evolved to the point that control over the state was no longer necessary to maintain control over economic power. An additional factor was that some groups who were dependent to some degree on state policies reached arrangements with the opposition for the state to continue policies favorable to their interests.

One such group was the organized crime mafias, those parts of the economic elite that had come into wealth with Milošević's blessing through circumventing the international sanctions regime. They had accumulated huge amounts of wealth during the period of war in Bosnia and the resulting international sanctions through their involvement in black market smuggling. Milošević had allowed them to operate in order to ensure that basic goods such as gasoline and cigarettes got into the country despite the sanctions. These groups thus represented a new elite sector in Serbia whose power was based on their control over illegal and clandestine distribution networks that were allowed to exist by the state.[118] By 2000, however, Milošević had reportedly begun trying to reduce the power of organized crime groups that he had allowed to flourish during the war. At the time of the elections, these groups, who were very closely tied to the special operations units of Serbian State Security, in effect defected to the opposition.[119] The opposition, in turn, apparently struck a deal with

[116] See Dragan Bujošević and Ivan Radovanović, *The Fall of Milosevic: The October 5th Revolution* (New York: Palgrave Macmillan, 2003), 27–28.

[117] For a detailed look at the events surrounding the protests, including the deals between the special police, mafias and opposition, see ibid.

[118] Thus in the realm of cigarette smuggling alone, smugglers earn US$1.2 million per day. Dragan Simeunović, Faculty of Political Science, University of Belgrade, "Corruption in Politics in Serbia and Montenegro and Problems Delimiting Possibilities to Uproot This Problem," unpublished paper.

[119] Obrad Kesić, "An Airplane with Nineteen Pilots," in *The Dysfunctional State: Serbian Politics and Society Since 1989*, ed. Sabrina P. Ramet and Vjeran Pavlaković (Seattle: University of Washington Press, forthcoming).

the mafias, promising to allow them to continue their illicit activities.[120] Thus a change in political structures, and even a transformation of the economy, would not necessarily have a negative impact on these groups, whose power was built on the private wealth they had accumulated, and whose control over illegal distribution networks would be allowed by the new government. (Đinđić would pay with his life for this deal; when he too tried to crack down on the mafias in 2003 he was assassinated.)

The other part of the elite who defected to the opposition is made up of those who are referred to as the "tycoons." These are people who had also accumulated enormous private wealth, but through enterprises that had been allowed to come into being by the SPS controlled state, referred to by Mladen Lazić above. The tycoons, too, reportedly struck a deal with the opposition, that they would support the overthrow of the SPS regime in exchange for the opposition allowing them to continue their businesses and continue the privileges and benefits they had received from the state under SPS rule.[121]

Thus the 2000 elections and the massive protests that accompanied the conservatives' attempts to reverse the results of those elections marked not so much a change in public sentiment—as we've seen, the population had wanted fundamental change all along—as it did a reconfiguration of the power dynamics. The regime itself no longer had a complete monopoly over power resources; it miscalculated in serious ways; and its moves led to the defection of key parts of the power structure, which struck their own deals with the opposition. The organization of *Otpor* and other opposition groups was important, but they were drawing on a very long tradition of citizen activism and anti-regime mobilization. Unlike in the previous cases of anti-regime mobilization, however, the strategy of demobilization was not available for the regime to save itself. The fact that crucial parts of the elite coalition were no longer dependent for their power on the SPS's continued control of the state also meant that the change of political power and the removal from power of the SPS and its allies no longer represented a significant threat to them.

---

[120] For references to this, see, for example, Bojan Dimitrijevic and Daniel Sunter, "Serbia: Red Berets Disbanded," *International War and Peace Reporting Balkans Crisis Report*, March 27, 2003. <http://www.iwpr.net/index.pl?archive/bcr3/bcr3_200303_418_2_eng.txt> (accessed October 17, 2003).

[121] Private communication with Dušan Pavlović, analyst at G-17 Plus Institute, Belgrade, October 17, 2003. Additionally, proposals by some in the opposition to pass a law on the origins of property, that is, to document how wealth and property had been obtained, were initially rejected by the new government. Such a law would have effectively overturned much of the insider privatization that had been undertaken under SPS rule. This had been the main means by which the "tycoons" had accumulated their wealth.

CHAPTER 5

CROATIA AND THE STRATEGY OF DEMOBILIZATION, 1990–2000

The nationalist policies of the Croatian government between 1990 and 1999, the wars in Croatia in 1991 and 1995, and the 1993–94 war in the Croat inhabited parts of Bosnia-Herzegovina have been explained in terms of ethnic hatreds, either ancient or recently constructed and mobilized. The main focus has been on Croatia as a land awash in nationalism and ethnic resentments between Croats and Serbs. From this perspective, Croatia was supposedly waiting to explode into nationalist bloodshed, hence providing fertile ground for ethnic entrepreneurs who mobilized Croats and Serbs (and in Bosnia, Croats and Muslims) into bloody warfare.[1]

This chapter shows that the violence in Croatia and in the Croat populated parts of Bosnia (so-called Herceg Bosna) was not the result of ethnic solidarity or hatreds, ancient or new. Rather, these wars were purposeful policies on the part of elites, namely, conservatives in the ruling party of Serbia who supported the extremist minority in the Serbian Democratic Party of Croatia and influential right-wing extremists within the HDZ—which from 1990 until 2000 was the ruling party in Croatia—and which was protected and supported by Croatian president Franjo Tudjman. Both of these groups were threatened by overwhelming public sentiment in favor of liberalization and democratization. And both responded by using strategies of violence as a way to *demobilize* the population.

[1] *New York Times* coverage of the war in Croatia, January–December 1991; Misha Glenny, *The Fall of Yugoslavia: The Third Balkan War* (New York: Penguin, 1992); Robert Kaplan, *Balkan Ghosts*.

These pressures for fundamental change in the structures of power were coming both from outside, from the IMF and western states, as well as from within Yugoslavia itself, at first from reformist forces within the League of Communists, then also from the Yugoslav federal prime minister, Ante Marković, who pushed for outright political and economic liberalization. From 1990 onward, moderates within the ruling party and the Croatian opposition parties were also calling for radical restructuring and liberalization of the structures of state and economic power in the republic. Throughout this entire period, these liberalizing forces were appealing to the values and interests of the wider population, and as in much of the rest of eastern Europe they attempted to mobilize that population against the status quo power structure.

The wars in Croatia and Bosnia-Herzegovina were the response of the status quo elites to this attempted popular mobilization. Faced with this threat, conservatives within the ruling nationalist parties in Croatia (the HDZ, and in Krajina, the SDS) pursued policies of violent conflict which they framed, explained, and justified in ethnic terms. Seeking to preserve its control over the structure of political and economic power in Croatia, the right wing of the HDZ sent paramilitary groups into ethnically mixed communities to terrorize and massacre civilians. The immediate purpose of this violence was to demobilize the wider population, to prevent a successful anti-regime mobilization from toppling the existing structures of power in the republic by shifting the focus of political discourse and action away from liberalization toward purported threats to the very existence of the nation newly defined in very narrow terms. The effect of the violence was also the construction of homogeneous political space, that is, political space within which were imposed anti-liberal, authoritarian notions of Croatness (and Serbness) in which the views of challenger elites and the wider population, which were not in line with the HDZ right, were defined as anti-Croat (or anti-Serb).

Simultaneously, status quo elites worked to shift the bases of their power from their positions in the old party-state system, which they had taken over in 1990, to new bases of financial wealth derived from privatized formerly socially owned economic objects. The violence and resulting homogenization of political space served to buy time for these elites in their efforts to transfer the bases of their power over to private property.

Thus, far from being caused by ethnicity or ethnic hatreds on the ground, the violence was an attempt to destroy the lived realities of the multiple and complex interactions that make up social coexistence. This violence also imposed a definition of groupness that did not correspond to the lived experiences of ordinary people and especially in the ethnically mixed regions of the country where the large majority of Croatia's Serb population lived.[2]

This strategy of violence framed in ethnic terms was successful in silencing, marginalizing, and demobilizing the large part of the Croat population that wanted fundamental change and allowed conservatives to impose their unpopular policies. The SDS right's similar policies had the exact same goal vis-à-vis Croatia's Serb population. (As we have seen, Belgrade's participation in this violence was aimed largely at the population of Serbia itself with the goal of preserving the structure of power within that republic.) The HDZ right's success lasted until the death of Franjo Tudjman in late 1999, which provided an opportunity for the population to reject the unpopular HDZ conservatives in the 2000 parliamentary and presidential elections. By this time, however, the structures and bases of power of much of the HDZ right and their allies had shifted to resources that were not as threatened by political change, while one of their major (and most unpopular) goals, the absorption of Western Herzegovina into Croatia, had been made impossible by the international community. Indeed, following its loss of power, the HDZ came to be openly dominated by the most ideologically hard right-wingers. As a result, its support plummeted even further, so that in Zagreb, for example, whereas in 1990 the HDZ won 48.7 percent of the vote, in the 2000 municipal elections it received only 11 percent. Despite this, the HDZ continued to try to use strategies of conflict to bring down the new government and the new president, but with no success.

In the case of the SDS right, their fate was so tied to Belgrade that, when it suited Serbia's conservatives, they were empowered to pursue violence as a way to silence and marginalize the ordinary Serb population, as well as moderate Serb elites. In the end, however, the entire Serb population of Krajina was sacrificed by Milošević and his allies in Serbia for reasons of self-interest, as they ordered the army and the civilian population to retreat in the face of the Croatian offensive in the summer of 1995. Nevertheless, from the perspective of the SDS right, their policies of provoking violence were aimed at the Serb population of Croatia, as a strategy to destroy what existed before, to silence and marginalize

[2] At the start of the war, the vast majority of Croatia's Serbs lived in ethnically heterogeneous communities. Only 24.8 percent of Serbs lived in Serb-majority (50 percent or more Serbs) municipalities, and only a little more than half of those (14 percent) lived in municipalities where Serbs made up 75 percent or more of the population. *Popis stanovništa 1991* (Zagreb: Republički zavod za statistiku, April 1992). The violence during the 1991 war was worst exactly in those municipalities with the highest level of heterogeneity, where Croats, Serbs, and others lived together: Vukovar, Beli Manastir, Osijek, Daruvar, Pakrac, Novska, Grubišno Polje, Benkovac, Obrovac, Karlovac, Slunj, Vrginmost, Gospić, Otočac.

political alternatives, and to impose unpopular policies. In this they too proved quite successful, at least until the 1995 invasion that marked the end of the Republic of Krajina.

This chapter will look at the pressures for change and the responses of the status quo elites in two periods: from 1990 until 1992, when the HDZ was in power and war was raging on Croatia's territory; and 1992 to 2000, when the HDZ right was facing greater and greater pressure from moderates within the ruling party and from the anti-regime opposition. In terms of both periods, this chapter will consider threats to the status quo elites that came in the form of proposals for liberalization mounted by their opponents and supported by the wider population, the response to these threats by the status quo elites, and the fact that the strategy of violence was not a reflection of sentiments at the local level.

The HDZ in Power: Ethnic Conflict as Political Strategy

The shift in Croatia from a one-party state socialist political system to a liberal democratic political system meant a shift in the politically relevant population. Now, rather than the SKH and its members, the entire adult population would be participating in formal politics. Especially given the policies coming from Belgrade that clearly threatened not only Croatia's autonomy but also the wider population's preferences for fundamental change, SKH conservatives seemed to be in a hopeless situation. Yet despite the seemingly favorable trends for radical change in Croatia, the structures of power in the republic changed relatively little over the following ten years.

The next section of the chapter explains this apparent puzzle by looking at how HDZ conservatives used a strategy of ethnic conflict in order to demobilize popular demands for radical change as well as to restructure Croatia demographically by constructing an image of Croat groupness that did not reflect the social realities of people in ethnically mixed communities. The result was to homogenize political space, imposing an authoritarian, conservative political line as the "correct" Croat position. The effect was to consolidate the HDZ right's tight control over the structures of power they had inherited from the SKH; indeed, the HDZ imposed a tighter and more authoritarian grip over society than had the SKH in the last years of its rule. The strategy of conflict was thus the means by which the HDZ right managed to stave off the kinds of change desired by the wider population and seen in other east European countries. In this they were greatly aided by the similar strategies of conflict used for similar purposes by conservatives in Serbia.

Croatian Society on the Eve of Elections

With the coming of multiparty elections in early 1990, suddenly the wider population mattered directly in the outcome of political conflicts. As shown in Chapter 2, by late 1989, Croatia was among the most liberal and open places in Yugoslavia, well placed for the kinds of fundamental changes being seen in neighboring Hungary. It also showed high levels of ethnic coexistence and little if any evidence that violence would break out based on ethnic relations within communities.

The stated preferences for Croatia's relationship to the rest of Yugoslavia were also very different from the image of the demand for immediate independence. In the months prior to the 1990 elections, 15 percent of Croats favored full independence, while 64 percent favored a confederal solution.[3] A different survey just before the election showed about 37 percent identifying Croatian independence as one of their top political priorities; this means that 63 percent of Croats did not list it as a top concern.[4] Of course,

[3] Nenad Zakošek, "Polarizacijske strukture, obrasci političkih uvjerenja i hrvatski izbori 1990," in *Hrvatska u izborima '90*, ed. Ivan Grdešić, Mirjana Kasapović, Ivan Šiber and Nenad Zakošek (Zagreb: Naprijed, 1991), 152. What is clear is that among Croats, the preferred solution was a looser confederation of republics, while Serbs preferred a more democratic federation. Indeed, even among supporters of the HDZ polled in 1990, only 30 percent called for total independence, "Croatia outside of Yugoslavia." Among supporters of the other, more moderate nationally oriented coalition, the KNS, only 6 percent supported full independence, while 84 percent supported a "confederation of autonomous states," a position similar to the status of the republics within Yugoslavia after 1974. Support for the confederation among Serbs was 11 percent, among "Yugoslavs" 31 percent, and among "others" in Croatia 46 percent. Ivan Šiber, "The Impact of Nationalism, Values, and Ideological Orientations on Multi-Party Elections in Croatia," in *The Tragedy of Yugoslavia: The Failure of Democratic Transformation*, ed. Jim Seroka and Vukasin Pavlovic (Armonk, N.Y.: M. E. Sharpe, 1992), 154–155.

[4] In this survey, carried out ten days before the election, respondents were asked to choose "the three most important problems of Croatian politics." "Croatian independence" was chosen by 29.3 percent of those polled while 32.6 percent chose "Yugoslav cooperation." Even assuming that all the Croatian independence responses were for Croats, that would represent 37 percent of all Croats. For the remaining 63 percent, independence was not among the top concerns. It should also be noted that the top choices here were "peace and security" (55.5 percent); social justice and security (42.5 percent); integration of Croatia into the EU (42.5 percent); and "national equality" (34.1 percent). "Anketa istraživanja IZBORI 1990, 1992, 1995, projekt 'Izbori, stranke i parlament 1990–2000'" (Polling Research Project Elections 1990, 1992, 1995), Faculty of Political Science, Zagreb University, online as "Rezultati longitudinalnog istraživanja političkih stavova birača 1990–1995," at <http://media.fpzg.hr/hip/stavovi.htm>.

peoples' expressed views on this subject were constrained by what was seen
as possible at that time. Nevertheless, a very significant number of people
were not so constrained and did support full independence. The fact that
they were a minority indicates that the desire for full independence was by
no means a unanimous sentiment among Croats, but rather that the subsequent events had a very substantial impact not only on what was perceived
as possible but also on what was perceived as desirable. In short, public
opinion or popular sentiment by itself provides no indication that independence was an absolutely predetermined, unavoidable outcome.

What is particularly striking about these findings on the state of Croatian society is that they represent opinion at a time when Milošević had
been actively putting pressure on Croatia, attempting to divide Serbs and
Croats by filling the airwaves and Serbia-based newspapers with strikingly provocative and negative images meant to undermine coexistence,
using various allies to undermine and destabilize the SKH leadership and
Croatia itself. This was an atmosphere that had been created *prior* to the
coming to power of the nationalist HDZ. Nevertheless, the social realities
in ethnically heterogeneous communities remained the dominant basis of
most people's views of interethnic relations.

Thus at the time of the first multiparty elections, those elites in Croatia who wanted to preserve the status quo power structures were facing
a wider population who desired fundamental change, a shift toward liberal democracy and radical economic reform, as well as a desire for continued peace and stability, but also the perception of threat coming from
the policies of Slobodan Milošević. At the same time, conservatives in
Croatia were facing the growing liberalization efforts of Ante Markovic,
the federal prime minister, whose policies of economic reform were not
only popular in Croatia but also very successful in reviving the Yugoslav
economy.[5] By his very success and popularity Marković posed yet another
very serious threat to elites who wanted to defend the existing structures
of power in Croatia and throughout Yugoslavia.

The 1990 Elections

The first multiparty elections in Croatia were won by the nationalist Croatian Democratic Union (Hrvatska Demokratska Zajednica, HDZ), which
won both the presidency as well as a majority of seats in the Croatian

---

[5] On the popularity of Marković and of his policies as prime minister, see Mihajlovski
and Bahtijarević and Milas in Bačević et al., *Jugoslavija na kriznoj prekretnici*, 59, 65 respectively.

parliament, the Sabor. This victory is usually interpreted as proof of the overwhelming importance of ethnic solidarity and sentiment among the population. But looking closer at the campaign and at the reasons the voters themselves gave for the electoral behavior, what becomes clear is that other factors were at least as important, and indeed in many ways more important, in the HDZ victory. In fact, the HDZ in general portrayed itself as wanting democracy and peace and as a moderate nationalist party.

The fact that the HDZ was the best financed and organized opposition party played a major role in its success. But the two key reasons for HDZ success were its campaign strategy, which focused on the threats coming from Belgrade and on the need for a change in governing parties after fifty years of communist rule and, in addition, the winner-take-all electoral rules drawn up by the SKH.

During the election campaign itself, the HDZ, using the specter of Slobodan Milošević, focused not on specific issues, but rather on demands for greater autonomy and sovereignty for Croatia, portraying itself as the party that would and could defend Croatia. Indeed, as SKH leader Ivica Račan noted after the election, "Milošević's aggressive policy was the strongest propaganda for Tudjman."[6]

In its campaign literature, at both the national and local levels, the HDZ stressed its desire for democracy, its opposition to "any kind of national exclusion and chauvinistic aggression," and its "guarantees to the Serbian people of all national, cultural, religious and other rights," in line with the values of the overwhelming majority of the Croat population. But alongside these guarantees, some within the HDZ attempted to link local Serbs to Milošević's strategy.[7] Such linkage, in effect, was an attempt to undermine the social realities in ethnically heterogeneous parts of the republic by equating local Serbs, who were not seen in negative terms, to Milošević, who was. Thus, while assuring Croats who were thinking of voting for the HDZ that they would ensure the rights of Serbs, the HDZ

[6] Quoted in Silber and Little, *Yugoslavia: Death of a Nation*, 84. For a similar argument see interview with conservative former head of SKH Stipe Šuvar, "Jugoslavija nije razbijena i neće biti," *Nedeljna Borba*, May 5–6, 1990, 12.

[7] Thus, for example, in one piece of campaign literature the HDZ warned that "Serbs cannot be the live coal by which Croatia is set on fire and destroyed from within" ("Za demokratski preobražaj," *Jedinstvo*, March 29, 1990, 3; "Za dostojan život svakog čovjeka," *Jedinstvo*, April 19, 1990, 4.) And Vladimir Šeks, an HDZ rightist, in a campaign speech in Dalmatia declared that "today, when the sovereignty of Croatia is threatened, the HDZ stands under the motto 'Never under Belgrade'" and that "the Croatian people have been silent subletters in their own country for enough, we have felt as foreigners in our own homeland long enough." K.M., "Konfederacija ali ne pod svaku cijenu," *Narodni list*, April 7, 1990, 4.

right was also appealing to anxieties about Belgrade's strategy of instrumentalizing the Serbian population in Croatia. The fact that it was making both types of appeals is an indication that appealing to resentment
and ethnic outbidding alone would get the support of only a small
number of voters, not enough to compete with the moderate nationalist
Coalition for National Agreement (KNS) and the SKH.

This dual message was also indicative of a deep split within the HDZ
itself. Indeed, the HDZ campaign featured moderate candidates who had
been mid and lower level SKH officials during the 1971 "Croatian Spring"
and had at that time been purged from the party. (The rival moderate
nationalist opposition party, the KNS, also gathered together people active
in the 1971 events, but these were the reformist leaders of the SKH at the
time of the Croatian Spring, and many of those who had been part of
the student movement at the time.) The hard-liners and Ustaša sympathizers were for the most part kept in the background and remained silent
during the campaign. In the final days of the campaign, before the second
round of voting (but after it was already clear that HDZ candidate Franjo
Tudjman had been elected president), Tudjman attempted to reassure voters that "there will not be revenge, the HDZ will come out for full equality of all citizens in Croatia," regardless of their ethnicity.[8] Clearly the HDZ
was appealing to the values and experiences of the large majority of Croats,
as described in the previous section.

The second major theme, one of the most effective parts of the HDZ
campaign and the one factor to which many local analysts attribute the
size of the HDZ's victory, was the fact that "its criticism of the [SKH] was
more specific and more radical than the other opposition parties."[9] Even
among HDZ voters, when asked why they voted against the SKH, 65 percent responded "responsibility of the SKH for the crisis and to give the
opportunity [to govern] to others," while only 14 percent responded "the
SKH does not sufficiently represent the interests of my nation [narod]."[10]
(Among those who voted for the Serbian nationalist party (the SDS), the
figures were 32 percent and 27 percent respectively.) As elsewhere in the
region, even reformist communist parties rarely survived the first election. In that regard, however, the SKH, with 34.5 percent of the vote, fared
better than any other reformist party in the region.

---

[8] See "Zbor HDZ u Karlovcu," *Karlovački tjednik*, May 10, 1990, 2.
[9] Dražen Lalić, "Pohod na Glasače: Analiza sadržaja poruka predizbornih kampanja
stranaka u Hrvatskoj 1990., 1992. i 1993. godine," in *Pohod na Glasače: Izbori u Hrvatskoj
1990–1993.*, ed. Srđan Vrcan et al. (Split: Puls, 1995), 247–248.
[10] Ibid.

The second major factor in the outcome of the election was the electoral system that the SKH had put in place wherein the country was divided into single member constituency districts. In districts where no single candidate won an absolute majority of the vote, a second round was held in which all candidates who received at least 7 percent of the vote in the first round participated. In this second round an absolute majority was not necessary: whichever candidate received the greatest support (plurality) was declared the winner.[11]

Given the subsequent course of events, what is most striking about the 1990 election results is the degree to which they reflect not an image of ethnic hatreds, but rather the values of coexistence expressed in the polling cited above. The Serbian nationalist party in Croatia, the SDS, which had been set up under the sponsorship of Belgrade writer Dobrica Ćosić and in coordination with Milošević's local allies, and which had portrayed itself as the defender of Croatia's threatened Serbs, received only 13.5 percent of the Serb vote.[12] It won only one seat in the parliament, in Knin, the base of Belgrade's allies in Croatia. Most of the rest of the vote of Serbs went to the SKH (46 percent).[13] This pattern of voting was also seen at local levels. For example, in the heavily Serb area of Lika, in the elections for općina assemblies (which were also single-member constituency elections), the SDS received only 24.8 percent of the mandates (although Serbs made up 49.5 percent of the population); the SKH received 34.2 percent.[14]

At the national level, the victor was clearly the HDZ, but the victory was far from overwhelming. Although the HDZ won 67.5 percent of the seats in parliament, this was the result of the electoral system rather than a reflection of votes: in the first round, the HDZ received 41.8 percent of the total vote (in the second round it received about same percentage). Given turnout of 84.5 percent, this means that the HDZ received the active support of 34 percent of all eligible voters, and 45 percent of all eligible

---

[11] In the 1990 elections, 36 percent of the seats were filled in the first round, and 64 percent in the second. For descriptions of the electoral system and outcomes, see Kasapović 1993.

[12] Overall election results from *Dopunski izvještaj o provedenim izborima za zastupnike u Sabor Socijalističke Republike Hrvatske* (Zagreb: Republička izborna komisija, 1990), cited in Cohen, *Broken Bonds*, 100. Figures on Serb votes extrapolated from population figures. In preelection polls, 23 percent of Serbs indicated that they would vote for SDS. Šiber, "Nacionalna," 99.

[13] Of the votes received by the SKH, 28 percent came from Serbs.

[14] Turnout was about 85 percent. M. Čuljat, "Završeni izbori," *Lički vjesnik*, May 15, 1990, 1.

Croat voters (53.5 percent of those Croats who voted, assuming all HDZ votes were cast by Croats).[15] Given the relatively small commitment of time and effort that voters need to take to cast votes, what is striking is that the HDZ was able to mobilize for voting only about half of all Croats. This is a strikingly different image than the usual one, which portrays the situation as one of massive and unified mobilization of Croats (and Serbs) behind the nationalist parties. The SKH received the votes of about 20 percent of Croats, and 52 percent of its overall votes came from Croats (17 percent came from "Yugoslavs").[16] Likewise, in the Lika region, in the elections for municipal (općine) assemblies (which were also single-member constituency elections), although Croats made up 46 percent of the population, the HDZ received only 17.8 percent of the seats.[17]

This overwhelming majority in the Sabor, and the fact that Tudjman was president, meant that between elections the major power struggles would take place within the ruling party rather than between parties. Yet the electoral results meant that, especially at election time, a major threat was also present outside the HDZ, since fewer than one-half of Croats had voted for the HDZ, a percentage that would only decrease over time; the SDS faced a similar threat, since over three-fourths of Serbs had not voted for that party. In addition, the desire of the population for fundamental changes in the structure of economic and political power continued to threaten key parts of the HDZ and SDS elite. Thus, even after the elections, the major axis of political conflict remained conservatives versus reformers.

The HDZ in Power: 1990–1992

Conflict between conservatives and reformers existed also within the HDZ itself. Indeed, the HDZ was more of a political movement than a political party, or in the words of Franjo Tudjman, a grouping of "all legitimate Croat political forces." At the time of the 1990 election, it covered a wide spectrum, ranging from moderate reformists who had been purged from the SKH in 1972 for nationalism but who were staunch advocates

---

[15] In the second round, the numbers were similar, with about 54.1 percent of those Croats who voted casting their ballots for the HDZ. Overall election results cited in Cohen, *Broken Bonds*, 100. Percentages of Croats voting extrapolated from population data.

[16] Šiber, "Nacionalna," 99–100.

[17] Turnout was about 85 percent. M. Čuljat, "Završeni izbori," *Lički vjesnik*, May 15, 1990, 1.

of democracy and economic reform; to technocrats and managers of socially owned firms who were interested in maintaining their autonomy and control of their firms, and whose priority was an efficient economy; to ideological hard-liners and nationalist fundamentalists who were very authoritarian and espoused the most ethnically chauvinistic and xenophobic views, and who would come to have enormous influence in the HDZ-controlled media and newspapers; to those with links to the Ustaša emigration, many of whom were from western Herzegovina and who sought to consolidate the HDZ's control over structures of power, who advocated authoritarianism, and who ended up having enormous influence on Croatia's policies, despite their small numbers and the lack of popular support for them and their policies. In addition, just before and after the 1990 elections a number of conservative SKH officials, especially at the lower levels of the party, joined the HDZ as a way to stay within local structures of power; so they too were committed to resisting fundamental political and economic reform.

Reflecting this spectrum, in the period from the 1990 election until the end of the war in Croatia in early 1992, HDZ policy was bifurcated between an officially approved moderate policy at the national level and a more hard-line policy in some localities. In this period, Tudjman publicly supported the moderate, reformist line on most issues, but privately he consistently protected and supported the minority hard-line conservatives and their policies.

At the national level, moderate reformists were in the forefront in terms of numbers and positions. Thus the prime ministers appointed by Tudjman in this period were all from the majority moderate wing of the party, and espoused policies in line with the preferences of the wider population. Indeed, what is striking about official HDZ policy at the national level is the question of the place of Serbs in Croatia and the response to provocations by Belgrade's allies, and the contrast between this official policy and the policies and actions of conservatives, especially at the local level.

As discussed, even before the SKH decided to hold multiparty elections, Belgrade had been working with local allies to create conflict along ethnic lines as a way to undermine the SKH, repeating the strategies that it had used successfully in Serbia, Vojvodina, and Montenegro. Unlike in those places, however, the result in Croatia had been to disempower SKH conservatives and to hasten the coming to power of a non-communist party committed on paper to policies that directly contradicted the Serbian conservatives' preferences.

In response to the election of the HDZ in Croatia, as well as to the threat posed by the increasing popularity of the reformist federal prime minister Ante Marković, the Serbian conservatives and the JNA shifted their strategy away from the earlier attempt to recentralize Yugoslavia, toward trying to destroy the federation through force and then to consolidate power in a smaller, Serbia-dominated state. As noted in the previous chapter, by June 1990 Milošević, Yugoslav President Borisav Jović, and Federal Defense Minister Veljko Kadijević had decided to "throw Slovenia and Croatia out" of Yugoslavia by using military force, thereby ensuring them and their allies a majority of the votes in the Yugoslav party and state presidencies.[18] Milošević's idea was "to undertake the 'cutting off' or 'severing' of Croatia such that the municipalities [opštine] in the regions of Lika, Banija and Kordun, which have created a separate community [zajednicu], will stay on our side. Then later the people there will decide in a referendum whether they want to stay or to leave."[19]

Very soon after this decision was made, the exact scenario Milošević had proposed began to unfold in the border regions of Croatia. Although prior to this the SDS in Croatia had been calling for "cultural autonomy" for Serbs in Croatia, either as individuals or in municipalities where Serbs were in the majority, now suddenly the head of the municipal council of Knin, a former local SKH official and now hard-line SDS member, Milan Babić, along with the head of the SDS, Jovan Rašković, announced the formation of a political entity, a "Free Serbian Joint Municipality" in Serb-majority municipalities in Lika and Knin, as well as in municipalities in the Banija region (the municipalities of Dvor, Kostajnica, and Glina) where non-Serbs were a significant percentage of the population. Soon the assemblies of the municipalities of Gračac, Donji Lapac, and Obrovac joined as well.

In an indication that this was a plan that had come about suddenly and was being imposed from outside, the heads of Kostajnica, Glina, and Dvor

---

[18] Jović notes that on June 27 he proposed to Veljko Kadijević "that I would most happily through the use of force throw [Slovenia and Croatia] out of Yugoslavia, by simply cutting the border and proclaiming that they created this situation through their own actions." He further proposed, and Kadijević agreed, that Serbs in Croatia would hold a referendum "on the basis of which it would be decided to undertake the redrawing of borders." On the next day, Jović proposed the same thing to Milošević, who "agreed to the idea of 'throwing out' Slovenia and Croatia from Yugoslavia" but worried about whether the army would follow such orders. Jović responded that he was not worried about that, but rather about how to ensure a majority in the SFRY Presidency for such a decision. Borisav Jović, Poslednji dani SFRJ: Izvodi iz dnevnika (Belgrade: Politika, 1995), 159–161.
[19] Ibid., 161.

municipalities expressed surprise, saying they had learned about this decision from the newspapers. The head of the Glina assembly, an SDS member, added that,

> Since the communists won in the recent elections in Banija and Kordun
> municipalities, I think that the SDS for now does not have in its plan that
> the općine in this area be included in the "Serbian community of munici-
> palities." We are of the opinion that linking on a political or national [eth-
> nic] principal does not have a real basis for Glina općina.[20]

Similarly, the presidents of the assemblies of Titova Korenica and Gospić
also learned about the initiative from the newspapers and had received
no official information about it.[21]

What is clear from these reports as well as from conversations with people who were involved in politics in this region at the time is that the hard-
line policy was being imposed on the local SDS organizations from above,
from Knin, which in turn was working in cooperation with and at the
behest of Belgrade. Indeed, although these moves were portrayed by Belgrade as a rebellion by local Serbs against threatening HDZ policies, Jović
himself indicates the stage-managed nature of these events in his memoirs, where he puts "rebellion" in quotation marks when he discusses the
"'rebellion' of Serbs in Croatia."[22] In short, it was a repeat of the stage-
managed demonstrations that led to the overthrow of the Montenegro
and Vojvodina leaderships.[23]

While there was no official announcement, unofficially people in these
regions knew that events were beyond their control, given that they were
being directed by Belgrade via Knin.[24] Hence weapons were being funneled

---

[20] Ž. Maljevac, "Banija ne podržava autonomiju," *Jedinstvo*, July 5. 1990, 2.

[21] A group of deputies in the Gračac assembly sought to postpone a vote on joining
the community, "because they had not received any kind of material on the basis of which
they could prepare for discussion and decision." "Što se događa u Lici?" *Lički vjesnik*, July
15, 1990, 3.

[22] "'Pobuna' srba u hrvatskoj," in Jović, *Poslednji dani SFRJ*, 178.

[23] Of course, this does not mean that the local Serbs were not fearful; one of the things
the SDS and Belgrade did was to play up the threat from the HDZ, claiming it was the
same as the Ustaša. In this the HDZ right aided the SDS right by insisting on policies
that were at a minimum reminiscent of some aspects of the NDH. Indeed, the HDZ right
publicly praised the NDH and the Ustaša, and many of them had links to the Ustaša of
World War II.

[24] Ž. Maljevac, "Autonomija bi štetila i Srbima i Hrvatima," *Jedinstvo*, July 12, 1990,
2. For example, a Serb acquaintance of the author's who was politically involved in the
Lika region was told by his brother, who was a member of SDS, that the situation was being
driven from outside and that the SDS was the only place to be in this coming scenario.

to the SDS from the Serbian Ministry of the Interior, via the JNA.[25] In response, the HDZ right began supplying arms to its local allies. The result was a rapid exodus of members and officials at the local level from the SKH toward the SDS and HDZ, even in municipalities where the SKH had a majority of seats, as they sensed which way the power was shifting; indeed, some of these newly minted nationalists, as they were called, became some of the hardest hard-liners in the nationalist parties.[26]

Over the course of July and August 1990, radicals allied with Belgrade continued to push toward confrontation, provoking violent conflict with Croatian police and setting up barricades along highways in the Knin area. In July, mass meetings were staged by the SDS in the Knin area, with hundreds of busloads of Serbs from Serbia and Bosnia in attendance; a "Serbian National Council" set up by the SDS adopted a "Declaration on the Sovereignty of the Serbian People," declaring the right to territorial autonomy for Serbs. On August 18, the SDS held a referendum on autonomy, in which any Serb in Croatia had the right to vote, although Croats living in the territories concerned were not allowed to vote. At the same time, the SDS sent women and children into Bosnia in expectation of a possible armed response by the Croatian government, a response that did not come.[27]

Faced with this increasingly tense situation, the HDZ at the national level, that is the government as well as Tudjman, pursued policies of compromise and negotiations. The most striking evidence of this is the response of Tudjman and the moderates to proposals by General Martin Špegelj to use military force to disarm the "rebellion." Špegelj had been a high officer in the JNA, and as commander of the JNA's Fifth Army had been in charge of all forces in Slovenia, Croatia, and Bosnia from 1985–1989.

---

[25] *Vreme*, September 30, 1991; and see stenographic notes of federal cabinet meeting at which this was discussed, in *Vreme*, September 23, 1991, 5–12.

[26] As one person interviewed by a regional newspaper noted, "Now suddenly, communists, former communists, are the most extreme in declaring their nationality, they are switching from the SKH into the SDS or HDZ," while another said "the bad ones are those individuals who do not want to give up their positions. Such ones go into SDS and HDZ only because of positions, only because of power." P. Opačić, "Zlo je ušlo među ljude i u ljude," *Narodni list*, July 21, 1990, 6. This shift of Serb SKH members into the SDS was apparently supported by the HDZ, who saw it as a way to further weaken the SKH. F.Š., "Milan Babić—Jedna karijera," *Vreme*, December 20, 1993, 16.

[27] This escalation was occurring at the exact time when the electoral campaign was underway in neighboring Bosnia, in which the reformist Ante Marković was presenting a formidable challenge to Milošević's conservative allies in that republic; the events in Croatia were highlighted in the SDSBH's arguments that Serbs were threatened by Croatia and that a vote for Marković would be a vote against protecting Serbs.

Although a member of the SKH, Tudjman appointed him as defense minister. Špegelj's knowledge of the JNA and especially of its weaknesses led him to counsel a preemptive attack to disarm the SDS's paramilitary forces, as well as the JNA in Knin, in order to prevent an all-out military attack on Croatia. He proposed such plans in July 1990, in September, in October, in December, and again in March 1991. Each time, Tudjman refused to approve the plans, noting that the government was pursuing negotiations with Serb leaders; Tudjman seems to have believed that the JNA would not attack Croatia, that he had some kind of assurances. He also said he did not want to provoke the army and provide them with a reason to attack.[28]

While it is difficult to determine Tudjman's exact motivations (belief that the JNA would not attack; or hope that it would, with a resultant shift to massive public backing for full independence), the negotiations, led by HDZ moderates Boljkovac and Degoricija, were seen by the HDZ moderates as the best way to resolve the outstanding issues surrounding the Serb question in Croatia. What comes out is the strong belief that the SDS would settle for cultural autonomy, which the HDZ moderates were apparently prepared to grant.

These negotiations continued throughout the summer and fall of 1990, even as the situation in Knin and then in other nearby areas became more threatening as more paramilitary forces flowed into Knin. The agreements reached between the HDZ moderates and the SDS moderates were substantial. In October, moderate SDS members from Slavonia, Baranja, Kordun, and Istria, in negotiations with Zagreb, received official recognition of the SDS as the legitimate representative of Croatia's Serb population and the promise that the draft Croatian constitution would not include the description of the republic as the "national state of the Croatian people," one of their main grievances. The new Constitution—whose text contained no mention of Croats as the country's constitutive people (although its preamble, which had no legal force, did, it also mentioned other peoples as constitutive)—was judged by the SDS negotiator Vukčević to be a good compromise. The HDZ delegation also promised to quickly resolve all other disputed questions.

At the same time that HDZ moderates were negotiating and pursuing policies of compromise at the national level, at the local level HDZ members were reaching similar agreements with local SDS leaders. Most common were agreements to force SKH deputies out of power in municipal

---

[28] See interviews with Špegelj in *Globus*, June 30, July 7, July 14, July 21, and July 28, 1995.

assemblies, even in places where the SKH received the greatest number
of votes, and then dividing up the positions between SDS and HDZ
supporters and members.

But the policies of moderates on both sides were undermined as the
SDS hard-liners, under directions from Belgrade, pushed for a full break
with Croatia. Thus the SDS hardliners from Knin denounced as traitors
the moderate SDS leaders who had negotiated with the HDZ moderates.[29]
Within local municipalities, the SDS used the familiar strategy of mob rallies to forcibly remove from power SDS members who were seen as moderates, or to remove Serb leaders who remained in the SKH. Prominent
Serbs in Croatia who refused to go along with the SDS hardliners were
threatened and belittled in SDS publications in quite menacing ways that
were clearly meant to silence them and to undermine their authority among
the Serb population.[30] In short, those who refused to go along with the
new harder-line allies of Belgrade, including their calls to distribute weapons
from the local arsenals to the population, were removed and silenced.[31]
At the same time, the SDS was continuing to carry out Milošević's plan
to dismantle Yugoslavia, as it moved to push local communities (*mjesne
zajednice*) that had Serb majorities but were located in Croat-majority municipalities (*općine*) to secede and join Serb-majority općine. In response to
this creeping ethnification of territorial power, Croat majority communities in SDS-controlled regions responded likewise.[32] In October 1990, SDS

[29] Miloš Vasić, "Labudova pesma dr Milana Babića," *Vreme*, February 10, 1992, 13–15.

[30] Some excellent examples of this threatening reportage can be found in the SDS pub-
lication *Zbilja*, which from September 1990 onward published articles, commentaries, and
letters that openly threatened Serbs who were either cooperating with Zagreb, who remained
members of the SKH, or who refused to go along with the SDS hard-liners. In addition
to threats, *Zbilja* also belittled these Serbs in an attempt to undermine their authority. Much
of the text took the form of rhyming couplets reminiscent of traditional Serbian folk epics
and songs. One example: in the December 1, 1990 issue, on page one, in large letters: "Warm
greetings to Dmitri Obradović, president of the Vrginmost municipality assembly:
PLEASE BE KIND ENOUGH TO COMMENT ON THIS PHOTOGRAPH?" (Capitals in original). The accompanying photograph showed the sign for the local self-defense force and municipality
offices on which a large "HDZ" was scrawled. Other notable examples can be seen in
almost all issues, often much more threatening.

[31] One example of this is Milan Đukić, who was head of government in the Donji Lapac
općina. A group of armed SDS deputies in October 1990 demanded that he leave his offices,
and he was quickly relieved of his duties, replaced by hard-line allies of Babić. "Smijen-
jen Milan Đukić," "Što je učinio Đukić," "Ponovo barikade," *Lički vjesnik*, October 15, 1990,
12, 1. In Titovo Korenica, the president of the općina assembly and all other općina level
officials were forced to resign "under the pressure of a group of citizens" who had gathered outside the općina administrative offices. "Ostavka općinskog vrha," *Lički vjesnik*,
October 15 1990, 3.

[32] "Traže izdvajanje," *Lički vjesnik*, October 15, 1990, 1.

hardliner Milan Babić ousted Jovan Rašković as head of the party and continued pushing the party in a confrontational direction.

Over this same period, the HDZ conservatives were similarly working to undermine the moderate policies being pursued by the national HDZ leadership, in many ways feeding into and reinforcing the fears that the SDS was trying to create. The most common strategy of local HDZ conservatives was to enforce policies that were either subtly or blatantly anti-Serb: removing Serbs from jobs, requiring loyalty oaths, sending in new poorly trained Croatian police officers to patrol Serb-majority regions, demanding that Serb police officers wear the šahovnica—an old Croatian symbol that had been used prominently by the Ustaša during World War II but that had been revived by the HDZ—on their caps. These policies were aimed to a large extent against non-political people, Serbs who did not necessarily have any ties to the SDS but were targets merely because they were Serbs, and they lent credence to the SDS right's claims that Serbs in Croatia were threatened by the HDZ. A further effect was to undermine the position of those moderate Serbs who were negotiating with HDZ moderates.

HDZ radicals were also simultaneously provoking violent conflict, further playing into the hands of the hardliners in the SDS, who used these HDZ policies to create fear among the Serb population in the Dalmatia, Lika, Banije, and Kordun regions. Indeed, one indication that the violence of the SDS extremists worked to further the goals of HDZ extremists came when the Croatian police captured Arkan in November 1990 in Dvor. Despite the fact that Arkan and his forces were clearly responsible for some of the worst violence and atrocities in this period, Tudjman decided to release him to Belgrade in June 1991, just as full scale war was about to break out in Croatia.[33]

The HDZ right also pushed the line of collective guilt, continuing their attempt to associate all Serbs in Croatia with Milošević's policies and portraying extremists in the SDS as typical and representative of all Serbs. They claimed that Serbs were over-represented in key sectors of government and thus were oppressors, while Croats were portrayed as innocent victims of a conspiracy stretching back to the previous century, but with its main high points in 1918 and then again in 1945 (the formation of the first and second Yugoslavias, respectively). The parallel with the Serbian nationalist portrayal of Serbia as victim was striking.

[33] Milošević reportedly paid Croatia one million DM for Arkan's release. "Hrvatski je vrh Arkana vratio Miloševiću za milijun marak," interview with Josip Boljkovac (Croatian Minister of Internal Affairs in June 1991), in *Slobodna Dalmacija*, January 17, 2000.

And indeed, just as the SDS hardliners pointed to Serbs' subaltern status in Croatia to justify their political control, so too the HDZ's tightening grip on society was justified by pointing to the Serbs who were said to control Croatia and who threatened to once again subordinate it to Belgrade. The anti-Serb policies of the HDZ right were portrayed as merely a question of justice, returning Croatia to Croats (though only HDZ Croats). The level of collusion between HDZ and SDS hard-liners from fall 1990 through spring 1991 was significant; both had an interest in constructing homogeneous political space; neither group was popular; and both faced pressure for fundamental change. For both, the response was to use fear and violence to change political space.

The crucial background to these events concerned the expectations of the Croatian population with respect to the elections and the introduction of democracy, the anticipation being that these would finally bring about the desired changes the SKH reformists had been pushing for prior to their electoral loss. This was reinforced by the success of Ante Marković's reforms at the federal level and by his popularity, but also by the growing economic crisis, especially in the poorer regions of the republic. For example, in Lika (one of the regions that had been incorporated into the SDS territory) unemployment was skyrocketing, and there was no unemployment insurance or any other governmental program to provide a minimum living standard; but nor was there any program to restructure those firms in the region that were losing money.[34] But as the SDS and HDZ extremists worked to push the country into conflict, issues of reform, as well as the moderates in both parties and in the opposition who were advocating fundamental reform, were pushed into the background and silenced by the growing focus on "ethnic conflict" and the images of threat being purveyed by both groups.

As already noted, even before the SKH decided to hold multiparty elections, Belgrade had been working with local allies to create conflict along ethnic lines as a way to undermine the SKH, repeating the strategies that it had used successfully in Serbia, Vojvodina, and Montenegro. In Croatia, however, the result was quite different than in these other places. SKH conservatives were disempowered and the coming to power of a non-communist party was hastened, a party committed on paper to policies that directly contradicted the Serbian conservatives' preferences.

---

[34] "Stečaj ili krah privrede," *Lički vjesnik*, November 15, 1990, 1.

Violence Imported from Outside

From the fall and winter of 1990–91 onward, extremists on both sides increasingly used violence to construct a climate of fear and to silence moderates who advocated a compromise solution. Thus as Tudjman and the presidents of the other Yugoslav republics were negotiating the future shape of the country, paramilitary groups infiltrating from Serbia into Croatia in cooperation with the JNA, along with HDZ hard-liners, were undertaking violent provocations. These had the effect of constructing a climate of fear in which people would be less able or willing to continue advocating either Croatia within a reformulated Yugoslavia or Serbs remaining within Croatia. The violence was coming not from below and was not an expression of ethnic hatreds. Nor was it a political strategy meant to mobilize the population. It was rather the policy of the small groups of conservatives and extremists on both sides who were seeking to impose their own political preferences on populations who had very different values and preferences.

A key moment on the Serb side came in February 1991. At a meeting of the SDS leadership that month, 38 of 42 members came out against the use of violence and for a policy of moderation, against Milan Babić, who with Belgrade's backing was advocating a hard-line confrontational and militant approach. The following day Babić formed his own party, the SDS Krajina. Rašković at this time stated that "for the first time I warned that this radical group which wanted to take over the SDS is a danger for us and that war will definitely result if they exacerbate things," and described this move as a "coup."[35] Babić was working closely with Belgrade, and as one Serb moderate pointed out, his group behaved "in a way very similar to the behavior of the communist political activists, aparatchiki and organizational secretaries."[36] Indeed, Babić's links to Belgrade became quite clear in March, when he continued to support Milošević despite the massive demonstrations in Belgrade.[37] Shortly after this, armed clashes between Serb paramilitaries and Croatian police broke out in Pakrac, in western Slavonia, and at the Plitvice Lakes national park in Lika. Croatian Serbs

---

[35] Interview in *Globus*, 14 February 1992, 14–15. His comment on the coup was published by Tanjug, June 8, 1991. See also the interview with Vojislav Vukčević, head of the SDS in Baranja and Eastern Slavonia, in which he confirms these events. "Odlazak pregovarača," *NIN*, April 19, 1991, 14.

[36] Interview with Vojislav Vukčević in *NIN*, April 19, 1991, 14.

[37] Srdan Radulović, "Naprsli štit srpstva," *NIN*, May 3, 1991, 15.

were increasingly pressured to toe the SDS hard line, and Croats in the SDS-controlled regions were besieged and pressured to leave.[38]

These moves by hard-liners in the SDS were mirrored in the actions of HDZ hard-liners, who took repressive actions against Serbs in areas where the ruling party controlled the local government; these actions were pointed to by Belgrade's allies as proof of the threat to Serbs. For example, in western Slavonia, hard-line HDZ members from Herzegovina, "formerly petty criminals," were put into the police force and began harassing Serbs, and even local Croats were frightened.[39] Likewise, as a Serb married to a Croat in the Pakrac region noted, "all the Serbs in my firm have been moved to bad positions," and of the thirty leaders in the Pakrac region, all were Herzegovinian Croats, none of them were local Slavonian Croats.[40] As a result, the SDS, which had little support in the region before, began to attract many Serbs.

This violence picked up in February and March 1991, especially in the regions near Knin, and in western Croatia. By May they had spread to Slavonia, in eastern Croatia. Again, the provocations were coming from extremists on both sides, including paramilitaries being sent into Croatia by the Serbian Ministry of the Interior and working with the JNA. The president of the Baranja SDS, Vojislav Vukčević, declared that "Belgrade has been exerting strong pressure on him because he is influencing Serbs in Baranja to act calmly and responsibly and not to cause incidents."[41]

The HDZ right-wingers for their part were doing everything they could to undermine the moderate Croats seeking to dampen down the rising fear. Most notorious was Gojko Šušak, who at the time was deputy minister of defense and very close to Tudjman. In April 1991, Šušak fired several missiles into the majority Serb village of Borovo Selo in Eastern Slavonia, a very mixed region, in an attempt to provoke a violent counter-response. The HDZ right continued to provoke violence, silencing moderates and even killing the moderate police chief of Osijek, Josip Reihl-Kir, who had been instrumental in dampening conflicts and fears on all sides.[42]

[38] The Croat-majority village of Kijevo outside Knin was besieged for eight months. Srđan Španović, "Čudo u Kijevu," *Danas*, March 12, 1991, 18–20.

[39] Zoran Daskalović, "Skupljenje povjerenja," *Danas*, March 12, 1991, 13–14; Milan Bečejić, "Forsiranje straha," *Danas*, March 12, 1991, 16–17.

[40] Milan Bečejić, "Forsiranje straha," *Danas*, 12 March 1991, 16–17.

[41] B. Pavlović, "Strength and Weakness of Reasonable People," *Borba*, April 5, 1991, 7, in FBIS-EE#073/91. Also cites Ilija Šašić, leader of SDS in Slavonia and Baranja who headed a delegation which held talks with Tudjman in March 1991, that "these events really have come to be led by extremists."

[42] See also Zlatko Kramarić, elected mayor of Osijek on the HDZ line, on hard-liners in the HDZ and their provocation of conflict, in *Gradonačelniče, vrijeme je . . .* (Zagreb: Mladinska knjiga, 1993).

What should be emphasized is that the violence that took place in Croatia throughout the winter, spring, and summer of 1991 was not a spontaneous eruption of ethnic hatreds. Indeed, the worst violence did take place in the most ethnically heterogeneous areas. But it was a violence that was imported from outside, that is, it was perpetrated largely by paramilitary groups who went in and slaughtered civilians, forced the rest of the civilians to divide themselves by ethnicity, and forced those on the "wrong" side to leave. The only way to destroy the realities of ethnically heterogeneous communities was through this kind of crude and blatant violence. Apparently, violence and threats were necessary to ethnicize a society that had until then not been divided along those lines.[43]

*   *   *   *   *

By June 1991, Milošević's strategy proved successful, as Slovenia and Croatia, in very large part as a response to the increased violence in Croatia's ethnically mixed regions, declared their intent to separate from Yugoslavia. As the violence increased, especially in the eastern part of Croatia, Tudjman appointed a coalition government of national unity, despite the opposition of the HDZ right. Yet while the right's goal of an independent Croatia was coming to be realized, the fact that Tudjman had ceded governmental authority not only to the moderates within the HDZ but also to the democratically oriented opposition, was seen by the HDZ right as a threat to its most basic goals. The response was an attempt by the HDZ right to oust Tudjman through a coup, which proved unsuccessful.[44]

The right also continued to use violence to achieve its goals. Thus from the summer of 1991 onward paramilitary formations linked to the HDZ right perpetrated atrocities against Serb civilians as part of an overall

[43] For example, hard-liners on both sides used threats and violence to destroy or break apart organizations that before then had not been organized along ethnic lines. One striking example of this, given the history and tradition of the Partisan movement, consisted of the attempts to force divisions along national lines in veterans organizations. The strength of the preexisting social realities can be seen in the response of the Section of the fighters of the Sixth Lika Proletarian division to attempts to divide the veterans association on national lines: the veterans denounced extremists in the SDS as well as HDZ actions that did not respect Serbs in Croatia, but they also harshly criticized Serbia's proclamations of Croats as genocidal. "Pogašena svjetla balkanske krčme," *Lički vjesnik*, November 15, 1990, 12.
[44] Josip Manolić, one of the founders of the HDZ who had been prime minister, describes how the HDZ right attempted through a conspiracy to overthrow Tudjman, because of his conciliatory strategy toward the opposition. Interview with Manolić by Davor Butković, "Nisam za opstanak HDZ-a pod svaku cijenu," *Globus*, September 10, 1993, 5–6.

strategy of "ethnic cleansing" that was hidden from the population and denied;[45] indeed, the argument used by the HDZ right to this day is that because Croatia was in a defensive war it was impossible for Croats to commit war crimes. The most notorious cases included the massacre of 24 Serb civilians in October 1991 in Gospić,[46] and the killing of a Serb family in Zagreb that included, among the dead, a twelve-year-old girl; yet even these crimes were just the tip of the iceberg when it came to the general terror against Serb civilians throughout Croatia, including even those who were not at all political.[47]

The stress in the HDZ right's discourse in this period was on the threats to innocent Croats, the bombing by the JNA and SDS paramilitary groups of Croatian cities and cultural monuments, expulsion of non-Serbs from areas under SDS control, and the massacre of civilians. In short, the HDZ right colluded with SDS hardliners to destroy those facts on the ground that contradicted the newly defined, hard-bordered political communities of "Croats" and "Serbs" that they had constructed in their discourse. The same goes for the SDS terror against moderate Serbs, and its policy of forcing Serbs to leave areas not under SDS control, under threat of death.[48] This violence was the greatest and the atrocities were the worst in exactly those municipalities, towns, and villages that prior to the war had been the most ethnically heterogeneous.

What is most striking about the war in Croatia is the discrepancy between, on the one hand, Western reports, which portrayed the war as a case of ancient hatreds bursting forth and as an expression of historical memories; and, on the other hand, the realities on the ground that revealed violence was clearly being imposed on those communities that had the longest traditions of positive coexistence and intermarriage. For both sides, the destruction of such communities was the key to marginalizing and silencing alternative visions of the future of Croatia and Yugoslavia.

[45] Citations on HDZ violence against Serbs: Human Rights Watch; Serbian Democratic Forum "Izvještaj o pojavama i oblicima kršenja ljudskih i nacionalnih prava srba u Hrvatskoj 1991–1995," Zagreb, June 1995; on SDS violence against non-Serbs, see Human Rights Watch, *War Crimes in Bosnia-Herzegovina.*

[46] Helsinki Watch, *War Crimes in Bosnia-Herzegovina,* 313–315.

[47] Typical is the case reported to me of a professor of Russian literature in Zagreb who was also a Serb. Her apartment was broken into by the Croatian police, who ransacked it and terrorized her, accusing her of being a "Chetnik" because of her cyrillic (Russian) books.

[48] A refugee from Voćin, a Serb-majority village in Western Slavonia, stated that "there were people [Serbs] who did not want to leave but the Četniks threatened them, and they butchered one person in front of his house," while at the same time they were promised wonderful conditions in the SDS controlled areas in Slavonia. Uroš Komlenović, "Voda gaji kukuruz," *Vreme,* May 23, 1994, 16–17.

To accomplish this, both sides used paramilitaries for purposeful and strategically targeted violence, the organized expulsions of populations of entire villages and regions, and the use of civilians as human shields. This violence was thus not the sudden outburst of hatreds, as the media portrayed it, but was the consequence of a very well-planned and organized policy of violence and terror against the civilian population in specifically targeted areas.

Despite the diplomatic intervention of the international community in July 1991, the war continued to escalate, as the JNA and paramilitaries targeted whole villages and cities for destruction. In October 1991, Lord Peter Carrington reached a compromise settlement for all of the republics of the former Yugoslavia, which was accepted by all except Serbia; Milošević pressured Montenegrin president Bulatović (who had been installed by Milošević in 1988) to withdraw his approval, which torpedoed the plan. But Croatian military forces put up a much harder fight than the JNA had anticipated, and by November and December they actually began retaking territories from the JNA and SDS forces. At that time, and under the threat of an internationalization of the conflict, Milošević finally relented and agreed to accept UN forces in the SDS-controlled parts of Croatia, so-called "Krajina."

By January 1992, the war in Croatia wound down, as the agreement to have United Nations troops patrol SDS-held territories in Krajina was implemented. Yet despite the presence of the UN on these territories, terror by SDS hardliners against moderate Serbs continued, as they were threatened, harassed, and even killed for speaking out against the hardliners. They also continued to expel non-Serbs from Krajina territory as the UN stood by. In short, over the next two-and-a-half years of the existence of Krajina, the SDS right continued to pursue a policy of violence and threats as a means to impose its authoritarian line in the territories under its control. Likewise in HDZ controlled territory, opposition journalists and politicians would bear the brunt of HDZ right-wing accusations against them as traitors, while Serbs, especially in rural areas of the country, faced continued violence and harassment.

1992–2000: The HDZ Right's Strategies of Conflict

Although the HDZ right—with the help of Belgrade's allies in the SDS—had managed to ethnically homogenize political space in Croatia, it was still faced with a population that had values and preferences that were

virtually unchanged from before the war and that were inimical to the
HDZ right's interests. The puzzle in this period is how, despite this unfa-
vorable situation, the HDZ right managed to hold onto power for
eight years and even to increase its grip on the party and its influence
over state policy. It is in the context of this puzzle that the HDZ-engi-
neered conflict in Bosnia and the violent retaking of Krajina must be
understood. Indeed, in this period the greatest challenge for the HDZ
right was to overcome those elites within the HDZ as well as outside of
it who were appealing to the wider population and calling for fundamental political and economic liberalization. Consistently over these
eight years, the HDZ right and its policies were unpopular. Just as
consistently the HDZ right resorted to a strategy of ethnic conflict,
provoking violent conflict in Bosnia and using violence to retake Serb-
held territories in Croatia as a way to demobilize and silence challenger
elites. This violence also served to help the HDZ consolidate its control over the structures of power within Croatia: over the HDZ itself,
which had previously had a large moderate wing; over formal political institutions, especially the Sabor, but also such key ministries as
defense and the police; and over the economy. In short, the HDZ right
used these eight years to hold off the opposition, including within the
HDZ, and to shift its power base from the old party-state system over
to private bases through insider privatization and the massive plunder-
ing of previously profitable firms.

The State of Croatian Society

By 1992 one-fourth of Croatia's territory was beyond the control of Zagreb,
and the majority of Croatia's Serb population were refugees in "Krajina" or in Serbia. Most of Croatia's major provincial capitals had been
bombed, villages and churches had been destroyed, Croats from Krajina
had been expelled from their homes and were refugees living in camps,
workers' barracks, and even disused railroad cars. These refugee camps
were politically organized and patrolled by HDZ right operatives. Indeed,
the HDZ right continued to pursue its goals of anti-democratic authoritarianism, and continued to purvey images of "others" as the enemy of
Croats and of the Croatian state, focusing on Serbs and Bosnian Muslims,
but including in that category, as well, opposition politicians, independent media, the international community, and even HDZ moderates. Serbs,
in particular, were singled out, however, and portrayed in the HDZ-right

controlled state media as collectively guilty for the war and the destruction that Belgrade and the SDS right had wreaked on the country.[49]

Yet despite months of conflict, enemy images, violence, and even
full-scale war, the sentiments of the Croat population were remarkably
unchanged on most issues. For example, despite a year of war and anti-
Serb propaganda, social science polling before the August 1992 elections
revealed that Croats had very strong democratic values and political
orientations, the antithesis of the HDZ right's authoritarian and anti-liberal sentiments.[50] When asked to identify the three most important problems of Croatian politics, the vast majority of respondents listed as
their top concerns issues of social justice and the poor economic situation; the least concern was expressed about those issues and themes that
were stressed by the HDZ right.[51] The public also had views of the Ustaša
regime of World War II that contrasted sharply with the generally positive views held by the HDZ right.[52]

Although there was a shift in attitudes toward Serbs, away from the very
positive evaluations that existed before the war to more negative ones in
questions dealing with personal interactions,[53] this shift was not simple

[49] Typical of this strategy were harsh denunciations of those who denied the concept
of collective guilt. See also columns in Vjesnik by Maja Freundlich in which she expressed
venomous anti-Serb sentiments as well as harsh denunciations of journalists critical of the
HDZ and its right wing. Freundlich went on to become a high official of the HDZ.

[50] For example, 96.6 percent agreed that everyone has the right to express his or her
opinion even if the majority thinks differently; 90.0 percent that true democracy is unthinkable without a strong opposition; 77.4 percent that every political party should have the
chance to come to power. HIP, Izbori 1992.

[51] Respondents' top concerns were social justice and security (50.3 percent); reducing
unemployment (39.7 percent); price stability (34 percent); ensuring individual rights and
freedoms (31.3 percent); and harmonious life of Croats and minority communities (28.5 percent). The choices "to build a stronger defense," "preserving national unity," and "spiri-
tual renewal"—all major themes of the HDZ right—received, respectively only 11 percent,
17 percent, and 8.8 percent. Polling undertaken by the Faculty of Political Science, University of Zagreb, available on website HIP, at <http://www.media.fpzg.hr/hip/stavovi.htm>.

[52] While the HDZ right saw direct continuity between the Ustaša Independent State of
Croatia (NDH) and the new Republic of Croatia (RH), and greatly admired the Ustaša, the
large majority of Croats rejected these positive evaluations. Examples from Globus polling,
April 14, 1995, 13: Do you consider RH to be successor to NDH? 70.1 percent no, 14.5 percent yes. Should April 10 be a state holiday? 65.4 percent no, 17.2 percent yes. What's
your opinion of NDH? 43.0 percent: expression of historical striving of Croatian people, but
under a criminal and quisling regime; 23.3 percent: NDH was a quisling and criminal state;
29.5 percent: NDH was expression of historical striving of Croatian people.

[53] Reflecting what may have been a partial success of the anti-Serb propaganda in
which the HDZ right blamed Croatian Serbs for the violence and atrocities carried out
by SDS paramilitaries, the JNA, and other allies of Belgrade against Croats and other non-
Serbs during the war, 53.4 percent of respondents said they did not want Serbs to live in

or straightforward. Indeed, when asked "what status should Serbs who are now refugees in Serbia have in Croatia," fully one-third (32.5 percent) advocated that Serbs be granted cultural autonomy in all of Croatia (as opposed to defining it in territorial terms), while 50.1 percent said that Serbs should have no special status but should enjoy the same rights as Croats. Only 14.3 percent advocated permanent emigration of Serbs to Serbia.[54]

Newspaper polling also showed the limits to the popularity of the HDZ overall. In the first half of 1992, Franjo Tudjman was receiving the support of between 33 and 36 percent of respondents, and the HDZ's support in this period ranged between 32 percent and 38 percent, which, while more than any other party, hardly represented overwhelming support. Just as in the earlier period, the HDZ benefited not from overwhelming popularity but from the fragmentation of the democratic political opposition and the electorate.

The first post-war elections, held in August 1992 for the lower house of the Sabor, the House of Representatives, confirmed this weakness. In the election campaign itself, the HDZ portrayed itself as bearing the sole responsibility for independence and for winning the war, and its messages "suggest[ed] the absolute domination of the ruling party on the political scene."[55] Yet despite this discourse which equated the HDZ with Croatia, and despite the fact that Croatia had indeed achieved its full independence with the HDZ in power, the HDZ received only about 37 percent of the vote (37.3 percent of the vote in the party list vote, and 36.9 percent of the vote in the single member constituencies). This represented about 28 percent of eligible voters, and not more than 29 percent of the vote of Croat eligible voters; in other words, fully 70 percent of the eligible voting population was not mobilized to support the HDZ even by giving it their votes. Elections for the upper house of the Sabor, the House of Counties, held six months later in February 1993, reinforced this conclusion. Here, although the HDZ received 42.6 percent of the vote, because of a significantly lower turnout rate (64 percent as opposed to about 78 percent in the August 1992 elections), this represented only 27.4 percent of eligible

---

their state; about 62 percent did not want Serbs as neighbors, co-workers, or friends; 79.3 percent did not want Serbs as relatives. It should be remembered that in this period there was a blanket demonization of all Serbs as collectively guilty for the war, the civilian victims, and the policies of Milošević, and the SDS right.

[54] Faculty of Political Science, "Rezultati longitudinalnog istraživanja političkih stavova birača 1990–1995." Part of website "Hrvatski Izborni Podaci," online at <http://media. fpzg.hr/hip/stavovi.htm> (accessed March 27, 2004).

[55] Lalić, "Pohod," 251–252.

voters, fewer votes than it received in August. This weakness was further confirmed in newspaper polling following the election, when the HDZ's support dropped to about 25–30 percent of those respondents who declared a choice, representing only about 12 percent of all respondents. By May 1993, the HDZ was placing second in popularity, behind the opposition Croatian Social and Liberal Party (HSLS).

While the popularity of the HDZ was not overwhelming, the HDZ right was even less popular, as newspaper polling showed it receiving a positive evaluation of only about 14.5 percent, as opposed to the HDZ moderates, who received about 44.8 percent.[56] In addition, in polling in this period, the HDZ conservatives consistently came out as the least popular political figures in the country.[57] The conflict between moderates and conservatives in the HDZ, which began to come out into the open in the fall of 1991, thus represented a real threat to the HDZ right, especially since the HDZ moderates vocally advocated policies that were antithetical to the HDZ right and were very critical of HDZ right policies.

The values and interests of the HDZ right were thus consistently threatened throughout this period, both from within the HDZ as well as from outside, a situation that culminated in the HDZ's loss of power in both parliamentary and presidential elections, in the first months of 2000, to parties and candidates promising not only to take on issues of the economy and of corruption, but to foster reconciliation with the Serb population.

The HDZ Right's Strategy of Conflict

In the face of this situation, the HDZ right and its sponsor, Franjo Tudjman, followed a multi-pronged strategy that included placing HDZ moderates up front, moderating policy lines in the period leading up to elections, changing electoral rules to favor the ruling party and to disadvantage the opposition, undermining the positions of the HDZ

[56] Respondents were asked: "If the HDZ fractions ran in an election, which would you vote for?" The "liberal" or moderate fraction received the support of 44.8 percent of respondents; the "conservatives" received 14.5 percent; and 18 percent of respondents answered "neither." Mirjana Kasapović, *Globus*, April 9, 1993, 3.

[57] For example, in the *Globus* poll of November 1993, the highest negative ratings were given to top HDZ rightists Šušak, Šeks, Đapić: when asked whether certain politicians deserved trust, they received about 34 percent negative; in the *Globus* poll of August 1994, when asked which political figures were most respected, HDZ rightists again came out on the bottom: Vukojević with -45.4 percent; Pašalić -40.8 percent; Šušak -43.2 percent, Šeks -41.8 percent. August 19, 1994, 10.

moderates, and taking control of the security apparatuses and the state-owned media. But perhaps the most important and certainly the most costly part of their strategy involved provoking war in parts of Bosnia-Herzegovina that were inhabited by Croats. This policy of warfare, and the related one of constructing enemy images, in concert with the above-mentioned strategies, effectively demobilized, silenced, and marginalized a large part of the population, allowing the HDZ right to dominate policy in a way that was not reflective of the values or interests of the wider population.

Such policies of violence worked to demobilize the population by shifting the focus of political discourse onto images of threats to Croats and away from issues around which challenger elites were appealing to the wider population, and which threatened the HDZ right's power—economic and political liberalization. By shifting political discourse in this direction, the violence and images of threat also justified the HDZ right's continuation of authoritarian policies in the face of quite different popular preferences. The effect was the construction of homogeneous political space, that is, the construction of a political discourse in which the only legitimately "Croat" position was the one taken by the HDZ right. Yet because of the strength of moderates in the HDZ itself, such homogeneity was not achieved until 1994, in large part due to the HDZ-right sponsored war in Bosnia.

Indeed, from 1992 onward the HDZ continued to present a moderate face. Publicly throughout the period under consideration, President Franjo Tudjman supported moderate members of the ruling party, as well as, at times, moderate policies advocated by these members. For example, all of the prime ministers appointed by Tudjman came from the moderate wing of the party; all were democratically and liberally oriented, calling for freedom of the press and political and economic liberalization.[58] They did not speak of Serbs as the collective enemy, and tended to favor a negotiated settlement to the Krajina question. Indeed, by late 1993 some political analysts were interpreting the outcome of the Second HDZ Congress as a victory for the moderates, who until spring 1994 were a force to be reckoned with in the HDZ leadership.[59]

---

[58] His first prime ministers were among the top HDZ moderates: Stipe Mesić and Josip Manolić; succeeding prime ministers likewise were from the moderate or democratically inclined "technomanagerial" wing of the party: Franjo Gregurić, Hrvoje Šarinić, Nikica Valentić.

[59] For example see Davor Butković, "Poražena desnica HDZ-a zapravo je zadržala vlast," *Globus*, February 18, 1994, 11–13.

In private, however, Tudjman supported the HDZ right and gave them enormous influence over policy. For example, the state-owned media, including television, were under the direct control of the HDZ right, and although over the course of 1993 Tudjman took steps to mollify the moderates, in the end he did nothing to prevent them from leaving the party.[60] Following that departure, the HDZ right became openly and fully dominant within the party, which explains in large part their loss in the 2000 elections.

Another factor in the HDZ's ability to retain power was its manipulation of electoral law. Before every election the HDZ rewrote those rules in a way that would maximize its number of deputies in parliament. Thus in August 1992, the HDZ was able to convert the 37 percent of the vote that it received into 72 percent of the seats in the lower house of parliament,[61] while in February 1993, with 42.6 percent of the vote it received 58.7 percent of the seats in the upper house of parliament.[62] This was a strategy that the HDZ followed before every election—1995, 1997, 2000— right up until the end of its rule. The most blatant manipulation came in 1994, when the HDZ-dominated Sabor granted to the "Croatian diaspora" 14 seats (out of 164 total) in the House of Representatives, a number of seats equal to each of the ten electoral districts in Croatia itself. Since these seats effectively were controlled by the HDZ of Bosnia (the vast majority of voters for these seats were in Bosnia), this provision gave the HDZ the security of an extra 14 seats. Since the number of voters in the diaspora was significantly less than the number of voters in each of the other 10 electoral districts, these diaspora voters were also relatively over-represented in the Croatian parliament. This kind of electoral engineering was a clear admission by the HDZ that its support among the wider

[60] The degree to which Tudjman's naming of moderate prime ministers was merely a political tactic could be seen in the comments of prime minister Hrvoje Šarinić, who in March 1993 resigned with the comment that his government "did not get the support from the HDZ that we expected to get." Interview by Davor Butković, in *Globus*, March 19, 1993, 3–4.

[61] The 124 seats in the House of Representatives in 1992 were divided into 60 seats to be determined by party lists, with the entire country representing one district and with a required minimum of 3 percent to gain representation; and 64 seats to be determined in single-member constituency districts, with the candidate receiving a plurality of the vote winning the seat. For the law, see *Narodne novine* 22 (1992) and 1 (1993). In the party list part of the 1992 election, the HDZ received 37.33 percent of the vote, which translated into 51.7 percent of those seats; in the single member districts, HDZ received 36.89 percent of the vote, which translated into 90 percent of those seats, for an overall total of 72 percent of the 164 seats in the House of Representatives. Before the next election the electoral system was changed yet again, with Croatia being divided into 10 electoral districts.

[62] Each county elected three representatives, and the city of Zagreb also elected three representatives.

population was limited in a way that put into question its ability to win elections fairly.

Once it was ensured of a majority in parliament, the HDZ right following the 1992 and 1993 elections was no longer constrained by the need to openly pander to moderate public opinion in the country; in fact, they actively worked to prevent political discussion of major issues. Indeed, in the two years of this parliament,

> more than 70 percent of legal drafts were accepted through emergency procedures . . . [due to the] desire to avoid debates about proposed laws in public, parliamentary working bodies and the sessions of both Houses of Parliament. Such longer procedures would enable the opposition to voice their objections and to engage in political activism and public exposure.[63]

This was possible because HDZ members of parliament were "a reliable voting machine for the government's proposals," showing "remarkable obedience to the party leadership."[64] Such tactics were necessary precisely because of the depth of unpopularity of the HDZ.

War in Bosnia-Herzegovina:
The HDZ Right's Strategy of Violence, Act II

Following the February 1993 elections, the HDZ right proceeded to foment full-scale war in neighboring Bosnia-Herzegovina. This war was not meant to increase the HDZ's support; nor was it meant to mobilize the population behind the HDZ; indeed, the official media lied about the nature of the war and denied reports about its true origins. In addition, the war was not a popular one, and the HDZ right's goal of joining "Herceg Bosna" with Croatia was opposed by a large majority. The HDZ's polling numbers plummeted during the course of the war, and the level of popular dissatisfaction remained incredibly high, due largely to economic problems. The war thus did not serve to mobilize people, nor did it change the main concerns of the population. Its main effect was the way in which it silenced and marginalized forces that had attempted to focus on these concerns.

The war was rather part of the HDZ right's response to the threats it was facing, as described above. Tudjman himself had long been an advocate of dividing Bosnia-Herzegovina. In March 1991, he had met with

---

[63] Grdešić, "Building the State: Actors and Agendas," 122–123.
[64] Ibid.

Milošević and is reported to have reached such an agreement with the Serbian leader. Much of the HDZ right strongly supported such a division because many of the hardest hard-liners came from western Herzegovina. Their goal was to incorporate that region, and other areas of Bosnia that they or the international community had designated as "Croat," into Croatia itself. The effect would have been to reinforce the construction of political space that had been underway since the summer of 1990: it would reinforce the image of political space as a specifically "Croat" space; it would serve to reinforce the image of "Croat groupness" as hard and clearly bounded, with "others," Serbs and Muslims as the enemy; and it would reinforce demographically the "Croat" nature of Croatia. It would also strengthen the HDZ right's hold on power within Croatia itself. Since Croats made up only about 18 percent of Bosnia-Herzegovina's population, and since the HDZ right was unpopular among the large majority of Bosnian Croats, the HDZ right's power would be very limited in a Bosnian state. Within Croatia, however, given their enormous influence within the ruling party, annexation of their home regions would only solidify their power. It would also bolster the support for the HDZ itself in elections and help ensure it a majority of seats despite its unpopularity within Croatia.

The Croat population of Bosnia-Herzegovina was widely spread throughout central and northern Bosnia. The only region where it was in a large majority was in parts of western Herzegovina, where Croats made up over 85 percent of the population, although they represented only one-third of Bosnia's Croat population. The other two-thirds of Bosnia's Croats lived in ethnically heterogeneous regions in Central and Northern Bosnia, and had a much different socially lived experience of interaction and coexistence than did the Herzegovinian Croats. Politically too the Bosnian Croats were moderate; the original leadership of the HDZ-BH reflected this moderation.

Over the course of 1991 and 1992, Tudjman, working with his HDZ right allies, had engineered a series of coups against the moderates who dominated the Croatian nationalist party in Bosnia-Herzegovina (the HDZ-BH), replacing them with hard-liners who, starting in late 1992, began provoking violent conflict in ethnically mixed Croat-Muslim regions. This strategy was undertaken in secret; even HDZ moderates were not aware of Tudjman's role in setting up and perpetrating the conflict, and they were vocally opposed to the war, which was carried out under the direct orders of Tudjman and implemented by his close advisor and Croatian Defense Minister, Gojko Šušak.

While Zagreb had been instrumental in the setting up of a Bosnian branch of the HDZ in 1990, Tudjman actively began to replace the moderate HDZ-BH leaders with hardliners from Herzegovina in the second half of 1991; in November of that year, the moderate Stjepan Kljuić was replaced by hard-liner and former local level SKBH official Mate Boban. Over the course of 1992, this enforced takeover of the HDZ-BH by Herzegovinian extremists continued, engineered from Zagreb.[65] During the summer of 1992 the HVO, the armed forces of the HDZ-BH, which were under the control of the HDZ right, also proceeded to use force to take over the political structures in areas where the HDZ had control of local governments, exacerbating relations with the Muslim population in the process.[66] In the second half of that year, after the elections in Croatia, the HVO began to provoke violent conflict, attacking Muslim villages and civilians. The HVO also in June 1992 assassinated Blaž Kraljević, the head of the HOS, a Croatian nationalist paramilitary group that included a large number of Muslims in its fight against the SDS and JNA in the Bosnian war; Kraljević had been one of the most outspoken proponents of a Croat-Muslim alliance, and stood in the way of the HDZ right's plans for a Croat-Muslim war.

In all of this, the HDZ right was especially forceful in using violence to impose its policies in areas that were ethnically mixed, in northern and central Bosnia, and went to great lengths, including covert but active cooperation with the Bosnian Serb party, the SDS, to achieve its goals. Tudjman went so far as to order local Croat forces to pull out of the Bosnian Posavina region and allow it to fall to SDS forces—thus sacrificing an area which had a large number of Croat and Muslim residents—in order to provide the SDS with a bridge or corridor between the lands they held in eastern and western Bosnia.[67] This fighting, which it must be remembered was taking place at the same time that forces operating under orders from Belgrade were ethnically cleansing "Serb

[65] Stjepan Kljuić, in interview by Željko Garmaz, "Rat hrvata i muslimana u BiH odavna su smislili neki moćnici u Hrvatskoj," *Globus*, October 29, 1993, 3–4.

[66] See the article by Anto Pejćinović, head of HDZ in Vareš, on HVO takeover and violence against Muslims in that municipality. "Hrvati srednje Bosne izdani su u Zagrebu," *Hrvatski i Bošnjački Tjednik* 10 (November 10, 1994): 10–11.

[67] As Manolić points out, there were no military reasons for Croatian forces to pull out of Posavina; this pullout he identifies as "one of the most important elements that shows the existence of an agreement of Tudjman and Milošević on the division of Bosnia-Herzegovina." He further pointed out that no one other than Tudjman could have ordered such a pullout. The pullout created a "corridor" for SDS forces between eastern and western Bosnia. Interview with Josip Manolić by Davor Butković, "Predsjednik Tudman naredio je da se hrvatska vojska povuče iz Posavine i da se taj koridor prepusti srbima," *Globus*, April 23, 1994, 7–10.

lands" in Bosnia, was portrayed in the HDZ-controlled press in Croatia itself as a defensive war, in which Croats were being victimized by Muslim extremists, Islamic fundamentalists.

This strategy of conflict in Bosnia was very controversial, and produced a very sharp rift within the HDZ itself. Indeed, in March 1993 the moderates threatened to leave the party, in large part over policy toward Bosnia. In response, Tudjman placated them by once again naming a moderate; Nikica Valentić, as prime minister. Valentić promised all the policies the moderates had been calling for, freedom of the press, liberalization both political and economic, etc.[68] Yet the policy of violence continued. Indeed, violent provocations picked up after this March 1993 meeting, culminating in the Easter Sunday attacks and massacres of Muslim civilians in the Lašva valley in central Bosnia, and then all-out war by the HVO against Muslim civilians, including massacres, expulsions, destruction of Muslims' homes, mosques, and other cultural objects identified with the Ottoman period. The goal was to create ethnically homogeneous territories in places that had previously been very heterogeneous, places with the highest levels of tolerance and positive coexistence.[69] This policy of massacres and expulsion of Muslim civilians, which continued until early 1994, was directed from Zagreb by Tudjman himself under the control of Defense Minister Šušak.[70] Indeed, Šušak arrived in the Lašva valley two days before the massacres began, demanding that the Croatian flag be hoisted in multi-ethnic Travnik. This violence was not coming from below, but rather was being imposed on these communities from outside, by forces directed from Zagreb, extremists in the HDZ and the HDZ-BH.

As mentioned above, one of the main effects of this war was intended within Croatia, where the HDZ right's policy of war was meant to bolster the right's own insecure position by demobilizing, silencing, and marginalizing the large degree of dissatisfaction and opposition to their rule by re-engineering the demographics of the territories they claimed in Bosnia, then incorporating those territories into Croatia, thereby giving them a sure bank of votes in future elections. These votes would be secure for the

[68] *Globus*, March 1993.

[69] For details, see reports given as evidence at the Hague Tribunal trials against Blaškić and others. For an on-the-ground view of how this happened in one village, see the documentary by anthropologist Tone Bringa, "We Are All neighbours," in which she and her film crew are present in a mixed Croat-Muslim village as the HVO is tightening its grip on the region; by the end of the film the majority Muslim population has been expelled and terrorized, while the Catholics have been silenced through fear.

[70] See documents cited in Jasna Babić, "Kaos u Šuškovoj Herceg bosni—Povjerljivi dokumenti o ustroju HVO-a," *Nacional* 181 (May 5, 1999).

HDZ right not because they were popular among Bosnia's Croats, but because in Bosnia the HDZ-BH, under HDZ right control, was in firm control of structures of power and could "deliver" votes regardless of the values and opinions of the population, through a reign of terror, intimidation, and silencing of Croats.[71]

Indeed, by October 1993 the HDZ had been trailing the opposition Croatian Social Liberal party (HSLS) in newspaper polling for about six months, with its support dropping to 26 percent of those who expressed a preference (a mere 12 percent of all respondents). This drop was almost wholly due to the bad economic situation and issues of corruption within the HDZ.[72] In May and June 1993, Dražen Budiša, the head of the HSLS party which was leading HDZ in the polls, had come out very critically against the HDZ's Bosnia policy, and squarely placed the blame for the conflict on the Croat forces. HDZ moderates were also publicly criticizing the right's policies in Bosnia.[73] Meanwhile, the peoples' expressed levels of dissatisfaction were skyrocketing.[74]

The war in Bosnia, though the target of criticism, also did have the effect of demobilizing people. Newspaper polling showed that especially in the first months of the war, when HDZ right controlled media portrayed it as purely defensive, people were supportive. Although the war was never at the top of the lists of peoples' political priorities, the discourse of innocent Bosnian Croats suffering at the hands of Islamic terrorists brought sympathy for the HVO's role in the conflict.[75] Yet there was very little support for incorporating Herceg Bosna into Croatia.[76] The effect of the HDZ's demobilization strategy was striking. In newspaper polling, over 50 percent of respondents were choosing not to respond (none of the above, don't know, don't plan to vote). As one independent political commentator noted, this level of non-response to opinion polling

[71] For example, in elections to the Croatian Sabor, the "diaspora" vote, 90 percent of which was from Herceg Bosna, 85 percent of that went to the HDZ, an extraordinarily high proportion that indicates minimal political competition.

[72] *Globus*, May 14, 1993, 44.

[73] See for example Josip Manolić's comments in interview by Davor Butković and Dubravko Grakalić, in *Globus*, June 18, 1993, 5–6.

[74] By January 1994, 54.5 percent of respondents said they were dissatisfied, and 38.9 percent said they were very dissatisfied, for a total of 93.4 dissatisfied. *Globus*, January 28, 1994, 2.

[75] For example in April 1993 polling, 56 percent of respondents supported the policies of HDZ-BH head Mate Boban and 56 percent did not believe that the HVO had perpetrated atrocities against the civilian population.

[76] A great majority of the respondents, 78.1 percent, preferred the two countries' relationship to be one of relations between independent countries. Only 14.9 percent favored joining in a confederation, and only 7.0 percent favored Bosnia joining Croatia.

shows a fear of politics, a great disappointment with politics and a certain psychological return to the communist times. Most people now say that the state should be led by experts, not by political parties. In the last few years of Yugoslavia, a state led by experts was the favored phrase of the liberal communist politicians.[77]

In addition to the war, however, Tudjman and the HDZ right continued their strategy of putting moderates up front. Not only had he named the moderate Valentić as prime minister, but he seemed to be appealing to the desire for a peaceful negotiated settlement on Krajina, as well, by pursuing the moderates' preferred policy on that issue. While the issue of Krajina was not high on peoples' lists of priorities—only 16 percent of respondents listed "unchanged situation in the occupied territories" as being one of their top three priorities[78]—the majority did support the policy of negotiations with the Krajina authorities.[79] When in January 1994 an agreement was reached, 60.4 percent of respondents polled in Croatia's major cities supported it, while only 24.0 percent opposed it.[80]

The HDZ's Second Congress, held October 15–16, 1993 saw an open clash between the power of the HDZ right and Tudjman's realization of the need to pursue a more moderate public policy. In party elections leading up to the Congress, the HDZ right was victorious, an outcome described by HDZ moderate Josip Manolić as "a real catastrophe" for the HDZ.[81] At the Congress itself, however, Tudjman managed to overrule the right, removing HDZ rightists from top offices in the party and imposing a moderate line as official policy. The degree to which he saw this policy as absolutely necessary for the HDZ's survival could be seen in the fact that he admonished the HDZ right that any refusal to support the official party line was the equivalent of an attack on Croatia itself.[82]

At the same time, however, the HDZ right was working behind the scenes to consolidate power within the party. While the right had been

[77] Davor Butković, "Predsjednik Tuđman opet bi bio izabran, a Budiša pada," *Globus*, November 19, 1993, 13–15.

[78] *Globus*, May 14, 1993, 44.

[79] For an interview with the Croatian government negotiator, HDZ moderate Slavko Degoricija, see *Globus*, May 21, 1993, 9–10; for polling, see ibid., 10.

[80] *Globus*, January 28, 1994, 4.

[81] Interview with Manolić by Davor Butković, "Nisam za opstanak HDZ-a pod svaku cijenu," *Globus*, September 10, 1993, 5–6.

[82] This way of ensuring discipline, by labeling critics of the official line as "political enemies," is strikingly reminiscent of how within the communist parties of eastern Europe dissident factions were forced to accept the official line. For a report on Tudjman's speech which gives a somewhat different analysis, see Mirjana Kasapović, "Drugi opći sabor HDZ-a: Dva sata anatomija doktora Tuđmana," *Globus*, October 22, 1993, 52–53.

excluded from top positions at the Second Congress, its members pursued a strategy that focused on taking control of local-level HDZ organizations and of the security apparatuses in the Ministry of Interior, the police, and the military.[83] The HDZ conservatives also attempted to discredit the moderates in the HDZ leadership by alleging corruption; and they sought to shut down independent media by bringing court cases against journalists and newspapers, charging them with libel for criticizing the policies and corruption of HDZ right.

The conflict in Bosnia officially came to an end in February 1994 when, under firm pressure from the United States, Tudjman signed the Washington Agreement that set up the Federation. But the sincerity of the agreement was seriously put in doubt because the people who were responsible for carrying out the policy of war were the same ones who were supposed to implement the federation agreement; the moderate Bosnian Croats were excluded because they were not part of the HDZ-BH power structure that the international community was dealing with.

Shortly afterward, in April 1994 came the final split of the HDZ, when moderates who had been founding members of the party and very close to Tudjman, including Josip Manolić and Stipe Mesić, left and formed their own party, the Croatian Independent Democrats (HND). The HND's goals were pointedly stated in terms that were opposed to the HDZ right:

> to struggle against all manifestations of totalitarianism in society as a whole, especially in state management, but also in its own ranks; . . . the struggle for full civil rights and freedom of each citizen of RH, regardless of national, religious, racial or political affiliation.

Once the moderates had left, the HDZ right's influence grew. They worked to purge the party of sympathizers of Manolić and Mesić.[84] And they continued to perpetrate violence against Serbs and others who disagreed with them.[85] The campaign of demonizing Serbs and other "enemies" of Croats and Croatia was stepped up in the state-owned media, as

---

[83] Davor Butković, "Poražena desnica HDZ-a zapravo je zadržala vlast," *Globus*, February 18, 1994, 11–13.

[84] See the experiences of the head of Orahovic općina, in Matija Biskupović, "Kad zafijuče HDZ-ov bič," *Bumerang*, February 23, 1995, 9.

[85] Human Rights Watch noted that "the most abusive elements of the Croatian government are the institutions responsible to the Ministry of Defense," under the control of Defense Minister Gojko Šušak." It pointed out also that "members of the more conservative wing [of the HDZ] defend the ministry and continue to be apologists for violence and crimes committed or tolerated by the government forces." Human Rights Watch, *Civil and Political Rights in Croatia* (New York, October 1995), 101.

well as in media that was owned by HDZ allies and supporters. So while Tudjman continued to keep moderates "up front" as prime ministers, the reality was that there was no longer a significant moderate faction in the HDZ. Ironically, this very victory of the HDZ right endangered the party's continuation in power. Over the next year, the HDZ's popularity continued to decrease, and Tudjman and other top HDZ rightists became more and more vocal about internal enemies who threatened the HDZ and thus Croatia itself.

The Retaking of Krajina: The HDZ Right's Strategy of Violence

The position of the HDZ right was bolstered when the United States moved in 1994 to support Croatia as a regional counterweight to Serbia in order to end what it perceived to be a military stalemate in Bosnia. The U.S. policy was in effect an unofficial military alliance with Tudjman's regime, and included sending the military company MPRI, run by retired U.S. generals, to train the Croatian army. This western alliance reinforced the hold of the HDZ right, who had consistently been very much in favor of a military solution and opposed to HDZ moderates' preference for a negotiated settlement. The HDZ right was also helped by the fact that SDS hard-liners in Krajina itself consistently undermined those Krajina Serbs who were working on a negotiated settlement, for example, denouncing and jailing those moderates who had signed the January 1994 agreement.

In the period leading up to the Croatian Army attack on Western Slavonia in early May 1995, the HDZ was facing serious challenges. In newspaper polling, opposition leader Budiša was by far outpolling any potential HDZ rivals for the post of presidency other than Tudjman himself;[86] and even against Tudjman he was running almost even.[87] The HDZ itself was facing the possible challenge of a coalition of parties that together would easily receive more support than the HDZ,[88] something that Tudjman

---

[86] Budisa, 33.1 percent; next nearest rival, Valentić had only 10.9 percent. *Globus*, March 24, 1995, 8.

[87] Asked whom they would support in the second round of voting, 35.5 percent of respondents said Tudjman, 30.3 percent Budisa. *Globus*, March 10, 1995, 10.

[88] In newspaper polling in March and April, HDZ was receiving support of about 32 percent, while HSLS about 27 percent, with the numbers moving away from HDZ. At this level, a coalition of the HSLS with either the SDP, the HND, or the HSS, or a coalition that would bring all of them together, would have presented a serious challenge to the HDZ. Polling in *Globus*, March 10, 1995, 10; April 21, 1995, 58. On the possible coalition, see Davor Butković in *Globus*, April 21, 1995, 4–5, 58.

harshly denounced as an attempt to destabilize the HDZ and thus also Croatia.[89] Levels of dissatisfaction were very high,[90] again because of the difficult economic situation and corruption; only about 10 percent of respondents gave the reason for their dissatisfaction as the Serb occupation of Croatian territory.[91] Tudjman himself was reportedly quite worried that the HDZ had shifted too far to the right, and there were indications in April 1995 that he was attempting to bring the party back to the center.[92] At the same time, he was warning about the dangers that Croatia faced, including attempts by the international community to push it back into some kind of Yugoslavia.[93]

Social science polling by the Department of Sociology of the University of Zagreb, as well as a separate poll conducted by the Faculty of Political Science at Zagreb, confirmed the consistency of democratic values in Croatia, as well as the overwhelming priority people put on economic growth rather than military strength.[94] This polling also showed that people were very skeptical about the HDZ's claims that Croatia was "the

[89] In his speech to the HDZ Central Committee, Tudjman denounced the proposed coalition of opposition parties (something that the United States and west Europeans had suggested to the opposition parties), warning about attempts to destabilize Croatia coming from outsiders who were working with internal forces: "In order to destabilize ... it is necessary first of all to destabilize the HDZ as the majority party in the Sabor." "Izvadci iz govora dr. Franje Tudmana, predsjednika Republike Hrvatske i HDZ-a," *Glasnik HDZ*, 184 (12 May 1995): 8–10.

[90] The percentage of respondents describing themselves as "very dissatisfied" was 56.3, whereas 29.6 percent described themselves as "dissatisfied," for a total of 85.9 percent. *Globus*, April 14, 1995, 47.

[91] Top reasons were "hard life, poverty, unemployment" 31.5 percent; abuse of power, privilege and corruption, 13.6 percent; wartime conditions, 12.5 percent; injustice and criminality in privatization, 13.8 percent; occupation of parts of Croatia, 9.0 percent. *Globus*, April 14, 1995, 44.

[92] Report by political analyst Davor Butković, pointing to a speech by Tudjman in April in Gospić which he describes as "the most untypical speech in the last two years, which was broadcast two times by Croatian television." In the speech, he sharply attacked the NDH and praised the partisan movement as the basis of the Croatian state; he also moved away from his earlier formula that the HDZ alone was responsible for the successes of Croatia, to giving credit for those successes to all political parties. "Predsjednik Tudman otpočeo je veliki obračun s desnom frakcijom HDZ-a?" *Globus*, April 14, 1995, 44–47.

[93] Speech to Sabor, in "Ostvarili smo najviši cilj hrvatskog naroda," *Vjesnik*, May 13, 1995, 2–3.

[94] For example, when asked what the main goals for the country should be, 71.1 percent responded a high rate of economic growth; 35.8 percent responded "having more say at work and in the community," and 25.8 percent responded "strong defense." "Svjetsko istraživanje vrijednosti; upitnik 1995," Odsjek za sociologiju, Filozoskog fakulteta Sveučilište u Zagrebu. The measure of democratic values was very little changed from 1992's results in the political scientists' polling. HIP, 1995.

most democratic country in the world."[95] In addition, it showed that the political spectrum in Croatia had shifted back to the left and that over three-fourths of the population was in favor of reforms.[96] Thus in terms of political forces as well as the basic priorities, interests, values and orientations of the wider population, the HDZ right was facing a series of serious threats.

It was in this context that the invasion of Western Slavonia and then of the rest of Krajina took place. The invasions were well-planned and not only took back all of the territory of "Sector West" of western Slavonia, and then in August of Sectors North and South, but also led to the vast majority of the Serb population fleeing. During the attacks, Tudjman broadcast assurances that the rights of Serbs would be fully assured, asking them to remain. But at the same time, the decision by the leader of the SDS during the May invasion to launch cluster bombs on Zagreb provided politically useful images for HTV of dead civilians in the heart of the capital. Meanwhile, the media was asking questions that amounted to: if they were really innocent, why would all the Serbs have fled? The invasions were accompanied by atrocities against Serb civilians that were at the least tolerated by the HDZ, while the homes of those who did flee were looted and burned by police, military, and civilians. The Croatian authorities made no attempt to prevent this.[97]

Since the territories were to be reintegrated into Croatia, which was also the goal of the international community, the HDZ right had to be concerned about the population of those territories. If the entire Serb population remained, that would be an additionally significant factor in future electoral contests, and given the margins by which the HDZ was barely slipping by, and the downturn in its fortunes, it would be in its interest to ensure that Serbs not stay. In addition, if the Serb population were to reach

[95] For example, when asked to evaluate the truthfulness of the statement, "elections in Croatia are free," 50.7 percent saw that statement as fully or mostly untrue; 63.3 percent did not agree that laws applied equally to those in power and to other citizens. Ibid. In a newspaper poll in September, when asked whether all parties would be treated equally by state television (HRT), only 26.2 percent of those surveyed responded yes, while 45.8 percent responded no. *Globus*, September 22, 1995, 14–15.

[96] Fifty-six and six-tenths percent self-identified as left and 40.3 percent as right. But 76.6 percent agreed that "our society should gradually be improved through reforms," and only 18.9 percent agreed that "our current society must be decisively defended from all changes that threaten it." "Svjetsko istraživanje 1995."

[97] Human Rights Watch report; also, for example, the Minister for Reconstruction and Engineering in May 2000 reported that he had seen with his own eyes Croatian soldiers burning Serb homes in Knin in August 1995. Reported in "Serb Refugees Given Hope," *IWPR's Balkan Crisis Report*, 143 (May 26, 2000).

8 percent of the total population, they would have the right to extra representation in parliament, further eroding the HDZ's majority.

In the short term, the invasions did boost the HDZ's popularity. The May invasion saw the HDZ's popularity increasing from about 32 percent to about 40 percent in newspaper polling. The August invasion saw a further jump in HDZ popularity, for the first time topping 50 percent through August and the first half of September.[98] The HDZ used this opportunity to call early elections for the House of Representatives (which had not been scheduled until 1997). The HDZ pushed the line that the invasion plus the taking back of most of Krajina meant that it would be unbeatable in elections, and top HDZ officials publicly talked about reaching a two-thirds majority in the Sabor, which would allow them to change the constitution unilaterally. Using this aura of inevitability, the HDZ in August and September attempted to recruit opposition deputies at the national and local levels into the HDZ. The incentives that were offered included not only being part of a fully dominant ruling party, but also such material benefits as better jobs, getting children into betters schools, and even a kidney transplant.[99] Especially targeted were deputies of the strongest opposition party, the HSLS.

The most striking aspect of this period of Croatian politics was the fact that the HDZ's invasion and liberation of Krajina provided only very short-lived advantages. Given that the liberation of occupied territories was well down on the list of priorities and causes of dissatisfaction for the vast majority of Croats, this should have come as no surprise. Thus following the invasions, dissatisfaction remained high, in very large part because of the economic situation.[100] The top priorities listed in social science polling prior to the October 1995 elections confirmed the consistency of opinion: when asked to identify the top three problems in Croatia, 66.9 percent listed social justice and security, 48.6 percent listed lower unemployment; 44.5 percent listed ensuring individual rights and freedoms. Social science polling before the 1995 election confirmed once again the

---

[98] The high point in *Globus*'s polling came in mid-August, when the HDZ was the choice of 54.4 percent of respondents, and Tudjman the choice of 63.1 percent. *Globus*, August 18, 1995, 5.

[99] See interviews with HSLS mayor of Osijek, Zlatko Kramarić in *Globus*, September 15, 1995, 54; and with Dražen Budiša in *Globus* September 22, 1995, 2–4.

[100] Dissatisfied and mostly dissatisfied responded 42.7 percent of the population, while mostly satisfied or very satisfied responded 25 percent. When asked why they were dissatisfied, responses were: hard living conditions, poverty and unemployment, 33.2 percent; abuse of power, privilege and corruption, 19.3 percent; unjust and criminality in privatization, 13.3 percent; occupation of parts of RH, only 6.9 percent. Ibid. 14–15.

strong democratic orientation of the population.[101] On relations with Serbs, the number of people who were in favor of emigration of Serbs to Serbia remained the same as in 1992, about 14 percent, while those who called for respecting basic human rights of everyone who lived in Croatia regardless of nationality, or the right to cultural autonomy in Croatia, also remained at about 83 percent.[102] In addition, the majority of respondents saw the calling of early elections as an abuse by the HDZ of the Oluja victory.[103]

Thus by mid-September, a mere month after the victorious "liberation" of the occupied territories, the HDZ's numbers had fallen again to about 30 percent. In addition, a group of parties, though not including the most popular opposition parties, joined together in a Coalition. In the election itself, the HDZ fell far short of its goal of a two-thirds majority, winning only 45 percent of the vote, which translated into 58 percent of the seats. If the 14 "diaspora" seats were not included, HDZ would have had only 53 percent of seats. In the election itself, the HDZ also lost its control of the local councils in every major city in the country, including for the first time in Zagreb, the capital. When Tudjman refused to recognize the opposition chosen mayor, and tried to block that move, the population was in very large part opposed to this attempt by the HDZ to hold onto power despite its loss.[104]

What this election underlined was that the base or core of the HDZ's support had been reduced to the poorest parts of Croatia and the oldest voters and those with the least education; the HDZ did least well in the most developed parts of the country.[105] These results are strikingly similar to the support base for Slobodan Milošević and the SPS in Serbia.

Indeed, this trend continued. In November 1996 Zagreb was rocked by street demonstrations for the first time since independence, with over 100,000 people coming out into the center of town to protest not over issues of ethnicity or nationalism, but rather because of the HDZ's control of local

---

[101] For example, in this poll conducted by the Faculty of Political Science, 96.8 percent of respondents agreed that everyone has the right to express their opinion, even if the majority disagrees; 88.8 percent agreed that real democracy is unthinkable without an opposition.

[102] The breakdown shifted, however, to 68.9 percent favoring basic human and political rights but with no specific national right; and 14.6 percent (down from 32 percent) favoring cultural autonomy in all of Croatia. HIP, 1995.

[103] When asked whether the HDZ was abusing the victory, 51.7 percent responded yes and 27.5 percent responded no; when asked whether they approved of early elections, 32.1 percent said yes, while 44.7 percent said no. Ibid.

[104] The percent of Zagrebers who thought the opposition should name the new mayor was 64.5. *Globus*, November 10, 1995, 5.

[105] Mirjana Kasapović, "Računice nedvojbeno pokazuju," *Globus*, 10 November 1995, 4.

media.[106] In newspaper polling, the HDZ's popularity continued to plum-
met, to the mid-20-percent range, and the coalition of parties was running
neck and neck with the HDZ. The April 1997 elections for the upper house
saw the lowest turnout yet, a mere 54 percent, 42.9 percent of whom voted
for the HDZ (representing 23 percent of eligible voters); because of electoral laws, HDZ won 41 of 61 seats. The presidential election, held in June,
also saw a low turnout, 54.6 percent. Tudjman easily won, with 61.4 percent (representing only 33.5 percent of eligible voters).

The End of HDZ Rule: The Elections of 2000

By the year 2000, little had changed. Political science polling before the
elections again demonstrated the basic value orientation of the electorate:[107]
54 percent opposed giving the vote to diaspora Croats; 53.3 percent of
respondents had a negative image of the HDZ, while only 21.6 percent
had positive opinion of the ruling party, and only 16.3 percent said they'd
vote for the HDZ (although 24.2 percent were undecided; 36.9 percent
supported the HSLS-SDP coalition). In addition, a majority of respondents
made it clear that they would oppose any coalition government that
included the HDZ; only 10 percent saw HDZ as capable of resolving the
problems that they identified as priorities for Croatia; 58.2 percent saw
their situations as worse than it had been in 1990, while only 18.3 percent
were better off; 55.5 percent identified as left, 35.5 as right; and the polling
showed a very strong orientation in favor of a strong socially oriented
state policy.[108] Forty-seven percent were dissatisfied with the state of
democracy in Croatia, only 21.5 percent were satisfied. Even Tudjman himself was not immune. In polling in September, he was running almost even

[106] According to former HDZ official Josip Manolić, hard-liners in the HDZ felt so
threatened by these street protests that they wanted to use force against the demonstra-
tors. Moderates in the party managed to prevent such a move. Interview with Josip Manolić in *Večernji list*, September 30, 2000.

[107] Faculty of Political Science and Croatian Academic Research Network, University of Zagreb, "Rezultati istraživanja političkih stavova birača 'Izbori 2000,'" part of website "Hrvatski Izborni Podaci," online at <http://media.fpzg.hr/hip/stavovi2.htm>.

[108] Thus 83.3 percent agreed and 5.2 disagreed that the state should ensure social security to every person regardless of their age and ability; 60.4 percent agreed and 12.5 percent disagreed that worker participation in decision making within firms results in greater
productivity; 55.5 percent agreed and 18.4 disagreed that the state should support firms
which, if they went bankrupt, would result in a large loss of jobs; 72.9 percent agreed and
11 percent disagreed that every society should strive for the least amount of material differences among people.

with Račan , getting about 26.3 percent support, due in part to his illness; indeed, half of respondents believed that Tudjman was not capable of being president.[109] But the HDZ was receiving in newspaper polling only 18.5 percent support, as opposed to the HSLS-SDP coalition, which had the support of 49.3 percent.[110]

On the nationalities question, strikingly given the events of the previous ten years, only 20 percent of respondents agreed with the statement, "The best is for members of individual nations to live together in their own state," while 62 percent disagreed. Attitudes toward Serbs remained unchanged from 1995.[111]

In the campaign itself, the death of Tudjman in late 1999 meant that the rightists who dominated the HDZ were not forced to present a moderate face to the electorate. The campaign was striking in that the opposition, which clearly was at an advantage in polling as well as in terms of the value orientations of the electorate, appealed to exactly those values. Despite the HDZ right's control of television, there was a limit on what the HDZ could do in the way of demobilizing through enemy imagery. Its room for maneuver in Bosnia was blocked by the international community, which had been putting tremendous pressure on the HDZ to respect the Dayton accords and the Federation agreement.

Subsequent revelations show that Tudjman and the HDZ had over the course of 1999 secretly and illegally gained ownership of the mass circulation daily *Večernji List*, thus not only gaining full and unaccountable control of an important media outlet but also, in Tudjman's own words, creating "the illusion of democratization privatization, etc."[112] The HDZ had also illegally skimmed $100 million from the sale of the Croatian telecoms company to Deutsche Telekom, with the money intended to help the HDZ in the upcoming elections.[113]

In the election itself, the coalition of HSLS and SDP won 51 percent of the votes, a higher proportion than the HDZ had ever won; the coalition of HSS, HNS, LS, and IDS won 17 percent; and HDZ won 29 percent. The HDZ lost in every single constituency except the diaspora and Eastern

[109] Polling in *Nacional* 200 (September 15, 1999).

[110] Ibid.

[111] Thus when asked about the status that Serbs living in Croatia should have, 13.6 percent thought Serbs should emigrate to Serbia; 68.3 percent that Serbs should be assured the same basic human rights as everyone else in Croatia without specific national rights; 14.6 percent were for cultural autonomy.

[112] Quoted in "Tapes Nail Tudjman Cronies," *IWPR Balkan Crisis Report* 138 (May 9, 2000), citing transcripts of tapes released by Mesić's office and published in *Jutarnji List*.

[113] Ibid.

Slavonia.[114] The presidential elections further confirmed the marginality of the HDZ. Although the popular HDZ moderate and long-time foreign minister Mate Granić was the party's presidential candidate, he did not even make it into the second round of voting, receiving only 22.5 percent of the vote.

The final victor was Stipe Mesić, who won 56 percent of the final vote in a campaign in which he stressed coexistence and reconciliation with Croatia's Serbs, and in which he fully distanced himself from and criticized the HDZ's policy toward Bosnia, making clear the HDZ-BH and HVO would no longer get support from Zagreb. He was also sharply critical of the HDZ as corrupt, criminal, and as protecting war criminals. In addition, in the run-up to the second round of voting, supporters of Budiša attempted to play the nationalist card against Mesić, including criticizing him for having a Serb wife. The results, with Mesić's 56 percent versus Budiša's 44 percent, were thus even more striking.

Indeed, once in power the government and president moved to make good on their promises; prime minister Račan introduced a new law on minorities, "which recognizes their languages and guarantees them representation in parliament." Despite attacks on this policy from the HDZ right, which equated the Serbs who wished to return with JNA killers, as well as violent attacks on symbols of anti-Ustaša monuments, Račan's government persisted and maintained "the support of the majority of the population."[115] Mesić too came under attack from the HDZ right for promising to use government funds to help Serbs rebuild their homes. But the only negative reaction came from the HDZ and other rightists, who despite public protests were not able to gain significant public backing for their anti-Serb stance.

The full measure of the HDZ's defeat could be seen in the subsequent Zagreb city elections. After the HDZ's defeat in the 2000 parliamentary and presidential elections, the party leadership was taken over by some of the most vociferous and hard-line rightists. The predictable result was the marginalization of the HDZ as a major political force; in the Zagreb elections, it received only about 10 percent of the vote.

Given the HDZ right's determination to stay in power over the previous ten years, perhaps just as puzzling as how it managed to do so is the question, why did they allow themselves to be defeated? Indeed, there

---

[114] Electoral results online at <http://www.izbori.hr/arhiva2000/index.htm> (accessed March 23, 2004).
[115] *IWPR Balkan Crisis Report* 143 (May 26, 2000).

was serious speculation about whether the HDZ would give up power, and even after the elections it was clear that the HDZ right was still ensconced in various parts of the state apparatus, including in the security apparatus.[116] In addition, the HDZ right may not have believed that it would lose. Its own propaganda and discourse on being authentic Croats may have led the membership to believe that they did indeed represent the true nature of Croats, and that there was no way they could lose. This view is supported by the fact that up until the very end, despite opinion polls to the contrary, the HDZ was publicly declaring that it would be the victor in the elections. Yet, the fact that they did put up moderate Granić (who subsequently left the HDZ) as its presidential candidate indicates that the leadership recognized that Tudjman's strategy of moderates up front was a necessary one, because in fact the HDZ right was out of tune with Croatian society (although there was quite a struggle within the HDZ, as hard-liners Šeks and Pašalić sought to minimize Granić's influence in the party).

Another reason for the loss could be that those who had the most to lose had defected to other parties, including much of the techno-managerial elite. More importantly, the process of privatization had shifted much of the basis of power in Croatia from political positions to actual ownership, or to wealth derived from such ownership.[117] Indeed, the HDZ elite had used their control over the state to shift state assets into the hands of its own loyalists and allies in ways that enabled them to gain control of capital at virtually no cost to themselves. This shift in the structure of power that occurred under the guidance of the HDZ meant that power now resided at least as much in actual ownership of private assets as it did in control over the state. The shift thus served to decrease the stakes for much of the elite, reducing the perceived level of loss that a HDZ loss of power would entail. Along these lines, further confirmation of this can be seen in the fact that by the end, the HDZ had come to be dominated by ideologues whose power was in fact dependent on HDZ control over the state, in particular, over the mass media and institutions of culture and information. For these hardliners, whose base of power was not transferable, the loss of power was disastrous. But these hard-liners were also the

---

[116] Attempts to clean it up failing, Mesić in May sent in troops to seal the building.
[117] Nevenka Čučković, "Siva ekonomija i proces privatizacije u Hrvatskoj, 1997–2001.," *Financijska teorija i praksa* (Zagreb) 26, no. 1 (2002): 245–271; Aleksandar Štulhofer, *Nevidljiva ruka tranzicije* (Zagreb: Hrvatsko sociološko društvo, 2000); Aleksandar Štulhofer, "Proces privatizacije u Hrvatskoj i hrvatska javnost 1996–1998: Povratak u budućnost?" in *Privatizacija i javnost*, ed. D. Čengić and I. Rogić (Zagreb: Institut društvenih znanosti "Ivo Pilar," 1999).

ones who had been overconfident in the degree to which the wider population supported their extremist positions.

Finally, it seems that, just as in Serbia, so too in Croatia the strategy of demobilization had gone as far as it could. The HDZ was limited in terms of the enemies that it could produce or the conflicts that it could provoke. Croatia was getting much international pressure to cooperate with the international community on Bosnia, on return of refugees. And while the HDZ right continued to portray the West as an enemy of Croatia, the population nevertheless continued to have a basically pro-western orientation. Thus even though in the post-election period the nationalist opposition, including the HDZ, accused Mesić of betraying Croatia by his promise to rebuild the houses of Serbs, and though they managed to hold a few demonstrations, the wider population was clearly not attracted to this nationalist discourse. Likewise, Mesić's and Račan's promise to bring Croatia into European institutions, long opposed by the HDZ right, proved very appealing to the electorate.

Conclusion

The violence undertaken by Croatia in this period, and the nationalistic policies of the government, were thus not the result of massive pressure from below, the response to nationalistic or ethnic hatreds, nor was it an attempt by the ruling party to mobilize the population behind them. Rather, it was part of a strategy to demobilize, silence, and marginalize the majority of the population who favored political and economic liberalization, and changes in the structure of power in Croatia. Indeed, what is most striking about Croatia throughout this entire period is the degree to which the basic value orientations and priorities of the population remained remarkably consistent over time, despite the war and the propaganda of the HDZ right.

Faced with their status as a small minority in terms of values and policy preferences, the HDZ right, under the protection of Franjo Tudjman, just as consistently used enemy images and violence as a way to construct and then reinforce their own version of political space, to alter it at both levels: in terms of who was a member of the political community, and who lived in the territory that was controlled by the Croatian state. The violence served to demobilize opposition to the HDZ right, and to enable them to carry out violent policies that changed political space. While they were partly successful, by driving out the Serb population of

Croatia and then the Bosnian Muslim population of "Herceg Bosna," the HDZ right were unable to fully realize their plans of redrawing political space, in large part because of international pressure.

They were nevertheless very successful in terms of their own power. By postponing fundamental changes in the structures of state and economic power, the HDZ right managed through their control of the privatization process to shift the bases of their power over from political positions in the HDZ and in the state, over to financial wealth, through insider privatization of some of the most profitable companies in the country. This shift enabled them to maintain their control over and access to resources in a liberalizing system. In part this was because of their control over enterprises; in part because they had used their time in power to extract wealth from those enterprises. Indeed, one of the biggest challenges facing the new government in 2000 was to deal with previously profitable firms that had been milked of profits and left as virtual wrecks.[118] Although the new government had promised to review all privatizations that had taken place under the HDZ, much of the damage was irreversible, and the new wealthy elite created under the HDZ rule—including the Tudjman family itself—seemed unlikely to be deprived of their gains. The cost in terms of economic hardship is being paid by Croatian society.

[118] For a summary, see R. Jeffrey Smith, "Croatians Find Treasury Plundered," *Washington Post*, June 13, 2000, p. A01.

YUGOSLAVIA AND THE MYTH OF ETHNIC WAR

When I began this project I knew that much of what was being written on the wars in Yugoslavia had the story wrong. There was virtually no evidence that the violence in Croatia and Bosnia-Herzegovina was the result of ethnic hatreds, despite the tenacity with which Western journalists clung and continue to cling to that story. The other major explanation, seen in the academic literature on ethnic conflict, focused on elites who pursued strategies of ethnic outbidding by provoking violence along ethnic lines in order to mobilize their populations to support them. Yet what was actually happening in communities in Serbia, Croatia, and Bosnia, both at the sites of violence as well as on the "home fronts," turned out to be very different from what one would expect in a mobilization scenario; in fact the massive popular mobilizations after 1990 were all focused on *non-ethnic* issues and were aimed *against* the ruling parties.

Dissatisfaction with the existing explanations led me to turn to work by sociologists, anthropologists and others who used a social constructivist approach. This approach makes clear that actively mobilizing people around issues of culture and identity requires more than simply appealing to history and symbols, or declaring a threat in ethnic terms. Indeed, the constructivist approach highlights the extent to which simple models of ethnic mobilization ignore the crucial role of immediate social context and personal, lived relationships in the construction of identity. This approach also points to the very problematic nature of fixed categories such as "ethnicity" and "ethnic group" as units of analysis. If we instead understand processes of ethnic identification in terms of the social construction of identities through lived experience, we open the door to a very different approach to these wars, an approach that recognizes that the violence was not a direct function of processes of ethnic identification.

The evidence shows quite clearly that the Yugoslav wars of the 1990s were the result of certain parts of the elite creating wars for their own purposes. As I have shown in this book, the violence was planned and carried out in very strategic ways by conservative elites in Belgrade and Zagreb, working closely with allies in the war zones. But the violence was not the result of mass mobilization, nor was it a response to pressure from below to remove ethnic others from particular territories. Indeed, looking in detail at the places where wars were actually fought—places with the highest pre-war levels of positive coexistence—the violence almost without exception was imported into those communities as the result of strategic decisions on the part of leaderships in Belgrade and Zagreb. But the wars were not a means by which elites sought to mobilize their populations, and they did not draw on or appeal to the lived experiences or processes of identification of people in the communities most affected by the wars. Their sources lie elsewhere.

As I have shown in this book, after 1990 neither the HDZ nor the SPS actively mobilized the majority of the population to support it, either in terms of street demonstrations or in terms of voting behavior. In both cases, the ruling parties managed to maintain control over the state only through extreme electoral gerrymandering or constitutional changes that gave the ruling party unfair advantages, and through the suppression of the opposition parties' ability to express their positions.

In their pre-campaign discourse both ruling parties portrayed themselves as moderate forces wanting ethnic peace and economic stability. The HDZ and the SPS also both portrayed the violence taking place in Croatia and Bosnia in very strategic ways. While to the international community they portrayed the wars as ethnic conflicts that were the inevitable result of ancient hatreds, cultural differences, and historical experiences, to their domestic audiences they portrayed the violence and the actions of their own armed forces as a story of good versus evil, of innocent women and children who, merely because of their ethnicity, were being unjustly victimized, expelled from their homes, raped, and killed by forces identified as the "ethnic other." The HDZ and the SPS vigorously denied accusations of war crimes leveled against their own forces. Anyone who questioned these stories or who criticized the president or the ruling party on the war or on domestic policies was demonized as being in league with the enemy, of not caring about the innocent victims of the evil others.

What I have argued in this book is that the strategies pursued by these elites had as their main goal not the mobilization but rather the *demobilization* of the population. In particular, these strategies were aimed against those parts of the population that were actively mobilizing against the interests of conservative elites and calling for fundamental changes to the structures of economic and political power within Serbia and Croatia. By constructing images of external threats and by provoking violent conflict along ethnic lines in their strategy of violence, the elites sought to shift the focus of political discourse away from issues of change toward grave injustices purportedly being inflicted on innocents, thus serving to demobilize—by silencing and marginalizing—those who posed the greatest threat to the status quo: the politically mobilized population and the opposition elites who were mobilizing them.

Of course there were some segments of the population in both Serbia and Croatia who were mobilized by these strategies and who actively supported the ruling parties. But they tended to be people whose own interests were also threatened by the proposed changes in structures of economic power, and they represented only a small portion of the overall population. Indeed, this base of support for the HDZ and SPS was strikingly similar: rural populations, pensioners, and other parts of the population that would be most negatively affected by a shift to a liberal economic system. The support that these people provided the ruling parties could thus just as easily be attributed to their economic interests as to their ethnic identities. The other much smaller segment that actively supported and participated in the strategy of violence included those for whom war represented glory and heroism or, conversely, the opportunity to partake in looting and bloody killing.[1]

This is not to say that people did not identify as Serbs or Croats, or that they did not identify with Croatia or Serbia as states. Many people did. But the meanings of those identifications varied by context. There is no evidence of an automatic or logical shift from such an identification to the kind of violence that took place in the 1990s. Understanding the behavior of those people who actually were mobilized by the violence thus requires a much more complex and nuanced approach than the typical ethnic mobilization scenario. The fact that most people in both places were *not* mobilized can be seen as evidence that for the large majority, the images of ethnic war that were purveyed by the ruling party were not drawing

---

[1] For more on this particular group and their role in the Yugoslav wars, see John Mueller, "The Banality of 'Ethnic War,'" *International Security* 25, no. 1 (Summer 2000): 42–70.

on or appealing to the lived experiences and meanings people attributed to their identification, either ethnic or national. Indeed, the evidence
points to the opposite: that conservative elites were using violence to demobilize people precisely because they were not able to use appeals to ethnic identity as the basis for mobilization.

The Goals of Demobilization

In both Croatia and Serbia the conservatives' strategy of demobilization
had short- and long-term goals. In the short term, the goal was to bring
an end to political mobilizations that represented an immediate threat to
the existing structures of power, especially the prospect that the ruling
parties would be ousted from power either through elections or through
street demonstrations. By using the image and discourse of injustices being
perpetrated against innocent civilians by evil others defined in ethnic
terms, conservative elites managed successfully to divert attention
away from the demands for change toward the question of these injustices. The violence thus served to silence and marginalize the proponents
of fundamental change.

In the medium term the wars served several functions. They satisfied
the goals of the allies of conservative elites in the regions of Croatia and
Bosnia where the wars were being fought; they served to change the demographic makeup of the population in those regions; and they served to
change the meaning of identifying as a Serb or Croat in places that had
previously been multiethnic.

Conservative elites who relied on this strategy of conflict faced a very
basic obstacle. Significant parts of their populations were identified with
the "enemy" (non-Serbs in Serbia, non-Croats in Croatia). In Serbia itself,
about one-third of the population were non-Serbs, while in Croatia about
25 percent were non-Croats. In the most basic electoral terms, these are
very significant numbers and clearly could change electoral outcomes.
Given that the ruling parties had declared the "ethnic others" as enemies,
it was almost a certainty that their votes would not go to the ruling parties, thus threatening those parties' control over state power. Similarly,
in the areas of Bosnia-Herzegovina claimed as "Serb lands," non-Serbs
represented about 50 percent of the population; in the areas claimed by
Croatia, Croats were actually a minority of the population. Given that the
stated goal of conservatives in both places was to absorb those areas of
Bosnia-Herzegovina into the "motherland," such demographics would

be additional threats to the ruling parties' electoral dominance, which was already tenuous.

Another factor here was that the heterogeneous communities in Croatia and Bosnia were areas where coexistence was the norm. In the parts of those republics where populations were very intermixed, the vast majority of the population did not want ethnic partition. They thus by their very existence contradicted the argument that coexistence was impossible and that ethnic partition was unavoidable. For example, Croats in ethnically mixed central Bosnia tended to be moderates who did not want an ethnically pure Croat state. Conservative Croats from relatively homogeneous western Herzegovina, along with Croatian president Tudjman, saw these attitudes of Bosnian Croats toward their Muslim neighbors as major obstacles to their long-term goals. The violence in central Bosnia was thus aimed just as much against Croats as it was against Muslims in that area. Similarly, it was conservative Serbs from areas that were homogeneously Serb who pushed for an ethnically pure enlarged Serbia and used violence not only to expel Muslims and Croats but also to change what it meant to identify as a Bosnian Serb.

This violence thus served to reconstruct territorial space in ethnic terms—to "ethnicize" territory— as well as to change the meaning of ethnic identification. The original goal seems to have been to prepare those spaces for incorporation into Croatia and Serbia without also increasing the number of non-Croats and non-Serbs.

But more important, the violence served to reconstruct *political* space at home, in Serbia and in Croatia, by disqualifying anyone who disagreed with the president or the ruling party as enemies of justice, as either dupes or tools of the evil forces responsible for these injustices, as traitors. The strategy of conflict thus sought to institutionalize the political demobilization of opposition forces by institutionalizing images of injustices and victimhood as the central political discourse.

The longer term goal of this strategy of demobilization was to maintain and consolidate control over existing structures of economic and political power, and to control the changes in those structures in such a way that the ruling parties and their allies would be able to maintain their access to and control over resources as the structures shifted to new forms. In both Serbia and Croatia conservative elites used the time that the strategy of demobilization bought them in order to shift their power from the resources that mattered in the old system—positions within the ruling nomenklatura structure and within the ruling party—to the resources that matter in a capitalist market system—ownership of economically productive assets and of capital, and control over distribution networks.

Indeed, while the imposition of a neoliberal version of capitalism was not what the vast majority of the population had in mind when they called for fundamental change,[2] in many ways it turned out to be the preference of conservative elites throughout the former socialist world. While in a reformed socialist system they would have been deprived of their bases of power, a transition to capitalism that they controlled allowed conservatives to privatize the bases of power and to maintain control of resources in a way that could not be threatened by formal politics. Thus throughout eastern Europe some of the most ardent advocates of privatization and neoliberal capitalism have been those who could be characterized as opportunistic conservatives in the old system. And also throughout eastern Europe, those who were in the forefront of the movement to democratize the socialist system—the main opponents of the conservatives in the old system—are also among the harshest critics of capitalism as it currently exists in that region, which they rightly see as being a continuity of the old system in terms of those who have power. The difference is that now the conservative elites have an unchecked kind of private power in which the powerful are responsible to no one but themselves.

By the time the SPS and HDZ lost power in 2000, this shift had been largely accomplished. So while the elections of that year brought opposition parties to power, thereby altering the face of politics in both places, they did not bring the same degree of change to the actual structures of power, or to control of those structures. The ruling parties' electoral losses were therefore much less threatening to significant parts of the conservative elite than they would have been had they occurred ten years earlier.

This analysis helps answer the question of why the ruling parties lost power. Indeed, after expending so much energy and effort on maintaining political power, what accounted for the electoral losses both parties suffered in 2000? There are three basic answers to this question.

[2] There is very little evidence that the wider population supported wholesale adoption of the kind of neoliberal capitalism that would come to dominate Western policy toward the region, with its focus on rapid and widespread privatization of state enterprises at the cost of jobs and social stability, and the reduction or elimination of state intervention in the economy. Their preference ranged from a more democratic and efficient form of the existing socialist system at the end of the 1980s to the desire for a social market system, that is, a capitalist economy but with the state assuring priority goals of social justice and full employment, by the end of the 1990s. For polling from 1988, see Bahtijarević et al., 1989. For polling from 2000, see Faculty of Political Science, "Rezultati istraživanja političkih stavova birača "Izbori 2000" Part of website "Hrvatski Izborni Podaci," online at <http://media.fpzg.hr/hip/stavovi2.htm> (accessed April 21, 2004), in particular question 29.

First, in both cases, the ruling parties had run out of options, making it increasingly difficult to use violent conflict as a way to demobilize the population. In Croatia, the HDZ was very limited in its ability to use the imagery of conflict and enemies after the international community began to crack down on hard-line Croat forces in Bosnia-Herzegovina. Clearly, an active strategy of externally oriented conflict would no longer be possible with the international military presence, and with the reintegration of areas of Croatia that had been occupied by SDS forces. In the case of Serbia, once the Kosovo war ended and NATO forces were present not only in neighboring Bosnia but also in Kosovo itself, the room for the provocation of violent conflict became very constrained (although if the international community steps back from that commitment such a strategy may again become viable). In addition, as pointed out in chapter 4, the strategy of demobilization in Serbia seems to have been exhausted by 1996 and the SPS had come to rely increasingly on overtly repressive and violent means to maintain its grip on power.

Additionally, both parties seem to have become overconfident, apparently believing that their strategies of conflict and demobilization had brought a fundamental change in the electorate and that their victories in the 2000 elections were therefore not in doubt. Given that confidence, there was less incentive to actively pursue the kinds of strategies that both the HDZ and the SPS had relied on in the past to demobilize the opposition. In the Croatian case, part of this overconfidence also manifested itself in the apparent belief by some top HDZ officials that the wider population was indeed more nationalistic and open to more extremist nationalist rhetoric than it actually was. In the case of Serbia, the ruling SPS and its allies seem also to have been overconfident in the extent to which the electorate identified with them as defenders of the nation, as well as the extent to which their repressive policies had weakened the opposition's ability to mobilize support. Milošević's decision to move up the date of the presidential election is but one indication of this overconfidence.

Overconfidence may have been in part a reflection of yet another factor that explains the loss of political power: shifts in the structures of power that occurred in both Serbia and Croatia over the previous ten years. These shifts meant that the loss of political power was not as great a threat as it would have been if it had occurred in 1990. In both Croatia and Serbia, significant parts of the elite had effectively used the 1990s and the demobilization of the opposition to solidify their control over the state and economy, as well as to transform those resources that had been the bases of power in the old system. In both cases, top officials of the ruling party turned out to be members of some of the wealthiest families in their respective societies, at a time when the wider populations were barely eking out a basic existence. The result was a breakdown of the conservative coalition. As parts of the elite gained other bases of power, their interests shifted and their stake in maintaining control of the state became less.

In Croatia, much of the economy had been transferred from state ownership into the hands of HDZ officials and their allies through a process of insider privatization. Others, in their capacity as HDZ-appointed managers, gained enormous wealth by draining state-owned enterprises of their value. These elites' access to and control over resources was thus by the 2000 elections not dependent on HDZ control of the state. An HDZ loss of political power was thus much less of a threat to their interests.

In Serbia too, while much of the economy remained under state control, between 1990 and 2000 major changes had taken place in the structures of economic power. Like the HDZ, the SPS had used insider privatization to reward its supporters, thereby creating a class of "tycoons," businessmen whose ownership of former state enterprises was due to their connections with the ruling party. In addition the SPS and Milošević had aided organized crime mafias in consolidating their power. By 1999 Milošević was apparently attempting to crack down on them; they therefore defected to the opposition coalition. They had gained enormous wealth through control over illegal networks of distribution during the international sanctions, so an opposition-controlled state represented much less of a threat to them. By 2000, control over and access to power resources thus no longer depended on controlling the state. So when elections signaled the end of SPS rule, large sections of the conservative elite were willing to acquiesce in a change of ruling party because such a change did not threaten their power. This fact proved crucial in the defection of parts of the military and police apparatus to the opposition. They seemed to have sensed that the opposition coalition had succeeded in mobilizing the population. But it should also be remembered that these defections were accompanied by assurances on the part of the opposition that they would be allowed to retain their positions and access to and control over resources in the new system.

The change in political power did, however, represent a continuing threat to those who remained dependent on positions within the ruling party and its allies. By 2000, however, more power had shifted to other parts of the elite. In the case of Serbia, it is notable that the deal allowing a shift of mafia forces to the opposition also meant that when prime minister Zoran Đinđić attempted to crack down on organized crime at the end of 2002 and beginning of 2003, they responded by having him assassinated. Clearly the coming to power of the opposition coalition in 2000 did not have the tremendous effect on the structures of power that such a turn of events would have had ten years earlier, precisely because of the changes in the structures of power that had occurred under the guidance of the conservative elites. The opposition victory was thus in part a reflection of changes that had already occurred.

Further evidence of the effectiveness of the strategy of demobilization can be seen in the response of opposition parties to the conservatives' strategies of conflict during the 1990s, as well as in their inability to overcome the conservative dominance until conservatives had themselves restructured power and consolidated their control over resources such that an opposition victory would not threaten that control. Consistently, the most extremist nationalist political figures and opposition parties received the smallest percentage of the vote. Yet some moderate opposition parties nevertheless tried to ethnically outbid the ruling parties. Consistently in every case the result was that those parties were marginalized. Similarly, the SPS and HDZ too had their worst showings when they took their hardest nationalist lines.

What both ruling parties seemed to realize was that the way to increase their share of the vote was not to take a more aggressively nationalist stance, but rather to portray themselves as moderate parties concerned with economic prosperity, peace, and stability. This is not to say that significant parts of the electorate did not value aggressive nationalist stances; in both places there appeared to be a hard core of about 15 to 20 percent who did (although as mentioned above, many of those people also were concerned with economic issues). What is striking however is that a much larger portion of the electorate held quite different priorities, congruent with the moderate positions the ruling parties attempted to take. Some opposition parties however seemed not to realize that the way to increase their support was to appeal to moderate values. The conclusion is that attempting to ethnically outbid the parties in power doomed an opposition party to failure.

Indeed, it is precisely the wider population's consistently moderate priorities and values that explains why the ruling parties had to rely on a strategy of demobilization. On the one hand, conservatives could not actively mobilize the population around their own conservative preferences for political and economic change, since those positions were highly unpopular. On the other hand, they could not mobilize people around issues of ethnic hatred and conflict, since this did not resonate with peoples' lived experiences. The remaining option was to demobilize people, that is, to prevent them from being mobilized by challenger elites around issues of fundamental change. To this end the ruling parties had to shift the focus elsewhere, toward the alleged threat from ethnic others, toward the egregious injustices being perpetrated by those ethnic others against innocent civilians.

In polities such as Serbia and Croatia, where the ruling party determines media coverage either through direct control or because the media is owned or controlled by forces in society that share the basic goals of the conservative elites, it may be difficult to challenge such a demobilization strategy. Indeed, in the case of Croatia in particular what was striking is how popular opinion turned against the HDZ when independent media were able to inform the public of the truth behind the HDZ's role in the war in Bosnia and the harsh crackdown on independent media that the HDZ subsequently pursued. When opposition parties yielded to the temptation of ethnic outbidding, or tried to appear more "patriotic" than the conservatives, these moves only reinforced the ruling party's framing of political discourse and thus actually served its strategy of demobilization. Such a move on the part of opposition parties yields no advantages in terms of winning votes.

As mentioned above, the desire of the wider population for changes in the power structures (especially economic liberalization) was not a desire for a neoliberal agenda. In both Serbia and Croatia polling made clear that supporters of the opposition valued continued state regulation of the economy to ensure high employment and social welfare. This fact has important implications that are already being seen in both countries in the post-2000 period. As the international financial institutions pressure both states to pursue neoliberal agendas, the former opposition parties that were identified with democratic change and that are now the parties of government are faced with the dilemma of no longer responding to the preferences of the population. While neoliberalism will indeed change structures of power and thereby create new elites, it also is setting the stage for a growing gap between the interests of those elites and the interests of the wider population. By depriving the newly elected governments of the ability to fashion an economic system that responds to the preferences of the wider population, for example in the form of a German-style social market system, the international community may be setting the stage for further conflict and destabilization in this region.

Lessons from the Yugoslav Cases

The cases of Serbia and Croatia in the 1990s open up a number of areas for further investigation. At the microlevel within Yugoslavia, much more research needs to be done to understand the interaction between local levels of party and economic power in the period both before and after 1990, and how local-level party officials (both SKH and HDZ) used their control over local resources, their connections to centers of power, and social networks to accomplish their goals. The evidence that I have seen indicates that this local level is a hugely important part of the overall story. Another level of interest concerns the republics, in particular the events of the 1980s within the communist party organizations of each of the Yugoslav republics. The key to a fuller understanding of the roots of the wars lies in this period. If and when party archives are fully opened, they will shed much light on the precursors to the conflict.

In this book I also argue for a reexamination of the attitudes toward this region on the part of the West, and why the ethnic hatreds thesis is so strongly held despite evidence to the contrary. We need to look at what it tells us about ourselves that the myth of ancient ethnic hatreds continues to hold such a strong sway over our imaginations.

These cases also point to the need to carefully examine all wars that are framed in a discourse of ethnicity or religion. Taking the social constructivist approach means not assuming the existence of "groups" as unitary actors with a common identity and single notion of groupness. It also means delving much more deeply into the processes related to social reality, recognizing and taking seriously the notion that identifications are contextual and fluid, and exploring how elites use their control over various resources in order to try to change, tap into, or homogenize those identities. Violence is clearly an effective way to create the image of hard boundaries where none existed before. It is also important to realize that the discourse of ethnic conflict is part of the ideology of the perpetrators of the conflict, part of their strategy of demobilization. The role of identification as a process is something to be tested and researched rather than assumed a priori. As the political scientist Charles King, a specialist on the eastern edge of the Balkans (Romania and Moldova), notes, "It is worth asking whether talking about a distinct category of violence called 'ethnic war' is as useful as [many scholars] think."[3] Indeed, the answer to

---

[3] Charles King, "The Myth of Ethnic Warfare: Understanding Conflict in the Post–Cold War World," *Foreign Affairs* 80, no. 6 (November/December 2001), 167.

the question posed by a workshop I organized in 1996, "Does Ethnic Conflict Exist?" could easily be answered in the negative, because as King notes, "viewing such conflicts as essentially different from any other instances of large-scale violence within a single state can be misleading."[4]

From this perspective, the Yugoslav wars can be seen as falling within a broader universe of cases where elites construct images of a threatening outside world as a means of demobilizing the politically relevant population. This universe includes not only conflicts that are framed in "ethnic" terms. Conflictual foreign policies, for example, may in fact be cases of demobilization. Elites who paint an image of a threatening outside world and who actively use violence against other states, may be doing so not for specific international goals but rather to achieve goals in the domestic arena. This is not a simple model of diversionary tactics; rather, it is one in which elites use their control over informational resources as well as over the apparatus of the state in order to create a context in which they attempt to affect processes of identification as a means of influencing the behavior of their population. Given the extent to which political debates within states are framed in terms of the interest of the population of the state, the contestation over defining that interest is central. Defining it in terms of an existential threat is clearly an effective way to demobilize, silence, and marginalize those who are pushing for changes in policies or in structures of power that would negatively affect status quo power elites. The fact that information about the world outside the borders of one's own state is filtered through media, which are themselves controlled by elites, makes foreign policy a prime area for strategies of demobilization.

Thus, for example, during the Cold War in both the United States and the Soviet Union, conservative forces constructed an image of the outside world and of the other superpower that can be seen as part of a strategy of domestic demobilization. In both superpowers, conservative forces were faced with opposition elites who were seeking to mobilize politically relevant audiences for fundamental changes in the structures of power. In the United States, the kinds of major changes that were implemented as part of the New Deal of the 1930s, and the concomitant mobilization of left forces, labor unions, leftist political parties, and the more progressive factions of the Democratic Party, were a major threat to the interests of conservative forces at the local and national levels. In response to this mobilization, and to the possibility of its continuation in the aftermath of

[4] Ibid.

World War II, conservatives used an image of an existentially threatening Soviet Union, targeting domestic opponents as agents of that external enemy. This shift came in about 1946 and successfully demobilized leftist forces in the United States. The result was that the Democratic party bought into this framing, and it shifted to the right. Many of the trends seen in the 1930s came to an end.

In the case of the Soviet Union, the politically relevant population was obviously different from that in the United States. It was limited to the members of the Communist Party of the Soviet Union (CPSU) and especially to officials in the CPSU at all levels. Here, in the aftermath of World War II, forces in the party were pushing for fundamental changes in how the party related to society, reducing the surveillance, control, and repression and shifting economic priorities toward consumer goods and the well being of the wider population. Conservatives in the CPSU who opposed this "New Course" policy used images of the United States as ultimately threatening, as seeking to destroy socialism, and they managed to demobilize reformist forces within the CPSU. Reformists attempted once again to mobilize the party under Khrushchev, and they were very successful in this, gaining the upper hand from the early to mid-1960s. In a scenario reminiscent of the strategy used by conservatives in the Serbian communist party, when the CPSU conservatives faced the elimination of key parts of the structure on which their power was based, they created conflict, most notably the Czechoslovak crisis, portraying it as proof of the aggressiveness of imperialism and demanding that armed forces be sent in to put an end to it. At the same time, they linked the reforms being undertaken within the Soviet Union, reforms of the CPSU as well as of the economy, to the dangers being seen in Czechoslovakia (as well as in Yugoslavia) and used the images of threat to demobilize and silence the reformist forces in the CPSU, thereby preventing substantive changes.

This approach also raises the question of whether the strategy of the Bush administration after the attacks of September 11, 2001, was motivated not so much by the desire for external security as by the desire to demobilize parts of the U.S. population. Indeed, the administration's rhetoric after that event focused on mortal threats to the nation, threats they claimed would keep the United States on a war footing for an indefinite period of time. In addition, there are other striking parallels with the demobilization strategies of the HDZ and SPS. Prior to September 11 the ruling party's standing among the wider population was plummeting and the opposition was strengthening, reflecting a long-term trend. Additionally, the agendas of the right-wing forces that had come to dominate the ruling party were considered to be extremist positions that did not have the support of a majority of the population.

Following the attacks the president and his party adopted a position of "you are with us or against us," and argued that any true patriot should rally unquestioningly behind the president and the ruling party in the time of crisis. Those who dissented or criticized the president were labeled as traitors who were siding with the enemy; indeed, there was an attempt to equate the United States with the ruling Republican Party and the person of George W. Bush, and to delegitimate any criticism of them. This move was justified with reference to the mortal danger now facing the U.S. population, the innocence of the United States and of the victims of the attacks, the characterization of the enemy in cultural terms as evil while identifying "our" side as the epitome of goodness. Those states which did not publicly support, or which criticized, the policies of the U.S. ruling party were denounced as enemies of the United States, as being motivated by hatred and jealousy and by anti-Americanism. This line was also repeated uncritically by Fox News and other right-wing media that were closely allied to the ruling party, and which repeated almost verbatim the inaccurate and deceptive lines about foreign and domestic policy that were put forth by the ruling conservatives.

The effects of this strategy were also very reminiscent of the cases of Croatia and Serbia, as the discourse of threat served to demobilize, silence, and marginalize criticism of the president by forces in society, in the ruling party, and in the opposition party. Even as information damaging to the administration began to be reported, the overwhelming tendency on the part of the media was to accept the arguments of the president at face value and to discount criticism as unimportant or illegitimate.

The ruling Republican party used the time bought by this demobilization to accomplish several sets of goals. In the short term, it used the silencing of opposition criticism to strengthen its hold on power by recasting the rules of the game to lock in its own advantage. Examples of this included setting up or redrawing electoral districts in ways to ensure Republican dominance regardless of overall electoral numbers; rewriting the rules within Congress to shut out opposition and even moderate Republicans from the legislative process; and the reduction of civil liberties resulting from the passage of the so-called Patriot Act legislation. At the same time, the ruling party was able to pass legislation that had nothing to do with September 11, and that would have had little or no chance of passing before those events because of their extreme nature.

While the cases of Serbia and Croatia are obviously quite different from the case of the United States, the demobilization approach, linking images of a threatening outside world to domestic political goals of conservative forces, nevertheless could provide an interesting way to understand the processes that the contemporary United States is undergoing and to understand apparently self-defeating foreign policy behavior on the part of the Bush administration.

Such an approach should also be able to explain noncases as well, that is, examples where elites do not pursue strategies of conflict. Hungary is a good example. In many ways Hungary structurally was comparable to Serbia and Croatia. It had a state-socialist system; a very significant number of Hungarians lived outside of its borders in neighboring states, and in some cases faced much worse conditions than Serbs or Croats in Bosnia, or Serbs in Croatia. Hungary also had a political party that used a discourse of conflict, pointing to the grave injustices being inflicted on Hungarians in Romania, Slovakia, and Serbia, and calling for a militant response. But Hungary did not pursue a strategy of conflict, and its political system was not marked by the strategy of demobilization the way Croatia and Serbia had been. One part of the explanation for this is that the interest of the elites in the Hungarian communist party were different from those of conservatives in the Croatian and Serbian ruling parties. The Hungarian party had instituted reforms over the thirty years before 1989 that, though gradual and evolutionary, had changed the structure of the economy and its relationship to the state in fundamental ways. Thus, by the time Hungary was facing multiparty elections, those elites who had been part of the state socialist structure were well placed and had the skills and knowledge to succeed as elites in a new, liberalized economic system. Indeed, many communist officials reportedly started their own businesses. Because there was not a significant part of the elite who faced the loss of everything in the transition to a new system, Hungary responded to the situation of Hungarians outside of Hungary in diplomatic ways. Hungary, like Serbia and Croatia, could have appealed to cultural symbols and historical memories and grievances in the pursuit of a conflictual strategy claiming to seek redress for the injustices suffered by the Hungarians in neighboring states. Yet the Hungarian government pursued a very different policy. Of course the international environment, the fact that international borders were recognized, and the fact that Hungary sought to join the EU made a difference. But it made a difference because the elites running Hungary saw the maintenance of good international standing as a priority, while conservative elites in Croatia and Serbia had other priorities in much of this period.

Another noncase that is structurally similar to the Yugoslav cases is that of the Soviet Union. In the waning days of the Soviet Union there were forces that structurally were parallel to the conservative forces in Serbia, that is, members of the ruling party, police, and army who were fundamentally opposed to the radical transformations Gorbachev was undertaking. These conservative forces, like Milošević, also used a discourse of grave injustices being inflicted on Russians outside of Russia. They painted liberal forces as traitors to these Russians, and they called for the use of force. Yet because they did not control the main information media, especially television, or the apparatus of the state, which was firmly in the control of Gorbachev and other reformers, these conservatives were unable to implement their strategy of conflict in order to demobilize the population's push for fundamental change.

These cases and noncases, preliminary and sketchy though they are, show the utility of this approach for understanding strategies of conflict that have as their goal demobilization of the population.

APPENDIX

A BRIEF OVERVIEW OF THE LITERATURE

Dominant Theoretical Approaches to Ethnic Conflict

The puzzles posed in this book about the Yugoslav wars cannot be satisfactorily answered by the dominant theoretical approaches that are used to explain conflicts described as "ethnic." Indeed, the puzzles bring into question both of the two broad ways of understanding these wars that predominate in the West. The first, which focuses on "ancient ethnic hatreds" and the premodern nature of the Balkans as the cause of the violence, has dominated journalistic coverage and continues to dominate the popular imagining of the Yugoslav wars.[1] Here hatreds of and resentments

[1] This characterization, which was very common during the war, continues to be seen in stories about the region. For examples see Thomas Friedman, "Not Happening," *New York Times*, January 23, 2001, 21, who argues that democracy is not working in Bosnia, because "ethnic identity and hatreds run so deep"; and Scott Anderson, "The Curse of Blood and Vengeance," *New York Times Magazine*, December 26, 1999, who argues that "when crisis came . . . it was to the primitive laws and passions of the village that these men reverted." In an appearance on PBS's *Newshour with Jim Lehrer*, political scientist and Eastern European expert Charles Gati, along with journalist Chuck Sudetic, in a discussion of Kosovo, declared that the violence could be explained because of the "backwardness" of the Balkans. Gati noted that "today Yugoslavia or the Balkans in general is inhabited by the sick children of the sick man of Europe," and confirmed his host's thought that the violence was "ethnic tribal nationalist," adding that this part of the world "has never known the rule of law." March 26, 1999 (transcript online at <http://www.pbs.org/newshour/bb/europe/jan-june99/balkans_3-26.html>, accessed October 12, 2003). The best selling book on the Yugoslav wars repeats this line. Robert Kaplan, *Balkan Ghosts: A Journey through History* (New York: Random House, 1994). For critiques of Kaplan's book, see Henry R. Cooper's review in *Slavic Review* (fall 1993): 592–593, and Brian Hall, "Rebecca West's War," *New Yorker*, April 15, 1996, 74–83.

against members of other ethnic groups, rooted very deeply in the culture and society of the region and submerged for fifty years, suddenly burst to the surface with the weakening of communist rule.

This approach distances the West from these horrors, in effect, constructing the Balkans as Europe's internal other, the irrational and primitive part of Europe, and thereby reinforces our self-image of the West as rational and civilized. While many academic works on ethnic conflict and on the Yugoslav wars in particular have rejected this approach, its tenacity in the public imagination as well as among some "experts" provides some clues to the West's inability to understand the nature of the violence in the Balkans. One explanation for this may be that ethnicity and the Balkans has replaced communism and the Soviet bloc as the uncivilized other that dominated the Western imagination in the years of the Cold War. Ironically, in those years Yugoslavia, because it was not part of the Soviet bloc, was seen as a more civilized part of eastern Europe. With the collapse of the Soviet bloc, Yugoslavia has shifted in the Western imagination from the more civilized part of the less civilized world to the epitome of the uncivilized.

A second way of understanding the conflict, occasionally seen in journalistic reports and very often in scholarly explanations, seems more reasonable and less disparaging. Rather than looking to ancient hatreds, this perspective sees the wars as the result of ethnic entrepreneurs who mobilize the population by playing the ethnic or nationalist card. Here, it is the power of symbols and the power of historical memory that are either driving the conflict, or that enable unscrupulous ethnic entrepreneurs to manipulate the masses into violent conflict.[2] Although this seems to avoid the historical inaccuracies of the ancient hatreds thesis, and fits into liberal rationalist images of interest group politics, in fact it is based on premises not so different from the ancient hatreds argument: that what we call ethnic conflict is at its heart about powerful ethnic or nationalist sentiments, either primordial or constructed. Political actors construct and/or tap into these sentiments by playing the nationalist card or pushing the ethnic button, thereby mobilizing ethnic groups to do their bidding. Ethnic groups thus mobilized then support previously unpopular regimes, fight wars, or even kill their neighbors.[3] From this perspective too the ethnic violence is a logical outcome of the power of ethnicity to mobilize people.

[2] See Stuart J. Kaufman, *Modern Hatreds: The Symbolic Politics of Ethnic War* (Ithaca: Cornell University Press, 2001); Donald Horowitz, *Ethnic Groups in Conflict* (Berkeley: University of California Press, 1985).

[3] Ironically, scholars who take a constructivist approach often tend to reproduce this logic. An example of this is Benadrine Arfi, "Ethnic Fear: The Social Construction of

Although both perspectives serve to distance the Balkans from the West, the location of this conflict alone made it difficult for western Europeans and Americans to completely ignore. Indeed, despite the horrors of World War II, such events were seen as impossible in late 20th century Europe, whose slogan "never again," if perhaps a bit optimistic for the non-western, developing world, was thought to apply at least to the European heartland. Additionally, exactly because they were deeply involved politically, economically, and militarily in the region even before the war, the West had a stake in this region that it did not have in central Africa or the Caucasus.

Given the importance of the region in terms of policy, the field of international relations has also been influential in shaping the thinking of policy makers about this conflict. Indeed, since the end of the Cold War scholars of International Relations have turned their attention to ethnic conflict as one of the major threats to international stability. The dominant perspective in the field of international relations, neorealism, draws in part on the literature mentioned above and in part on its own assumptions about the behavior of state actors and therefore portrays ethnic conflicts as clear cut wars between ethnic groups. Just as states face security threats from other states, so too ethnic groups are said to be threatened by other ethnic groups. Neorealists thus discuss ethnic conflicts in terms of security dilemmas, commitment problems, and other dynamics drawn from their understanding of interstate relations. Especially in situations when pre-existing states become weak or collapse, ethnic groups are said to find themselves in an anarchic situation where they have to focus on their very survival.[4] For people who

---

Insecurity," *Security Studies* 1.8, no. 1 (Autumn 1998): 151–203. Arfi, though taking a constructivist approach, assumes the existence of ethnic groups, speaking in unproblematized ways about Croats, Serbs, and Muslims as undifferentiated groups. She also reproduces the logic of the ethnic mobilization approach, in her claim, for example, that "the same groups then turned to killing each other." This not only assumes the existence of clearly bound groups, but also does not problematize the image of "groups" killing each other. As this work shows, it was not just "Croats" killing "Serbs," but very specific individuals who identified as Croats killing not only people they identified as Serbs, but also others they identified as Croats, for very particular reasons. Arfi thus limits the usefulness of the constructivist approach by reproducing the conceptual framework of rational choice as well as primordialist approaches that assume the existence of corporate identities.

[4] See Barry Posen, "The Security Dilemma and Ethnic Conflict," *Survival* 35, no. 1 (Spring 1993): 27–47; James Fearon, "Commitment Problems and the Spread of Ethnic Conflict," in *The International Spread of Ethnic Conflict*, ed. David A. Lake and Donald Rothchild (Princeton: Princeton University Press, 1998); John Mearsheimer, "Back to the Future: Instability in Europe after the Cold War," *International Security* 15, no. 1 (Summer 1990): 5–56; Steven Van Evera, "Hypotheses on Nationalism and War," *International Security* 18, no. 4 (Spring 1994); Chaim Kaufmann, "Possible and Impossible Solutions to Ethnic Civil Wars," *International Security* 20, no. 4 (Spring 1996).

think within this framework, the existence of clearly bounded ethnic groups with objective and identifiable interests vis-à-vis other such groups, and in which "ethnic interests" predominate, is assumed and unproblematic. That is, just as they reify states into real actors, so too are ethnic groups reified despite the fact that such "groups" do not even possess the institutional realities that states do. There is some disagreement among neorealists about whether ethnic groups exist before a conflict, or whether violence creates ethnic groups. But in both cases the war itself and the post-conflict situation can be understood in terms of a dynamic between ethnic groups.[5]

Based on its assumptions, the logical neorealist solution is to "clean up" ethnically mixed regions, partitioning them and transferring populations to "their" homelands, which, as could be expected, confirms the ideological arguments and projects of the perpetrators of violent conflict.[6] By taking the discourse of ethnic conflict at face value and acting upon it, neorealists—and policy makers who base their decisions on neorealist assumptions—set up a self-fulfilling prophecy, and ensure instability in the societies as well as the regions concerned.

Neorealists thus define the ethnic group on the assumption of a common ethnic identity; the group's interest vis-à-vis other groups is determined by this common ethnic identity; and these different ethnic identities in turn lead to conflict. Besides the tautological nature of this approach, this focus on the ethnic group as the unit of analysis reduces culture to merely a one-dimensional monolithic attribute of a supposedly clearly defined and pre-existing group. This assumption prevents neorealists from understanding the dynamics of conflicts described and justified in ethnic terms, driving them to the conclusion that differences in ethnic culture by themselves are the cause of violent conflict. Neorealism seems unable to countenance a situation in which the conflict has as its goal to produce cultural difference, to change the essence of groupness. Nor can neorealism see that such difference, though perhaps produced at the level of discourse, may not reflect in any way social relationships on the ground. Indeed, terms such as "ethnicity" have their main meanings within communities: most definitions of ethnicity and culture

[5] This reification of ethnic groups and of their purported interests is strikingly similar to the reasoning of the perpetrators of ethnic cleansing, who also speak of ethnic groups as clearly bounded, natural entities, who also use the language of security threats from other ethnic groups: the need to be armed to be secure.

[6] On Bosnia, see John Mearsheimer and Robert Pape, "The Answer: A Partition Plan for Bosnia," *New Republic*, June 14, 1993, 22–28; on partition as the only answer for stability, see Chaim Kaufmann, "Possible and Impossible Solutions to Ethnic Civil Wars," *International Security* 20, no. 4 (Spring 1996): 136–175.

focus shared meaning, language, history, and systems of communications. In addition, cultural boundaries are never as clear-cut as state borders and so the term "ethnic group" is much less defensible as a unit of analysis than the term "the state."

The other main approach, International Relations (IR) Liberalism, including arguments about the global spread of democracy, accepts in many ways the premise of the neorealists, although liberals are more optimistic about peaceful outcomes. Liberals, like realists, tend to focus on ethnicity and culture as an interest, albeit one that is not rational. Particularly striking is how experts on global democratization portray examples of ethnically defined violence as evidence that the countries in question are not yet ready for democracy. From this perspective, the wars in Yugoslavia are seen as manifestations of the will of the people: as the country democratized, citizens could finally express their interests. Since violent conflict along ethnic lines broke out at the same time as the country was democratizing, the conclusion is that such violence was an expression of long pent up interests or passions, thus revealing that the "real" or natural fault lines of interest in society were ethnic.[7]

Thus, until this irrational or emotional factor of ethnic hatreds is dealt with, true liberal democracy is impossible. In Fukuyama's words, such societies are still "in history" and have not yet realized the futility of such behavior.[8] One key implication of this analysis is that ethnic homogeneity is a prerequisite for stable democracy, and that the societies in question need to be taught democracy by Americans or western Europeans.[9] This kind of assumption also leads liberals to focus on the need to institutionalize ethnic interest, that is, to provide an institutional mechanism to ensure the interest of the "ethnic groups" is taken into account (or compartmentalized) as a way to overcome the negative effects of ethnic sentiment on liberal democracy. The most common "solution" proposed by liberals is to construct ethnically homogeneous sub-spaces within the larger polity. This kind of institutionalization,

[7] For an example of this kind of argument, see Donald Horowitz, "Democracy in Divided Societies," in *Nationalism, Ethnic Conflict, and Democracy*, ed. Larry Diamond and Marc F. Plattner (Baltimore: Johns Hopkins University Press, 1994), 35–55. Such reasoning is also implicit in arguments such as those of Thomas Friedman ("Not Happening," *New York Times*, January 23, 2001, 21) who claims that democracy is not working in Bosnia because "ethnic identity and hatreds run so deep."

[8] Francis Fukuyama, *The End of History and the Last Man* (New York: Penguin, 1992); see also Richard Rosecrance, *The Rise of the Virtual State* (New York: Basic Books, 1999).

[9] For a critique of this kind of policy, see V. P. Gagnon, Jr. "International NGOs in Bosnia-Herzegovina: Attempting to Build Civil Society," in Sarah Mendelson and John Glenn, eds., *The Power and Limits of NGOs: A Critical Look at Building Democracy in Eastern Europe and Eurasia* (New York: Columbia University Press, 2002).

in the form of consociationalism or ethnic territorialization (as, for example, in an extreme but by no means unique way in the Dayton Agreement that ended the war in Bosnia) is seen as a way to remove the supposedly nonrational ethnic factor from politics and allow these societies to move forward to the more modern or rational interests that are the mainstay of liberal democracy.[10] Another, related option, one put forth forcefully by some liberals in the context of America and western Europe, is the need for assimilation, or for limits on the immigration of peoples from cultures that are "too different" from the host culture.

The dominant approaches to ethnic conflicts thus see ethnicity itself as the main cause of war. The solutions they put forward thus focus on ethnic difference, calling for the removal of ethnic difference and the creation of ethnically pure states, or at best ethnically defined states with "minority" rights for others. But what if ethnicity and ethnic pluralism is not the main cause of violence? What are the effects and costs of constructing ethnically pure territories in formerly plural communities? Do such moves lead to stability, or are they, by ignoring the actual causes of the violence, in fact reinforcing those factors, a recipe for instability?

An exception to this focus on diversity as the cause of violence comes from scholars, many of them in the fields of sociology and anthropology, who take social realities seriously. There are a number of works on the former Yugoslavia and beyond that show a clear understanding of the dynamics of violence that has come to be labeled "ethnic conflict."[11] This work follows in this tradition, and attempts to apply it to the intersection of politics and society as a way of understanding the Yugoslav wars of the 1990s.

[10] Donald Horowitz, *Ethnic Groups in Conflict* (Berkeley: University of California Press, 1985); Milton Esman, *Ethnic Politics* (Ithaca: Cornell University Press, 1995). Of course this institutionalization of ethnicity merely serves to reify ethnic groups, creates institutional interests defined in ethnic terms, and thus ensures that conflicts will be described and justified in such ethnic terms. In that sense, consociational "solutions" merely become a self-fulfilling prophecy about the basically ethnic nature of politics in ethnically heterogeneous polities. For a critique of the logic of this kind of thinking in the context of liberal societies, see Kalpana Ram, "Liberal multiculturalism's 'NESB women': A South Asian post-colonial feminist perspective on the liberal impoverishment of 'difference,'" in *The Teeth Are Smiling: The Persistence of Racism in Multicultural Australia*, ed. Ellie Vasta and Stephen Castles (St. Leonards, NSW: Allen and Unwin, 1996), 130–144.

[11] See Tone Bringa, *Being Muslim the Bosnian Way: Identity and Community in a Central Bosnian Village* (Princeton: Princeton University Press, 1995); Eric Gordy, *The Culture of Power in Serbia: Nationalism and the Destruction of Alternatives* (University Park: Penn State Press, 1999); Ger Duijzings, *Religion and the Politics of Identity in Kosovo* (New York: Columbia University Press, 2001). See also David Campbell, *National Deconstruction: Violence, Identity, and Justice in Bosnia* (Minneapolis: University of Minnesota Press, 1998); Georgi Derluguian, *Bourdieu's Secret Admirer in the Caucasus* (Chicago: University of Chicago Press, 2005).

SELECTED BIBLIOGRAPHY

Journals/periodicals

B-H Dani (Sarajevo)
Borba (Belgrade)
Bumerang (Osijek)
Danas (Belgrade)
Danas (Zagreb)
Front Slobode (Tuzla)
Glas (Banja Luka)
Glasnik HDZ (Zagreb)
Globus (Zagreb)
Hrvatski i Bošnjački tjednik
Jedinstvo (Sisak)
Karlovački Tjednik (Karlovac)
Lićki Vjesnik (Gospić)
Nacional (Zagreb)
Narodni List (Zadar)
Naša Borba (Belgrade)
Naše Teme (Zagreb)
Naši Dani (Sarajevo)
Oslobođenje (Sarajevo)
Politika (Belgrade)
Slobodna Dalmacija (Split)
Srpska Reč (Belgrade)
Start (Zagreb)
Sveske (Institute for the study of national relations, Sarajevo)
Valter (newspaper of the students of the University of Sarajevo)
Velika Srbija (newspaper of the Serbian Radical Party, Belgrade)
Vjesnik (Zagreb)
Vreme (Belgrade)
Zbilja (newspaper of the municipal branch of the Serbian Democratic Party [SDS],
    Karlovac)

Books and Articles

Antonić, Slobodan, Milan Jovanović, and Darko Marinković. *Srbija između populizma i demokratije: Politički procesi u Srbiji 1990–1993*. Belgrade: Institut za političke studije, 1993.

Artuković, Mato. *Ideologija Srpsko-Hrvatskih Sporova (Srbobran 1884–1902)*. Zagreb: Naprijed, 1991.

Arnautović, Suad. *Izbori u Bosni i Hercegovini '90.: Analiza izbornog procesa*. Sarajevo: Promocult, 1996.

Baćević, Ljiljana , Štefica Bahtijarević, Vladimir Goati, Goran Milas, Milan Miljević, Stojmen Mihajlovski, Dimitar Mirćev, Dragomir Pantić, Nikola Poplašen, Niko Toš, and Mirjana Vasović. *Jugoslavija na kriznoj prekretnici*. Belgrade: Institut društvenih nauka, 1991.

Bahtijarević, Štefica, and Mladen Lazić. *Položaj Naroda i Međunacionalni odnosi u Hrvatskoj*. Zagreb: Institute for Social Research, 1991.

——. "Javno mnijenje Zagreba '88." *Naše teme*, 33, no. 7–8 (1989): 1955–2022.

Bakić, Biljana. "Constructed 1990s Yugoslav Reality." M.A. thesis, University of Pittsburgh, 1994.

Bakić, Ibrahim. "Stavovi mladih Bosne i Hercegovine prema naciji i religiji." *Sveske*, nos. 24–25 (1989): 371–406.

Bakić, Ibrahim, and Ratko Dunđerović. *Građani Bosne i Hercegovine o međunacionalnim odnosima*. Sarajevo: Institut za proučavanje nacionalnih odnosa, 1990.

Baletić, Milovan, ed. *Ljudi iz 1971. Prekinuta Šutnja*. Zagreb: Vjesnik, 1990.

Banac, Ivo. "The Fearful Asymmetry of War: The Causes and Consequences of Yugoslavia's Demise." *Daedalus* (Spring 1992): 141–174.

Begić, Kasim I. *Bosna i Hercegovina od Vanceove misije do Daytonskog Sporazuma (1991–1996.)*. Sarajevo: Bosanska Knjiga, 1997.

Bogosavljević, Srđan. "Bosna i Hercegovina u ogledalu statistike." In *Bosna i Hercegovina između rata i mira*, edited by Bogosavljević et al., 31–47. Belgrade: Institut drutvenih nauka, 1992.

Bogosavljević, Srđan, Vladimir Goati, Zdravko Grebo, Jasminka Hasanbegović, Dušan Janjić, Branislava Jojić, Zoran Slavujević, Paul Shoup. *Bosna i Hercegovina između rata i mira*. Belgrade: Institut društvenih nauka, 1992.

Bosanski Muslimani: Čimbenik mira izmedju Srba i Hrvata: Interview Adila Zulfikarpašića. Zürich: Bosanski Institut, 1986.

Bougarel, Xavier. "Bosnie-Herzégovine: anatomie d'une poudrière." *Hérodote* 67 (1992): 84–147.

Branković, Srbobran. "Social Class and Political Affiliation." In *Challenges of Parliamentarism*, edited by Goati, 69–91.

Bringa, Tone R. "Averted Gaze: Genocide in Bosnia-Herzegovina 1992–1995." In *Annihilating Difference: The Anthropology of Genocide*, edited by Alexander Hinton. Berkeley: University of California Press, 2002.

——. *Being Muslim the Bosnian Way*. Princeton: Princeton University Press, 1995.

——. "Nationality Categories, National Identification and Identity Formation in 'Multinational' Bosnia." *Anthropology of East Europe Review* 1.11, nos. 1–2: 69–76.

——. "The Peaceful Death of Tito and the Violent End of Titoism." In *Death of the Father: An Anthropology of the End in Political Authority*, edited by John Borneman. New York: Berghahn Books, 2003.

Bujošević, Dragan, and Ivan Radovanović. *The Fall of Milosevic: The October 5th Revolution*. New York: Palgrave Macmillan, 2003.

Burg, Steven. *Conflict and Cohesion in Socialist Yugoslavia*. Princeton: Princeton University Press, 1983.

Burg, Steven L., and Paul Shoup. *The War in Bosnia-Herzegovina: Ethnic Conflict and International Intervention*. Armonk, N.Y.: M. E. Sharpe, 1999.

Cohen, Lenard J. *The Socialist Pyramid: Elites and Power in Yugoslavia*. Oakville, Ont.: Mosaic Press, 1989.

Cvitković, Ivan. "Nacionalno i vjersko u odnosima naroda, narodnosti i religijskih zajednica u Jugoslaviji." *Sveske*, 26–27 (1989): 76–82.

Čučković, Nevenka. "Siva ekonomija i proces privatizacije u Hrvatskoj, 1997–2001." *Financijska teorija i praksa* (Zagreb), 26 (1) (2002), 245–271.

Dević, Ana. "Nationalism and Powerlessness of Everyday Life: A Sociology of Discontents in Yugoslavia Before the Breakup." Paper presented at "Living with the Beast: Everyday Life in Authoritarian Serbia," Clark University, Worcester, Mass., April 2000.

Dizdarević, Raif. *Od smrti Tita do smrti Jugoslavije: Svedočenja*. Sarajevo: Svjetlost, 2000.

Dugandžija, Nikola. "Domet Nacionalne Zaokuplenosti." In *Položaj Naroda i Medunacionalni odnosi u Hrvatskoj*, edited by Štefica Bahtijarević and Mladen Lazić, 101–114. Zagreb: Institute for Social Research, 1991.

——. "The Level of National Absorption." In *Croatian Society on the Eve of Transition*, edited by Katarina Prpić, Blaženka Despot, and Nikola Dugandžija, 135–152. Zagreb: Institute for Social Research, 1993.

Duijzings, Ger. *Religion and the Politics of Identity in Kosovo*. New York: Columbia University Press, 2000.

Đukić, Slavoljub. *Izmedu slave i anateme: Politička biografija Slobodana Miloševića*. Belgrade: Filip Višnjić, 1994.

Faculty of Political Science and Croatian Academic Research Network, University of Zagreb. "Rezultati longitudinalnog istraživanja političkih stavova birača 1990–1995." Part of website "Hrvatski Izborni Podaci," online at <http://media.fpzg.hr/hip/stavovi.htm> (accessed March 27, 2004).

——. "Rezultati istraživanja političkih stavova birača 'Izbori 2000.'" Part of website "Hrvatski Izborni Podaci," online at <http://media.fpzg.hr/hip/stavovi2.htm> (accessed March 27, 2004).

Gagnon, V. P., Jr. "Ethnic Conflict as Demobilizer: The Case of Serbia." *Institute for European Studies Working Paper* 96.1 (May 1996).

——. "Ethnic Nationalism and International Conflict: The Case of Serbia." *International Security* 19, no. 3 (Winter 1994–95): 130–166.

——. "Historical Roots of the Yugoslav Conflict." In *International Organizations and Ethnic Conflict*, edited by Milton Esman and Shibley Telhami, 179–197. Ithaca: Cornell University Press, 1995.

Goati, Vladimir, ed. *Challenges of Parliamentarism: The Case of Serbia in the Early Nineties*. Belgrade: Institute of Social Science, 1995.

——. "Politički život Bosne i Hercegovine 1989–1992." In *Bosna i Hercegovina izmedu rata i mira*, edited by Bogosavljević et al., 48–61. Belgrade: Institut društvenih nauka, 1992.

——. *Političkog anatomija jugoslovensog društva*. Zagreb: Naprijed, 1989.

Golubović, Zagorka, Bora Kuzmanović, and Mirjana Vasović. *Društveni karakter i društvene promene u svetlu nacionalnih sukoba*. Belgrade: Filip Višnjić, 1995.

Gordy, Eric. *The Culture of Power in Serbia: Nationalism and the Destruction of Alternatives.* University Park: Pennsylvania State University Press, 1999.

Grdešić, Ivan. "Izbori u Hrvatskoj: biraši, vrednovanja, preferencije." In *Hrvatska u izborima '90,* edited by Ivan Grdešić, Mirjana Kasapović, Ivan Šiber, and Nenad Zakošek, 49–97. Zagreb: Naprijed, 1991.

——. "Building the State: Actors and Agendas." In *The 1990 and 1992/93 Sabor Elections in Croatia: Analyses, Documents and Data,* edited by Ivan Šiber, 103–134. Berlin: Sigma, 1997.

Grdešić, Ivan, Mirjana Kasapović, Ivan Šiber, and Nenad Zakošek, eds. *Hrvatska u izborima '90.* Zagreb: Naprijed, 1991.

Hansen, Lene. *Western Villains or Balkan Barbarism? Representations and Responsibility in the Debate over Bosnia.* Copenhagen: Insitute of Political Science, 1998.

Hodson, Randy, Garth Massey, and Duško Sekulić. "National Tolerance in the Former Yugoslavia," *Global Forum Series Occasional Papers, Center for International Studies, Duke University,* Occasional Paper 93–01.5 (December 1993).

Human Rights Watch. *Civil and Political Rights in Croatia.* New York: Human Rights Watch, October 1995.

Inayatullah, Naeem, and David Blaney. *International Relations and the Problem of Difference.* New York: Routledge, 2004.

——. "The Westphalian Deferral." *International Studies Review.* 22, 2000: 29–64.

Izetbegović, Alija. *Čudo bosanskog otpora: Odabrani govori, interjui, izjave (decembar 1993–decembar 1994).* Sarajevo: BIH Press, 1995.

Janjić, Dušan. "Građanski rat i mogućnosti mira u Bosni i Hercegovini." In *Bosna i Hercegovina između rata i mira,* edited by Bogosavljević et al., 100–139.

——. *Religion and War.* Belgrade: European Movement in Serbia, 1994.

Karajić, Nenad. "Javnost u hrvatskoj tranziciji—između države i tržišta." In *Socio-Kulturni kapital i tranzicija u Hrvatskoj,* edited by Matko Meštrović and Aleksandar Štulhofer, 173–204. Zagreb: Hrvatsko sociološko društvo, 1998.

Kasapović, Mirjana. *Izborni i stranački sustav Republike Hrvatske.* Zagreb: Alinea, 1993.

——. "Strukturna i dinamička obilježja političkog prostora i izbora." In *Hrvatska u izborima '90,* edited by Ivan Grdešić, Mirjana Kasapović, Ivan Šiber, and Nenad Zakošek, 15–48. Zagreb: Naprijed, 1991.

——. "The Structure and Dynamics of the Yugoslav Political Environment and Elections in Croatia." In *The Tragedy of Yugoslavia,* edited by Seroka and Pavlović, 23–48. Armonk, N.Y.: M. E. Sharpe, 1992.

Kasapović, Mirjana, and Nenad Zakošek. "Democratic Transition in Croatia: Between Democracy, Sovereignty, and War." In *The 1990 and 1992/93 Sabor Elections in Croatia: Analyses, Documents and Data,* edited by Ivan Šiber, 11–33. Berlin: Sigma, 1997.

Klučnih pet: intervjui Gorazda Suhadolnika sa lanovima Demokratske alternative. Ljubljana: Mladina, 1990.

Kraljačić, Tomislav. *Kalajev Režim u Bosni i Hercegovini 1882–1903.* Sarajevo: Veslin Masleša, 1987.

Kramarić, Zlatko. *Granonačelniče vrijeme je . . .* Zagreb: Mladinska knjiga, 1993.

Krstić, Slobodan. *Niški liberali u jugoslovenskoj politićkoj zbilji.* Niš: Gradina, 1993.

Lalić, Dražen. "Pohod na Glasače: Analiza sadržaj poruka predizbornih kampanja stranaka u Hrvatskoj 1990., 1992. i 1993. godine." In *Pohod na Glasače: Izbori u Hrvatskoj 1990–1993.,* edited by Srđan Vrcan et al., 203–280. Split: Puls, 1995.

Lazić, Mladen. "Introduction: The Emergence of a Democratic Order in Serbia." In *Protest in Belgrade: Winter of Discontent,* edited by Lazić, 1–30. Budapest: Central European University Press, 1999.

Lazić, Mladen, ed. *Protest in Belgrade: Winter of Discontent.* Budapest: Central Euro-
pean University, 1999.
——. *Razaranje društva: Jugoslovensko društvo u krizi 90-ih.* Belgrade: Filip Višnjić, 1994.
Livada, Svetozar. *Etničko čišćenje - Zločin stoljeća.* Zagreb: Prosvjeta, 1997.
Mamula, Branko. *Slučaj Jugoslavija.* Podgorica: CID, 2000.
Marković, Vera. "Odnos prema političkom sistemu u SFRJ 1980–1990." *Gledišta*
1–6(1994): 111–130.
Mesić, Stipe. *Kako je srušena Jugoslaviju.* Zagreb: Mislav Press, 1994.
Mihailović, Srećko. "Parlamentarni izbori u Srbiji 1990, 1992, i 1993." *Gledišta* 1–6
(1994): 33–42.
Mihajlovski, Stojmen. "Informisanost i informisanje građana o programu reformi
Saveznog Izvršnog Veća." In Baćević et al., 39–55.
——. "Predstave javnosti o Saveznom Izvršnom Veću." In *Jugoslavija na kriznoj prekret-
nici*, edited by Baćević et al., 56–64. Belgrade: Center for Political Research and
Public Opinion, Institue of Social Sciences, University of Belgrade, 1991.
Milićević, Aleksandra Sasha. "Joining Serbia's Wars: Volunteers and Draft-dodgers,
1991–1995," Ph.D. diss., University of California at Los Angeles, 2004.
Miljević, Milan, and Nikola Poplašen. "Politička kultura i međunacionalni odnosi."
In *Jugoslavija na kriznoj prekretnici*, edited by Ljiljana Baćević et al., 133–168. Bel-
grade: Center for Political Research and Public Opinion, Institute of Social Sci-
ences, University of Belgrade, 1991.
Miller, Nicholas J. *Between State and Nation: Serbian Politics in Croatia before the First
World War.* Pittsburgh: University of Pittsburgh Press, 1997.
Oliveira-Roca, Maria. "Demografski profil hrvata, srba i jugoslovena u Hrvatskoj."
In *Položaj Naroda i Međunacionalni odnosi u Hrvatskoj*, edited by Štefica Bahtijare-
vić and Mladen Lazić, 183–263. Zagreb: Institute for Social Research, 1991.
Omeragić, Sejo. *Dogovoreni Rat.* Sarajevo: Proton, 2001.
Pantić, Dragomir. "Nacionalna distanca građana Jugoslavije." In *Jugoslavija na kriznoj
prekretnici*, edited by Baćević et al., 168–186. Belgrade: Center for Political Research
and Public Opinion, Institute of Social Sciences, University of Belgrade, 1991.
——. "Voters' Value Orientations." In *Challenges of Parliamentarism*, edited by Goati,
93–140.
Pašić, Najdan. *Razgovori i rasprave o političkom sistemu.* Belgrade, 1986.
Pavlović, Dragiša. *Olako obećana brzina.* Zagreb: Globus, 1988.
Pavlović, Dušan. "Spoljna politika SR Jugoslavije 1992." *Gledišta* 1–6 (1994): 141–158.
Pavlović, Vukašin, ed. *Potisnuto civilno društvo.* Belgrade: Eko Centar, 1995.
Perović, Latinka. *Zatvaranje Kruga: Ishod rascepa 1971–1972.* Sarajevo: Svjetlost, 1991.
Petrović, Ruža. *Etnički mešoviti brakovi u Jugoslaviji.* Belgrade: Institute for Sociologi-
cal Research, Faculty of Philosophy, Belgrade University, 1985.
Prpić, Katarina, Blaženka Despot, and Nikola Dugandžija. *Croatian Society on the Eve
of Transition.* Zagreb: Institute for Social Research, 1993.
Pupovac, Milorad. "Stavovi govornika hrvatskog ili srpskog prema jeziku i pismu."
In *Položaj Naroda i Međunacionalni odnosi u Hrvatskoj*, edited by Štefica Bahtijare-
vić and Mladen Lazić, 165–181. Zagreb: Institute for Social Research, 1991.
Pusić, Eugen, Josip Kregar, and Ivan Šimonović. "SK u razvoj komunalnog sistema
grada Zagreba." *Naše teme* 32, no. 12 (1988): 3009–3041.
Radulović, Sran. *Sudbina Krajine.* Belgrade: Dan Graf, 1996.
Šarinić, Hrvoje. *Svi moji tajni pregovori sa Slobodanom Miloševićem 1993–95 (98).* Zagreb:
Globus International, 1999.

Šiber, Ivan. "The Impact of Nationalism, Values, and Ideological Orientations on Multi-Party Elections in Croatia." In *The Tragedy of Yugoslavia: The Failure of Democratic Transformation*, edited by Jim Seroka and Vukašin Pavlović, 141–171. Armonk, N.Y.: M. E. Sharpe, 1992.

——. "Nacionalna, vrijednosna, i ideološka uvjetovanost stranačkog izbora." In *Hrvatska u izborima '90*, edited by Ivan Grdešić, Mirjana Kasapović, Ivan Šiber, and Nenad Zakošek, 98–130. Zagreb: Naprijed, 1991.

Šiber, Ivan, ed. *The 1990 and 1992/93 Sabor Elections in Croatia: Analyses, Documents and Data*. Berlin: Sigma, 1997.

Šiber, Ivan, and Christian Welzel. "Electoral Behavior in Croatia." In *The 1990 and 1992/93 Sabor Elections in Croatia: Analyses, Documents and Data*, edited by Ivan Šiber, 80–102. Berlin: Sigma, 1997.

Slavujević, Zoran Dj. "Election Campaigns." In *Challenges of Parliamentarism*, edited by Goati, 159–181.

Spasić, Ivana, and Milan Subotić, eds. *Revolution and Order: Serbia after October 2000.* Belgrade: Institute for Philosophy and Social Theory, 2001.

Špegelj, Martin. *Sjećanja vojnika*. Zagreb: Znanje, 2001.

Stambolić, Ivan. *Put u bespuće*. Belgrade: Radio B92, 1995.

——. *Rasprave o SR Srbiji 1979–1987*. Zagreb: Globus, 1988.

Štulhofer, Aleksandar. *Nevidljiva ruka tranzicije*. Zagreb: Hrvatsko sociološko društvo, 2000.

——. "Proces privatizacije u Hrvatskoj i hrvatska javnost 1996–1998: Povratak u budućnost?" In *Privatizacija i javnost*, edited by D. Čengić and I. Rogić. Zagreb: Institut društvenih znanosti "Ivo Pilar," 1999.

Tašić, Predrag. *Kako sam branio Antu Markovića*. Skopje: Mugri 21, 1993.

Todorova, Maria. *Imagining the Balkans*. New York: Oxford University Press, 1997.

Tripalo, Miko. *Hrvatsko proljeće*. Zagreb: Globus, 1990.

van Beek, Martijn. "Beyond Identity Fetishism: 'Communal' Conflict in Ladakh and the Limits of Autonomy." *Cultural Anthropology* 15, no. 4: 525–569.

Vrcan, Srđan. "Izbori 1990–1993. Između demokratizacije i tehnologije vladanja." In *Pohod na Glasače: Izbori u Hrvatskoj 1990–1993*, edited by Srđan Vrcan, 139–202. Split: Puls, 1995.

Vujošević, Ljubiša. *Interesi i delovanje Saveza komunista Jugoslavije: istraživački projekti CKI*. Belgrade: Izdavački Centar Komunist, 1986.

Zakošek, Nenad. "Polarizacijske strukture, obrasci političkih uvjerenja i hrvatski izbori 1990." In *Hrvatska u izborima '90*, edited by Ivan Grdešić, Mirjana Kasapović, Ivan Šiber, and Nenad Zakošek, 131–187. Zagreb: Naprijed, 1991.

Zulfikarpašić, Adil, Vlado Gotovac, Miko Tripalo, Ivo Banac, *Okovana Bosna: Razgovor*. Zürich: Bošnjački Institut, 1995.

INDEX

CPSIA information can be obtained
at www.ICGtesting.com
Printed in the USA
LVHW090919171121
PP17022900002B/4